IN
THE
GAME

SUNY series on Sport, Culture, and Social Relations

CL Cole/Michael A. Messner, editors

IN THE GAME

Gay Athletes and the Cult of Masculinity

Eric Anderson

STATE UNIVERSITY OF NEW YORK PRESS

Published by
State University of New York Press, Albany

For information, address State University of New York Press,
90 State Street, Suite 700, Albany, NY 12207

Production by Marilyn P. Semerad
Marketing by Fran Keneston

Library of Congress Cataloging-in-Publication Data

Anderson, Eric.
  In the game : gay athletes and the cult of masculinity / Eric
Anderson.
    p. cm. — (SUNY series on sport, culture, and social relations)
  Includes bibliographical references and index.
    ISBN 0-7914-6533-0 (hardcover : alk. paper) — ISBN 0-7914-6534-9
(pbk. : alk. paper)
  1. Gay athletes. 2. Masculinity in sports. 3. Sports—Social
aspects. 4. Homophobia in sports. I. Title. II. Series.

GV708.8.A43 2005
796.086′64—dc22

                                                            2004021367

10 9 8 7 6 5 4 3 2 1

To my partner, Grant Tyler Peterson

Contents

Acknowledgments

After coming out of the closet as an openly gay high school track coach in 1993, I was urged by my friend to read Patricia Nell Warren's *The Front Runner*. Depressed after a poor performance at the California State Cross-Country Meet, I asked my assistant coach to drive the six hours home so that I might read the novel that I had purchased the night before. I read with speed at first, simply trying to get through the novel so I could return to the "more important" stack of nonfiction books I had waiting for me at home. I read the story of Harlan Brown, a gay coach at a premier distance running university. His sexuality is discovered, he is jeered, and his name blackened. I periodically cried the entire drive home, for the struggle he and his athletes endured was both an accurate representation of my life and a foretelling of my future.

I was so inspired after reading *The Front Runner* that I penned my own autobiography, *Trailblazing: The True Story of America's First Openly Gay High School Coach*. Also, in an attempt to understand my experience and the extreme hostility my athletes and I withstood, I returned to graduate school to earn my PhD in sociology so that I might better understand the nexus of men, sport, and homophobia.

It was at the University of California, Irvine that I found a sharp gender scholar as a mentor. Francesca Cancian supervised my intellectual growth and supported the public dissemination of that knowledge. She encouraged me to spread out from our sociology department and suggested that I read and contact the author of *Power at Play: Sports and the Problem of Masculinity*, Michael Messner of the University of Southern California. I found in Messner both a friend and mentor, and I am extremely grateful to both Francesca and Michael for their support and friendship.

As a burgeoning academic, I discovered a wealth of knowledge and support at the annual meetings of the North American Society for the Sociology of Sport, but none more so than from the only other openly gay male member and author of *The Arena of Masculinity: Sports, Homosexuality, and the Meaning of Sex*, Brian Pronger. Brian's groundbreaking book was the first detailed theoretical exploration into the relationship between homosexuality and sport. Brian and I quickly united as friends, sharing similar ideology over many social and academic terrains. Brian encouraged me to think in new directions and supported my every move. His influence can be found in every page of this book. Finally, as a young graduate student, I came across Pat Griffin's *Strong Women, Deep Closets: Lesbians and Homophobia in Sport*. As a brazen second-year graduate student, I wrote to her and said, "I'm going to write your book, but for gay male athletes." Her book has largely served as the model for this research.

These authors, of course, are just a few of those who have intellectually inspired and socially promoted me. I am in great debt to Judy Treas, Pat Walsh, David Meyer, David Frank and the faculty of the Sociology Department at the University of California, Irvine; Susan Zeiff at San Francisco State University; Sharon Guthrie at California State University, Long Beach; Michael Kimmel at the State University of New York, Stony Brook; Gail Kligman at the University of California, Los Angels; Ellen Staurowsky of Ithaca College; Donald Sabo at D'Youville College; and many of the members of the North American Society for the Sociology of Sport. I also thank Jim Buzinski and Cyd Zeigler for their passionate, persistent, and important work on the website Outsports.com. Their website has morphed from one about sport statistics to important social issues, and their expertise in the world of gays in sport was called upon numerous times for this book. I'd also like to recognize the pioneering efforts of all of those involved with the Gay and Lesbian Athletic Foundation. Finally, I would like to thank Priscilla Ross at the State University of New York Press for taking an interest in this project and helping me prepare it and Dave Prout, who not only copyedited the book but taught me a great deal in the process.

Of course, the intellectual stimulation and support from my peers would be useless if it were not for the support of those at home. I am profoundly lucky to have come from parents, Raymond and Margaret Anderson, who supported me in my academic and personal lives, and even though my father passed away years ago, I know he would have been proud. I am also indebted to my mother for her support in my decision to return to graduate school at the age of twenty-nine, and her assistance through it. I am also thankful to my new parents through my partner, Vic and Judy Peterson, and the support their family provides to my partner and me. Most importantly, I thank my life-partner, Grant Tyler Peterson, who has, since 1997, been my strength through everything. I am grateful to have his intellect, his theoretically prudent mind, and for the volumes of proofreading he has done for my academic works.

Grant supported me in the research and writing of this book, which took place simultaneous to the research and writing of my dissertation on another topic. It was through what essentially amounted to writing two dissertations at once, while also trying to maintain my activist work and public speaking in our conservative county that I owe him a nice, long vacation. At times it was tough. I often felt alone in my struggles and occasionally doubted my ability. During one particularly bad span in which I felt as if I was fighting uphill battles all alone, he brought home a gift and said, "You've told me that you feel like you're running up an endless hill, that you're the only one around here pushing for change." He pulled out an eight-inch statue of a man straining against the pressures of the world. He then presented me with a second statue, one of a man pushing the other way. "And this one is me, just so you remember I'm always there—pushing with you." The statues sit on my desk, serving as bookends, a perfect match from a perfect partner.

Introduction

I took delight in the 1992 presidential election of Bill Clinton over George Bush. Clinton had advocated for gays and lesbians to openly serve in the U.S. Armed Forces and sparked national debate around the issue. Although he failed to secure a safer space for America's[1] gay and lesbian soldiers, and ultimately betrayed them by failing to sign an executive order before leaving office, the discourse regarding the "gays in the military" issue proved beneficial for gay liberation politics in general and for gay male athletes in particular. It was, for example, this dialogue that helped shift attitudes regarding homosexuality in the United States in the early 1990s. I wasn't a sociologist at the time, and I had no idea of the shifting cultural attitudes on the issue. All I knew was that, as a closeted high school coach, for the first time I began to hear discussions of homosexuality around me. Whereas before there seemed to be unanimity in disgust at who I was, I began to see slivers of light crack through what we call the "Orange Curtain," which metaphorically surrounds Orange County California and keeps it seemingly free of liberal thinking. It was the first time I heard honest discussions about gay men in which not everybody found homosexuality abominable. Years later I would learn that studies confirmed my feelings, that, indeed, a significant decrease in cultural homophobia had occurred during this time. It was a trend that continued throughout the 1990s.[2]

Not only was the issue of gays in the military important for raising general discussion about homosexuality, but the discussion also made Americans aware that gay men *did* exist in the highly masculinized arena of war-making. And while I doubt most people thought of this in more complex terms, the mere fact that the question was raised also meant to me that homosexuality was compatible not only with masculinity, but with hypermasculinity. As a closeted athlete, and as a closeted athletics coach, this gave me hope. It meant that if gay men could exist within the highly masculinized and homophobic armed forces, they might also exist in other highly masculinized institutions—like the institution I had devoted my life to as a way of hiding my sexuality from others—institutions like sport.

Because of these reasons, 1993 was also the year that I came out of the closet as an openly gay distance running coach at a rather conservative high school in Southern California.[3] As an openly gay coach, I experienced just how important sexuality is in America. Whereas before I was a privileged, white, middle-class, athletic (some would say) good-looking, young, ostensibly heterosexual male, things changed after coming out of the closet. Overnight I had gone from being known as the hilarious teacher and revered coach to the faggot teacher and the faggot coach. My athletes went from being the pride of the school (we were quite successful) to the shame of the school, affected by a guilt-by-association process relating to my stigma. In other words, because their coach was gay, they too were considered gay. My athletes and I began to face the discrimination that went hand in hand with the stigma of the time. Athletes ceased to join my team, and those remaining found themselves immersed in daily battles with ignorance. Some that even threatened their safety.

My status as the first publicly recognized gay male coach in the United States went relatively unnoticed until 1996, when a football player brutally assaulted one of my heterosexual athletes who he assumed to be gay because he was on my team. We had had several problems with the football team before. In fact, we had been moved from one locker room to the next in order to protect my team from football-player harassment. After a near fight, in which several football players decided that we could no longer use "their" locker room, we finally ended up moving into a small, locked bathroom, effectively segregated away from the rest of the athletic community. The brutal attack saw the football player knock my runner to the ground, where he sat atop him and began pounding at his face. The assailant even tried to gouge my athlete's eyes out. When a bystander begged him to stop the beating, he proclaimed, "It ain't over until the faggot's dead." My runner knew that he had to escape.

Although his vision was bloodied, he managed to squirm from beneath the large football player and run away. He climbed a fence that the pursuing football player was too large to scale and got away. He was left with four broken facial bones and for the rest of his life will have two screws through his palate. The police department reported the incident as "mutual combat," *not* a hate crime or aggravated assault, and the assailant received no time behind bars. Essentially, it seemed that he largely got away with it.

It was clear to me that the incident did not "just happen." The beating was influenced by factors, people, perhaps even institutions. Immediately I suspected that his actions were covertly encouraged by what seemed a lack of administrative action against those who previously displayed hostility toward my team. Why had his parents not been called the day he physically prevented my athletes from entering the locker room? Why had he met no punitive measures? Essentially, the high school administration may have sent an institutional message of support for the continuation of violence. Such homophobia is, of course, not surprising, especially when one considers that the assailant had been socialized into the homophobic language of masculinity embedded in combative team sports. Perhaps his training served as a powerful socialization into the norm of violent masculinity. It is this socialization, and America's blind obsession for sports, that I maintain is responsible for *most* of America's social ills. Masculinity in America, I maintain, is a public health crisis.

In addition to a predictable anger that lingered for years, I was also left with an intellectual angst over not fully understanding how such intense homophobia could develop within an individual and how educated people like the school principal could dismiss such violence as simply a fight. I was not satisfied with the "boys will be boys" or "people hate what they don't understand" rationalizations. I sensed the matter was much more complicated and that the beating was attributable to the manner in which the assailant was socialized into masculinity, the value of physical brutality he learned in sport, and the culmination of many years of growing aggression and hostility that largely went uncontested by the administration. Essentially, I was more clear in understanding why he assaulted my runner; what I was less clear about was why the school's administration had been so unwilling to stop the harassment before it got to the point of serious bodily injury.

My master's in sport psychology had equipped me to understand how to help athletes negotiate personal waters in society, but it failed to explain the origins of social problems in the first place. For example, I had been trained to help athletes negotiate the pressures of competition, but not to examine our cultural addiction for competition. Realizing that my training was insufficient to fully understand the social dynamics that culminated in this beating, I returned to school to earn a doctorate in sociology.[4]

As a sociologist, I now better understand the operation of hegemony. I understand the near-seamless manner in which groups of people can maintain power by policing ideologies through the threat of force and the willing compliance of those oppressed. I have grown to understand the complex role that sport plays in society, particularly in the production of a violent, homophobic form of masculinity. I now have a much better understanding of the unfortunate circumstances by which the structure of sport in society influences many boys to develop such a narrow sense of masculinity, as well as a strong hatred for homosexuality. I understand the role sport plays in teaching boys to accept risk, to out-group others, and to use violence in order to gain masculine capital by physically subjugating other men.

Throughout my intellectual growth, and as a result of my research, I slowly saw my love for sport dissolve. It is not that I don't enjoy the thrill of a close competition anymore, or that I don't cherish my long runs with friends in the hills. It is not that I don't see many of the positive attributes of sport, it is mostly *how* we do sport in this culture that bothers me. I no longer see sport in the problem-free manner that I used to. I now understand the relationship between sport and men to be a complicated and highly contentious one, and I have a better and more disturbing understanding of that relationship.

The years since Clinton's election, and the years since my athlete was beaten, have continued to bring tremendous cultural and institutional gains for gay Americans. Vermont passed civil unions in 2000, giving gays and lesbians the rights of marriage in that state, and in the summer of 2003, the U.S. Supreme Court ruled that the thirteen states with remaining sodomy laws could no longer enforce them. Just five months after this landmark ruling, the Massachusetts State Supreme Court granted gays and lesbians the right to marry, opening the door to constitutional challenges for gay marriage across the nation.

These court cases, and myriad other legal municipal and state rulings, have sparked public debates regarding the status of gays and lesbians in nearly every American institution, including cherished American institutions like the Boy Scouts (which has come under increasing fire for its discriminatory practices), and most Judeo-Christian churches (which frequently fracture over issues pertaining to homosexuality) as well. Furthermore, gays and lesbians are increasingly represented on television, gaining popularity not only in a large number of shows with gay and lesbian characters, but also with shows *about* gays and lesbians (like *Queer as Folk*). *Queer Eye for the Straight Guy* even features five gay men schooling heterosexual men in the ways of fashion and culture.[5] It seems that in the new millennium Americans (particularly urban Americans) are increasingly less tolerant of both institutional and cultural homophobia.

Going into this research, I wondered how the decreasing homophobia in American culture might affect men and what it meant for gay athletes. Was sport as homophobic as it was when I coached in the mid-1990s? Would my athlete have been beaten today? It was these questions, centering around the relationship between homosexuality and masculinity, that lead to the research for this book.

It should be noted that this book primarily addresses the issues of *gays* in sport. This is, however, not to say that I am not interested in the experience of bisexual men, lesbians, or bisexual women in sport. I am. However, I have necessarily limited the scope of the research in order to make the work manageable and in order to be able to draw generalizations about the group studied. The experience of women, and particularly lesbians, in sport is a worthy subject that deserves a broad and comprehensive investigation of its own. Fortunately, many of those studies have already been conducted and an excellent book has been written on the relationship between lesbians and sport. On this subject, I highly recommend Pat Griffin's (1998) *Strong Women, Deep Closets*. In fact, it is the book I modeled this research on. Still, there are many important similarities between the experiences of lesbians and gays in sport and they are discussed in chapter 8.

Readers should also note that while this research is conducted on openly gay athletes, in no way am I trying to essentialize or reify the term *gay*. I fully recognize that as an identity category, gay and homosexual are socially constructed and historically fluid. I also recognize that the term *gay* can be used in order to describe one's sexual behaviors, one's sexual desires (sometimes called sexual orientation), and one's sexual identity. For example, one can see that it is quite possible for a man to engage in heterosexual sex, but desire sex exclusively with other men. In this case we might say that his behavior was heterosexual, while his orientation is homosexual (gay). Wouldn't that pose an interesting question as to what his "identity" was? Finally, the same categorization and fluidity can be found when it comes to gender. There exists great fluidity in what it means to biologically be a man, and fluidity in what it means to act masculine. Combined with the fluidity of sexuality, the possibilities are endless.

This book serves as a deconstruction of masculinity. It does not, however, attempt to deconstruct sex, sexuality, sexual orientation, gender, or gender identity. Therefore, in order to avoid post-structural complications, I've solely relied on the informants' self-identification of sexuality. That is to say that these athletes are considered gay by self-proclamation and self-categorization. I have avoided complicating affairs by only including men who self-identified in this way. Thus, I do not account for self-identified bisexual men, heterosexual men, or men who consider themselves MSM (men who sleep with men). In this way, the informants represented in this work maintain a sexual orientation, identity, and behaviors that are consistent with *their* notion of gay.

Along those lines, my theoretical positioning falls in line with strategic empiricism and strategic essentialism. While I agree with the tenets of post-structuralism in that there are no categories and no obtainable truths in the world, it is also my contention that as long as people are oppressed by categories that don't really exist, I will go about pretending that they do exist. In other words, to me, the important debate is not whether something called homosexuality or heterosexuality exists or not, it is whether people's lives are adversely affected by the simple belief that these categories exist. To this extent, at a purely intellectual level I agree that they do not, but at a practical level, they do.

Finally, it should also be noted that I am a firm believer in identity politics. While I truly understand the limitations of identity and regret the exclusive nature of identities, I have settled upon its limitations and embraced its power in constructing social change for the liberation of oppressed people. This position might appear obvious in the pages of the text, but be assured that it has not influenced me to exaggerate the positive findings and downplay the negative. I've been as true to my data as possible.

OVERVIEW

There are not a lot of openly gay men in sport today. But if gay men are present in any significant numbers in sport, then the declining degree of cultural homophobia that has led gay men to come out in the larger society might exacerbate the emergence of gay men from the sporting closet as well.[6] This book examines the stories of those who have both come out and those who remain closeted in sport. It examines their stories from a sociological perspective, which is to say that while I am interested in their individual stories, I am more interested in their collective stories. I am interested in what similarities occur among gay athletes.

This book examines the issue from a variety of perspectives. Not only does it tell the story of openly gay athletes in sport, but it examines the effect that coaches, institutions, and broader concepts of masculinity play in shaping their experience. It also examines homophobia from a number of perspectives, and realizes that there is no one reason for homophobia. For example, homophobia may be socialized in a top-down process in which athletes simply adopt homophobia in order to win the adoration of peers and coaches; it may stem from the denial of their own same-sex desires; or it may represent a prejudice with roots in religious intolerance. These various sources of homophobia imply that there is no one "cure" for the problem of homophobia in sport. In fact, even though homophobia seems to be on the ever-increasing decline in American society, the collective stories in this book imply that sport remains a bastion of hegemonic masculinity, homophobia, and misogyny. That is to say that sport remains an arena that reproduces a desire for the toughest form of masculinity, an attitude in which "men are men;" an arena in which homosexuality, femininity, and other assumed "weaknesses" are not perceived as being conducive to the ultimate quest for victory. What this research does question is whether the criteria for masculinity are softening. Is the notion of conservative masculinity growing less conservative?

These stories suggest that it is. The athletes in this book also illustrate that hegemony is never seamless, that there are cracks of resistance in every social system. Many of the athletes in this book represent that crack. The boys and men studied for this book have begun to challenge sport as a site of orthodox masculine construction. Sometimes they simply contest sport by simply being honest about their sexuality; and other times they fight for institutional equality through legal challenges or media coverage. Although (at present) it is mostly white, highly valued athletes (that is to say those who are the best on their teams) with strong social support from their friends and coach who seem to feel safe enough to publicly emerge from the closets in any real numbers, this research clearly proves that homosexuality is not antithetical to athleticism; that gay athletes are in the game and can beat heterosexual men at their own game.

I suggest that the openly gay, trailblazing athletes researched for this book also help undo years of socialized fears for other gay and straight athletes. As this book goes to print, I am beginning to see evidence of this. In other words, when a gay athlete comes out on his team, not only does he make it safer for other gay athletes to come out, but he makes it safer for his heterosexual teammates to admit that they are not as homophobic as they previously portrayed themselves to be, or that they frequently (and quickly) lose their homophobia altogether. This will eventually help lower caliber athletes to also emerge from the sporting closets, and will help homophobia as a whole to wither away.

Unfortunately, not all is rosy with this research. This research also shows that the institutions that govern sport have been virtually non-respondent in addressing homophobia in athletics. Institutions are generally slower to change than individual attitudes, but the institution of sport may be even slower to change because it represents a closed-loop system. It is important to remember that those who run the institution of sport (coaches, managers, and administrators) were at once athletes themselves, schooled in the language of violent, homophobic masculinity, and they tend to reproduce themselves. This, combined with the fact that there is no formal education required to be a youth, high school, or professional coach, and only minimal education required to be a university coach, enables orthodox notions of masculinity to be constructed and reproduced in the same manner that they were during the early part of the twentieth century. Essentially, conservative attitudes are passed down from generation to generation without much intervention. Just as women have done so for the past thirty years, however, gay male athletes are beginning to challenge the ability of sport to continue to do business as usual. Because of their contestation of sport as a masculinizing institution and because of the threat that gay athletes pose to the "business as usual" attitude, this research shows that gay male athletes are hotly contested at all levels of organized sport.

How gay male athletes are contested proves to be nuanced. For example, this research found virtually no overt violence against gay athletes. That is to say that none of the athletes in this study were beaten or physically harassed. This, however, is not to say that gay athletes are treated as equals on the sporting turf. This book highlights the complex processes by which gay athletes are overtly and covertly discriminated against, and even how gay athletes cooperate in their own oppression through the prolific use of discourse. Oppression largely appears in the form of don't ask, don't tell, a covert system of stigmatization that attempts to nullify the gay athlete's agency and visibility. Furthermore, the scarcity of openly gay athletes is exacerbated by the fact that once an athlete does come out, he generally feels that he no longer needs the representation of heterosexuality that sport once provided him and usually drops out of sport.[7]

Finally, and of particular use to the gay athlete, this book also highlights that while homophobia in sport presents itself in nuanced and complex ways, it remains predictable along a number of variables. These variables can be strategically shaped in order to promote a culture more conducive to gay athleticism. To help gay athletes navigate their teams, the final chapter is designed to help apply the research findings to one's actual experience. It is a how-to that is free of academic jargon and is based on my extensive involvement in helping athletes come out to their families and teams.

In addition to proving helpful to gay athletes, and interesting to gay men, this book is significant to the field of sociology. While it is not the first to discuss the relationship between homosexuality and sport, it is the first with a sufficient sample size to thoroughly examine the lives of *openly gay* male athletes. It is therefore important to the understanding of masculinities in contemporary America because the mere fact that this research can now be conducted signals that something is changing in our culture in regard to homosexuality and masculinity. It contests dominant theories regarding the relationship between homosexuality and masculinity and it adds theoretical insight into our understanding of sex and gender. This book is particularly useful in helping us better understand the relationship between homophobia and the construction of rigid, masculine boundaries. Ultimately it serves as evidence to my contention that significant changes to our sex/gender system are underway in American society, and that American masculinity is perhaps growing less rigid in recent years.

OUTLINE

Chapter 1 lays the foundation for the discussion between gay athletes and sport by examining notions of American masculinity and homophobia. It familiarizes the reader with terms that will be used throughout the book and generally lays the groundwork for the book. It also explains the context and methods in which this research took place.

Chapter 2 illustrates the use of homophobia in the construction of masculine hierarchies, and how those hierarchies center on athleticism among boys and men. It examines the construction of heterosexual masculinity and how the dominance and oppression of other boys and men are used to establish masculine worth among peers. It also examines the relationship between homosexuality and masculinity, and the threat that homosexuality poses to the maintenance of patriarchy. It clarifies different forms of masculinity, and highlights how they operate in the masculinized culture of team sports. In doing so, it lays down the framework necessary to understand the relationship that gay male athletes maintain to both masculinity and the institution of sport.

Chapter 3 examines the current relationship between gay male athleticism and sport. It looks at why homosexuality is often thought to be incompatible with masculinity and examines sport as a masculinizing institution. It theorizes why gay men may be attracted to or repelled from sport, and asks whether athletes may be over or under-represented in sport as compared to the broader population. Most importantly, this chapter examines the role that gay athletes play in challenging sport as a masculinizing, and homophobic, institution.

Chapter 4 examines the structures that have enabled the institution of sport to resist change and remain a bastion of conservative sexual and gender ideology. It asks how, in a time of greatly decreasing cultural and institutional homophobia, institutions of sport have remained steadfast in their production of a homophobic and conservative gender ideology. It shows that there are three interwoven factors. The first is that sports are a near total institution in which athletes find it difficult to escape a single-minded way of viewing sex and gender. The second is that sports are a segregated institution that prevents heterosexual men from hearing the narratives of women. And the third is that the institution of sport is a closed-loop system in that it lacks critical self-examination. When taken together, these factors enable sport to near-seamlessly reproduce itself as an institution of orthodox masculine expression.

Chapter 5 examines the fears that athletes have about coming out, and explores their coming out narratives. It shows the release of their fears and the sense of elation that most feel after coming out. The chapter also shows, however, that this elation may also blind them to some negative aspects of their coming out.

Chapter 6 examines how gay athletes attempt to refute the stigma of effeminacy that is associated with gay men and become more accepted into the sporting realm. Primarily, it examines the raising of masculine capital in order to mitigate the stigma of being gay. Although it is recognized that gay athletes do not fit the definition of hegemonic masculinity because of their sexuality, they may still raise their masculine capital by acting in accord with the other tenets of orthodox masculinity. This is to say that by being "a big wheel" and "giving them hell" a gay male athlete can potentially mitigate some of the stigma associated with his sexuality.

Chapter 7 discusses the culture of silence that pervades gay athletes and their teams through a don't ask, don't tell culture that is similar to the official don't ask, don't tell policy of the U.S. Armed Forces. It clearly shows that the transformative potential of gay athletes in sport is mitigated through the silencing of gay discourse, identity, and behaviors; and it shows that a gay identity is also nullified through the normalization of homophobic discourse, such as the prolific use of the word *fag* in sport.

Chapter 8 examines many of micro/macro variables that are also likely to influence the homonegative or homopositive attitudes on any given team. It looks at the attitude of the coaches, the help of team-mates, the particular problems that gay athletes of color face due to the intersection of marginalized identities, and the attitudes of the institution to which the team belongs as having an impact on the attitudes on a team. It also theorizes that American-originated sports might carry more homophobia with them than sports of European origins.

Chapter 9 examines what Michael Messner calls "the center of sports," the world of professional sports and professional closets. It highlights the institutionalization of homophobia in professional athletics and asks tough questions about the relationship between professional sports and gay athletes. One question it does not address, however, is whether gay athletes at this elite level of sport *exist* or not. We know they do. In fact, three of them were interviewed for this book. Rather, some of the important questions that this chapter examines are in what numbers do they exist, why don't they come out, and how will they come out.

The final chapter helps gay athletes, and those concerned with the culture of sport, to put to use the lessons of the book. It is a how-to that helps the athlete come out to his team, and helps him secure the best possible reception once he does. The recipe for coming out is based on the years of experience I have in helping athletes come out, as well as the empirical evidence that this research shows makes a difference. It also provides gay coaches with practical advice on how to come out, and it should be equally as useful for heterosexuals who desire to make a difference in the athletic setting.

1

Warming Up

THE LINK BETWEEN SPORT AND HOMOPHOBIA

Sport is theorized to be one of the last bastions of cultural and institutional homophobia in North America. The institution produces an orthodox form of masculinity that is rigid and exclusive for many types of men and most women. It is predicated upon homophobia and misogyny and is even theorized to be crucial to the reproduction of patriarchy in American culture.[1] In fact, sport remains so homophobic that many (ostensibly heterosexual) athletes maintain that the hypermasculinity exhibited in sports nullifies the possibility of gays even existing in their space, even though they are well aware that gay men exist in large numbers in the culture at large. To them, homosexuality is synonymous with physical weakness and emotional frailty, and the term *gay athlete* therefore remains an oxymoron (although gay is often used as a synonym for homosexual pertaining to either gender, in this book I use gay to contrast with lesbian).[2]

But the presence of extreme homophobia in sport does not necessarily mean that gay boys and men would be driven away from competitive team sports. In his influential book *The Arena of Masculinity*, Brian Pronger said (1990, 4), "Not all homosexual men and boys avoid athletics because of its masculine significance."[3] In fact,

Pronger theorizes that gay men might actually be drawn to sport because of the veneer of heterosexuality it provides gay males. Competitive team sports, he argues, are a great place to hide one's sexual orientation, as athletes are shrouded in a cloud of scripted heterosexuality. He even maintains that some gay athletes might be inclined to stick with sport in an attempt to continually rectify the feeling of femininity that comes with the stigma of homosexuality.

Gay men might also be drawn to competitive athletics because the sporting arena remains one of the most gender-segregated institutions in Western cultures. Men's sporting teams beam with young, toned, sexualized, and highly masculinized bodies. These bodies serve as a homoerotic enticement for gay boys and men, and Pronger suggests that they bring out latent homoerotic desires from heterosexual men as well. He suggests that, as an artifact of this extreme homogenization, homophobia may appear as a way to nullify the homoeroticism of the sporting arena. Extreme homophobia prevents men from acting upon their stigmatized desires.

Attitudes toward homosexuality, however, are quickly changing in North America. Indeed, data shows that between 1988 and 1991 only 14 percent of those surveyed said that "homosexuality is not wrong at all," but in 1994 that number dramatically increased to 23 percent.[4] Throughout the latter half of the twentieth century, Americans have steadily grown more aware that homosexuality exists, and by the late 1990s three-quarters of all Americans knew a gay or lesbian personally.[5] This has helped reduce homophobia because studies show that the most effective way to reduce homophobia is by having a gay or lesbian acquaintance.[6] Perhaps more significantly, there has been a well-documented and remarkable decrease in disapproval of same-sex relations since 1998 (Widmer et al. 2002, 349–65). Gary Gates, a demographer at the Urban Institute in Washington, D.C., says, "The stigma of being gay is disappearing. This is a huge change. Gay people in general are feeling more comfortable in society, and society is feeling more comfortable with gay people."[7]

Theoretically, the trend of rapidly reducing cultural homophobia may have a profound impact on both the American sex/gender system and the manner in which masculinity is constructed. If masculinity is predicated upon homophobia, and homophobia is the chief policing agent against behaviors coded as feminine, then the reduction of cultural homophobia would lead to a significant change to the manner in which masculinity is both constructed and maintained. For example, reduced policing of masculine boundaries should allow men to occupy feminized social space with fewer stigmas. In other words, the cultural reduction in homophobia may lead toward a softening of masculinity through the less rigid policing of its gendered borders. Other research suggests that this may already be occurring in some contexts.[8]

In an exploration of masculinity-related issues throughout two hundred American cities, researchers found that American men aged twenty-one to forty-eight were in an emerging wave of men who chafed at the restrictions of traditional male roles.[9] The data (focusing on masculine attitudes toward consumerism) show that men are increasingly buying products and services that are culturally perceived as feminine. For example, the findings demonstrate that heterosexual men are increasingly visiting day spas and buying designer clothing. The research received a great deal of media attention for introducing the term *metrosexual* into the lexicon. A metrosexual is said to represent a heterosexual male who permits himself to act in culturally ascribed "gay" ways. The tremendous popularity of the television show *Queer Eye for the Straight Guy,* which features a heterosexual man being instructed by five queer men on how to groom, decorate, and entertain in a cosmopolitan manner, highlights the phenomenon.[10]

Furthermore, some of my other research suggests that decreasing cultural homophobia has enabled the creation of an inclusive form of masculinity in highly feminized institutions. My (2004) work on heterosexual male cheerleaders and heterosexual male nurses shows that while a good number of men still establish their masculinity in opposition to homosexuality and femininity, an equal number of men have begun to construct their masculinity around a more inclusive model. These men do not base as much of their masculinity on homophobia or misogyny, and they are much more likely to associate with gay men and women. The form of masculinity they perform is also more inclusive to gay men.

Highlighting the affect that the cultural reduction of homophobia may have on attitudes within what Michael Messner calls "the center of sports" (team sports such as football, basketball, and hockey), a 1998 anonymous survey of 175 National Football League first-year players found that attitudes in the NFL are *not* monolithically homophobic, nor are all players resolute that their teams are entirely heterosexual.[11] While none of the 175 players admitted to being gay (and all think that less than 7% of the NFL is gay), 43.4% believed that there are at least some gay players on their teams, and 8.3% claimed to be aware (or reasonably sure) of gay players on their team. Five of the 175 first-year players even indicated that they were "friends with a homosexual player," a surprisingly high number when one considers that these were players who had only been in the NFL for a year and had therefore not yet been able to develop social networks of trust. Similarly, one closeted professional athlete told me that he had met at least eleven other professional gay hockey players in his career.

When one considers the high degree of homophobia that team sport athletes are reputed to maintain, it is astounding that 76.4% of first-year NFL players reported that they would have no problems playing next to a gay teammate. While the number decreases the more intimate shared space becomes (58% indicated that they would be comfortable sharing a locker next to a gay teammate, and 42.7% indicated that they would be comfortable sharing a hotel room with a known gay player), these statistics indicate that homophobia in the NFL may be on the same trajectory as homophobia in the culture at large—rapidly decreasing.[12]

If the softening of masculinity continues, the older conservative form of masculinity may be less alluring, and the masculinizing context of sport may have to adjust to the new version of masculinity or risk losing its effect on socializing boys and men in the culture as a whole. In other words, if everything changes around sport, sport will either have to change or it will lose its social significance and be viewed as a vestige of an archaic model of masculinity. I argue that our culture *may already* be seeing the beginning stages of this. I argue that although the institution of sport has lagged behind mainstream culture, it has been impacted by the larger social climate. In short, the research data disseminated in this book leads me to maintain that the hegemony sport once maintained over the production of orthodox masculinity is not seamless and that it is under contestation. Gay athletes represent that challenge.

As a sociologist, I examine all social arrangements with a critical eye. Questioning metanarratives, myths, stereotypes, and hegemonic processes of social matters enables sociologists to better comprehend sport and its relation to society—apart from whatever the dominant culture beliefs might be. I use social-feminist thinking, including viewing power and stratification as being embedded within institutions, in order to ask critical questions about the relationship between sport, gender, and homosexuality. Specifically, I am interested in understanding how homophobia operates within the institution of sport, how it is reproduced within the institution, and how gay men negotiate this homophobic space both in and out of the closet. I question whether the presence of openly gay athletes undermines hegemonic masculinity or whether the collective adherence to masculinity enables the institution of sport to resist gay male participation by instead masculinizing these men into complicity. I examine the relationship between homosexuality and sport so that we might better understand the variables that influence the concealment of homosexuality and the celebration of heterosexuality in sporting culture.

I examine sports that are considered to be at the center of masculine production (such as football and basketball), those in the semiperiphery (such as soccer, tennis, and track), and those at the periphery of sport (cheerleading, bowling, and figure skating) in order to see if homophobia operates differently throughout the stratification. Also, in order to better understand the operation of homophobia throughout the institutional progression of sport, I interview athletes from high school, college, and the professional ranks. As Michael Messner (2002) has theorized, the more competitive the sport, the less elbow room there is for variable conceptions of athletic masculinity. But because I was not able to locate and interview enough professional gay athletes from which to generalize, in chapter 9 I draw upon a number of secondary sources in order to better understand the operation of homophobia in professional team sports.

METHODS

I used qualitative methods to analyze the institution of sport from an institutional, interactional, and gendered perspective. Using grounded theory as a way of generating theory from qualitative data, I analyze the relationship between the hegemonic process of masculinity and the social realities created by human actors.[13] I interviewed a total of sixty gay male athletes from North American high schools, colleges, and professional sporting teams, intentionally limiting the study to school-based and professional sports. I obtained informants through convenience and snowball sampling. About half of those athletes came to me after visiting my website devoted to gay athletes, www.EricAndersonPhD.com, and others came to me through a posting on www.OutSports.com. I used snowball sampling to acquire more informants from some of these contacts.

Athletes included in this study were actively playing or had played within one year of the interview. I did not include athletes from recreational or club-level sporting teams, athletes who strongly identified as bisexual, athletes who identified as heterosexual, or athletes who identified as being heterosexual but have sex with men. All athletes were between the ages of seventeen and twenty-five with the exception of the professional athletes, and most were middle class. The sample contained only nine athletes of color, not because I specifically desired to study white athletes, but because white athletes were the majority of openly gay athletes that I was able to locate. Because of the small numbers of athletes of color, there may not be enough evidence to draw general conclusions about the intersectionality between race and sexual orientation, but a thorough discussion of the intersectionality of race with homosexuality is presented in chapter 8. All athletes' identities have been protected, regardless of whether they were original or secondary sources, with the exception of those who are public figures (such as professional athletes who have publicly revealed their homosexuality).

The sixty interviews sometimes occurred in person but most often were telephone (taped and transcribed) interviews that lasted from 60 to 120 minutes. In these interviews I questioned athletes about their socialization into sport, what variables have led to their coming out or remaining closeted, how they negotiated cultural stereotypes in the production of their own gendered and sexual identities, and how they may have attempted to publicly mitigate the stigma of their sexual identity. Of these sixty athletes, forty were out of the closet on their teams, meaning that they had either explicitly told (at least three) members of their team or that there was an assumption about their sexuality from some other method of public declaration. Openly gay athletes represent all hierarchical levels of sport, although there were fewer informants that were out of the closet in college than high school and very few who were out of the closet as professional athletes (and all from marginal or peripheral sports).

The remaining twenty closeted athletes were also represented by sports from throughout the masculine and institutional hierarchies of sport, including two active professional team sport athletes (football and hockey). These athletes were interviewed to better understand the social circumstances that led some athletes to come out to their teams and to understand the operation of fear in the self-silencing of gay athletes.

I also used dozens of secondary sources to acquire data about the experiences of gay male athletes in sport, as well as a number of interviews with heterosexual athletes, coaches, and female athletes. I read autobiographies by ex-professional athletes, articles written in popular press books or magazines, articles written on Outsports.com and other gay athlete websites, and accounts of the experiences of gay athletes from several other academic investigations. Also, in order to better understand the institutional effect on homophobia in athletic culture, I conducted three hundred hours of participant observation in the sport of cheerleading, where gay male athletes are represented in large numbers (approximately twenty percent).

The compilation of data from interviews, participant observation, secondary sources, and popular press has given me a better understanding of the complex relationship between homophobia, masculinity, sport, and gay male athletes. In the chapters that follow, the reader learns to view this relationship in a more nuanced perspective, seeing that sport is not monolithically homophobic and understanding under what conditions a gay athlete is given more leeway in a highly masculinized arena.

2

Sport, Masculinity, and Hegemonic Oppression

ONE ATHLETE'S STORY:
DALE, HIGH SCHOOL FOOTBALL PLAYER

In 1997 I received a lengthy e-mail from an individual too afraid to tell me his name, or where he went to school, writing only, "I am a high school football player and I am really good." He continued:

> I've always known I liked guys. I never really liked sports, but I really have no choice. I was pushed into sports by my dad because he wanted his son to grow up to be a real man.... High school football is all about manliness and toughness. It's a true hell on earth for me, and the homophobia is unbelievable. My coaches try to motivate us to hit harder, crunch more, or throw farther by calling us fags all the time. And if you can't do something, or mess it up, you get called a fag. My teammates call all the guys fags, but I think that if they really knew I was, I'd get beaten up. So I just go about trying to prove I'm straight by dating women and talking about girls all the time.

The tone of the e-mail soon changed to the genre of a confessional, particularly when it came to highlighting his part in the production of homophobia. In addition to expressing victimization and personal distress over the profusion of homophobia within his sport, he also reported active engagement in it:

> I have to call other guys fags, especially other athletes. I am ashamed to admit it, but I am one of those guys calling the runners and swimmers fags. I mean, if I don't, then the guys on my team might think I am gay. So, basically, I have to call them fags, or fear being called one myself.

The final paragraphs of the e-mail reflected the athlete's depression. "I lie on my bed and cry at night. I pray for an answer but there is none. I have parents who are proud of me, and I have friends and respect at school. I seem to have it all, but in reality I feel like I have nothing." He concluded with, "You wouldn't know it if you met me, but inside, I'm just so afraid. Anyhow, thanks for listening, Coach." The letter went unsigned.

I e-mailed him back, and we began corresponding. I learned that his name was Dale, and eventually I met him in person. Dale graduated from the oppressive, hypermasculine environment of high school football and used the bittersweet laurels to earn a college scholarship, where he "played" for a U.S. military academy, enslaving himself to masculine and homophobic enterprises throughout college. He graduated the academy and was contractually obliged to enter the military, where he remains a willing prisoner of narrow masculine expression.

The military gives Dale a few weeks off each year, and in those fleeting moments he attempts to absorb a year's worth of gay life—taking a deep breath of freedom before again submerging back into the depths of homophobia. On leave, however, he is visibly ecstatic, like an animal escaped from its cage. The question, of course, is why. Why does Dale continue to enchain himself to hypermasculine, homophobic, and violent institutions such as football and the U.S. military?

Dale has spent his life attempting to live up to the expectations of other men. He is well versed in "taking one for the team" and doing what one is told. Although he wanted to be in his elementary school's band, his father forced him into football, believing it would make him a real man. A man who is emotionless, yet prone to rage; in control, yet trained to follow; physically robust, yet willing to risk health; ostensibly heterosexual, yet unable to prove it. Through the tragedy of talent, high school football took him to college and college to compulsory military service, symbolically graduating from one boxing ring to the next. Dale's masculinization in sport, it would seem, has strongly helped influence him to live between the narrow sheets of masculine acceptability. It is a location that hegemonic forces have taught him to occupy, and after all these years, perhaps this is where he wants to be.

MASCULINITY AS HEGEMONIC OPPRESSION

This chapter examines the construction of heterosexual masculinity and how hegemonic processes of dominance and oppression are used in the process. It examines the relationship between homosexuality and masculinity and the threat that homosexuality poses to the maintenance of patriarchy. It clarifies different forms of masculinity and highlights how they operate in the masculinized culture of team sports. In doing so, it lays down the framework necessary to understand the relationship that the gay male athletes maintain to both masculinity and the institution of sport.

Sociologists recognize that there are various forms of masculinities found among differing cultures, and that there is no one way of being masculine within any given culture.[1] We recognize that the definitions of what it means to be masculine shift within the same culture over time in response to social forces, and that not all masculinities are treated equally. In his book *Masculinities* (1995), Robert Connell gives an excellent discussion of the various and often competing forms of masculinities in Western cultures, especially in regard to understanding the operation of hegemony as it relates to masculinity.

Hegemony, a concept developed by Antonio Gramsci (1971), refers to a particular form of dominance in which a ruling class legitimates its position and secures the acceptance—if not outright support—from those classes below them. While a feature to Gramsci's version of hegemony is that there is often the threat of rules or force structuring a belief, the key element to hegemony is that force cannot be the causative factor in order to elicit complicity. Rather, people must believe that their subordinated place is both *right* and *natural*. For example, hegemony is fortified when a slave believes his rightful place is that of slave (a racist society), when a woman believes she should be subservient to a man (a sexist society), when a poor person believes that he does not merit wealth (a classist society), or when a gay man believes he is undeserving of the same rights as a straight man (a heterosexist society).[2] Hegemony has therefore been a key concept in understanding oppression of women, racial and ethnic minorities, and the lower classes in American society. Of relevance to this research, the concept of hegemony has only recently been applied to a more nuanced understanding of how men and their masculinity and sexuality are stratified in society.[3]

Much of the study of masculinities centers on how men construct hierarchies that yield decreasing benefits the farther removed one is from the flagship version, something known as hegemonic masculinity. This form of masculinity is privileged in social structures, particularly in the institution of sport. While it is difficult (perhaps impossible) to come up with an archetype of what *exactly* hegemonic masculinity is, psychologist Robert Brannon (1976) has come up with four rules that have influenced but not limited the definition I use in this research. Brannon's rules are (1) no sissy stuff; (2) be a big wheel; (3) be a sturdy oak; (4) give 'em hell.

While Brannon's definitions foremost include not acting in ways associated with femininity, data from this research suggest that the primary element toward being a man in the hegemonic form in contemporary culture is first and foremost, not to *be, act,* or *behave* in ways attributed to gay men, something gender theorists have largely overlooked. This means that North American masculinity is based on gender-exclusive heterosexual behavior—a homophobic ascription similar to the one-drop rule in which a person of mixed racial background is ascribed as being black by having even one distant black ancestor. When applied to masculine sexualities, the one-drop rule asserts that one homosexual act necessarily defines one as a homosexual. This homophobic ascription conflates behaviors with identity. In other words, homosexual *acts* in American culture, whether active or passive, have been uniquely, and publicly, equated with a homosexual *identity,* despite the fact that self-identified heterosexual men frequently engaged in same-sex behavior while publicly and privately maintaining the identity of heterosexuality.[4]

Hegemonic masculinity not only requires that a male maintain 100 percent heterosexual desires and behaviors, but that he must continually prove that he is heterosexual. In a homophobic culture this is best accomplished through the sexual objectification of women and the public discussing of heterosexual "conquests" (something often exemplified in locker-room talk).[5] But this is also accomplished through the use of homophobic discourse. Frequent use of the words *fag* and *faggot* as well as the expression *that's so gay* are used to disassociate oneself from homosexuality even though only about half the men who use it mean it in a derisive manner (Burn 2000). Sociologist Tim Curry (1991) maintains that it is often not enough for heterosexuals to simply say that they are not gay; he posits that they must also behave in *vehemently* homophobic ways if they desire to cast off homosexual suspicion.[6] In this way homophobia can be used as a vessel toward the continual maintenance of a defensive heterosexual identity in an attempt to prove that the speaker is not gay.

Furthermore, Brannon and other gender scholars assign primary importance to a durable sociological understanding that contemporary masculinity is strongly based on patriarchal opposition to femininity.[7] Feminist gender scholars such as psychologist William Pollack (1998) and sociologist David Plummer (1999) have suggested that North American men avoid effeminacy because it is associated with homosexuality, maintaining that this rigid contention carries with it a measurable cost that begins as early as the first grade. Pollack maintains that fear of homosexual stigmatization limits males from engaging with anything that is designated feminine.[8] Sociologist Michael Messner says that men must, therefore, avoid at all cost emotion, compassion, and the appearance of vulnerability, weakness, and fear. If one becomes too emotionally open, he risks being labeled a sissy or a fag.[9]

In this aspect, homophobia and misogyny work together in the construction of men as "masculine." However, in order to ascend the masculine hierarchy toward the most esteemed version of hegemonic masculinity, one must also maintain a host of ascribed variables (things that one is born with, such as skin color); and one must behave in accord with a number of achieved variables too. One of the achieved variables that Brannon points out with "be a big wheel" is that men must be better than and/or be in charge of other men. This is also something described as being the top dog. Sports, of course, provide a perfect venue for the establishment of this sort of hierarchy. Sports are an arena in which men can literally battle for supremacy. Highlighting this attitude, professional baseball player Billy Bean (who came out after retiring in 1999) reports in his autobiography that his father (an ex-marine) used to tell him, "Remember, it's just you and him, and you're better" (2003, 22). His father's encouragement, although designed to reflect support to his son, instills the value of competition and *dominance* among boys and men.[10]

Brannon's other attributes, "be sturdy as an oak" and "give 'em hell," are also reflected in sporting culture. Athletes, of course, are not permitted to show fear or weakness and a stone-cold stoic game-day face must be learned. It is a performance that children learn from early childhood. One that is nicely captured in the phrases *game face* and *never let them see you sweat.* Perhaps, "give 'em hell" is the *essence* of almost any pregame pep talk, half-time speech, or motivational words from coaches and fathers. "Give them the whole nine yards"; "show them who's boss"; and "go for the throat" epitomize these attitudes.

Together, these aspects are embedded into the scripts of American men, and the more a man adheres to them, the more worth he is said to have in masculine peer culture. Similar to the ways sociologists describe human capital as the worth one has because of his skills or education, I describe this as *masculine capital.*[11] The more a male adheres to these traits, the more he raises his masculine capital—his worth among other boys and men.

MASCULINE CAPITAL, ORTHODOX MASCULINITY, AND HEGEMONIC MASCULINITY

While (1) not associating with homosexuality, (2) not associating with femininity, (3) being a big wheel, (4) being a sturdy oak, and (5) giving them hell will raise the masculine worth of an individual, they alone do not qualify one as *hegemonically* masculine. As mentioned earlier, in order to gain this status, certain ascribed variables must also be possessed. These variables are out of the locus of an individual's agency because they are primarily ascribed traits that fall in line with dominant power positions in current culture. For example, white Americans are privileged over blacks; youth is valued over the elderly; abled over disabled, and so on.

Therefore, for the purposes of this research, I use the term *orthodox masculinity* as a way to describe someone who fits all of Brannon's aforementioned tenets, but who does not necessarily maintain the ascribed traits to be considered hegemonically masculine (including not being gay). Hegemonic masculinity, by contrast, describes men who have not only achieved all of these tenets, but who also possess the ascribed variables of the dominant form of masculinity, in whichever status or context it currently exists. That is to say, men who possess hegemonic masculinity in North American culture are white, abled, heterosexual, athletic and attractive, *and* their masculine behaviors meet Brannon's tenets. Although Goffman (1963) did not use the words *hegemonic masculinity*, he effectively described such a male by saying, that in America, there is only

> one complete, unblushing male. A young, married, white, urban, Northern heterosexual, Protestant, father, of college education, fully employed, of good complexion, weight and height, and a recent record in sports. Every American male tends to look out upon the world from this perspective. . . . Any male who fails to qualify in any one of these ways is likely to view himself . . . as unworthy, incomplete, and inferior. (128)

If we were to attempt a project of describing a hegemonic male today, we might exclude the Northern, urban, and married variables; this highlights Connell's (1995) notions that hegemonic masculinity shifts according to broader social trends.

In short, if a male acts in accord with the five tenets mentioned above, he can be described as attempting to raise his *masculine capital*. If he raises his masculine capital enough, he is said to be acting in accord with *orthodox masculinity*; and if he happens to be white, good-looking, and so on, then we might say he represents *hegemonic mas-culinity*. It is important to understand these differences because they involve the intersectionality of race and other ascribed variables. For example, a black athlete could be described as meeting all of the man-dates of orthodox masculinity (and therefore maintaining extremely high masculine capital) but not be described as being hegemonically masculine because (at present) we still live in a society that favors and privileges whiteness.[12] Thus, the intersectionality of a male who repre-sents orthodox masculinity but is also of color still results in a margin-alized masculinity.

MAINTAINING MASCULINITY: HOMOPHOBIA AT WORK

Once a social space is created for or claimed by men, the maintenance of that space is collectively policed by the social sanctions placed on men's identities and behaviors as a whole. Consequently, the con-struction of masculinity is reproduced through the policing of both collective social space (such as sport) and an individual's gendered behaviors. Divergence from the stated and unstated masculine behav-iors is interpreted as subversive, for transgression undermines the desired level of masculine cohesion in the maintenance of patriarchy. Men are, therefore, ever vigilant in maintaining individual masculin-ity through near-total homosocial patrolling, as they are under the con-stant scrutiny of other men.

Sociologist Michael Kimmel (1994, 128) maintains that other men "watch us, rank us, and grant or deny our acceptance into the realm of manhood."[13] This homosocial policing is evident from early childhood, as Barrie Thorne (1999) has shown that elementary school play-grounds have been shown to be highly contested social terrains in which children explicitly define an activity or group as gendered.[14] Social sanctions already serve their purpose of intimidating boys from transgressing gendered space (or behavior) by the second grade, as boys begin to adhere to the mandates of orthodox masculinity mod-eled to them by older males.

Primarily fearing gay stigma, boys (gay and straight) rigidly police their gendered behaviors to best approximate orthodox mas-culinity, something Pollack (1998) describes as attempting to be "a real boy." He suggests that, in an attempt to displace homosexual sus-picion, boys at a very young age learn not to ask for help, hide weak-ness, and disguise fear or intimidation. They learn that they must fight when challenged and that they must sacrifice their bodies for the sake of the team. Pollack (1999, 6) calls these mechanisms a "boy code," which he maintains "puts boys and men into a gender straight-jacket that constrains not only them but everyone else, reducing us all as human beings, and eventually making us strangers to ourselves and to one another."[15]

McGuffey and Rich (1999) show that those who cross the boundary (especially boys who move into female space) risk being ostracized and accused of being a sissy or like a girl, or being (directly) accused of homosexuality.[16] Thus, transgression is met with the violent language of homophobic and misogynistic discourse. Terms like *fag* are employed to police and pressure the individual to devalue their behaviors and return to conventional masculinized space and/or behaviors, thereby securing men's privilege over women as a whole.

Athleticism is the primary axis of masculine stratification among school-aged boys, even though athleticism (or the ability to physically dominate others in sport) has little practical value in modern society outside the athletic arena. The most athletic boys occupy the top positions within the masculine hierarchy and the least athletic the bottom. Michael Messner says that, "Every elementary or high school male knows that the more athletic you are, the more popular you are" (1992, 152). High status boys stand to gain considerably from the hierarchy as they earn social prestige and secure resources for themselves. This hierarchy is maintained in high school and university cultures.

Boys with the most masculine capital are provided with many social privileges, including near immunity from homosexual suspicion. This effect is largely a product of the association between athleticism and masculinity. Because masculine capital is achieved through athleticism, and because masculinity is thought to be incompatible with homosexuality, it follows that athletes must not be homosexual. Another way to examine this is to say that the better the athlete is—and the more masculine the sport he plays—the less homosexual suspicion there is about him. Consequently, football players are provided near immunity from homosexual suspicion, while band members are inundated with it. From the top of the hill, the male is able to marginalize others, by using homonegative discourse, and his derision is legitimated because he has earned the respect of peers.

Surprisingly, boys at the top of the masculine hierarchy are actually provided more leeway to transgress the rigid gender boundaries, because few other boys would be willing to challenge their sexuality for fear of social or physical reprisal. For example, the masculine elite boys on elementary school playgrounds have been shown to possess more freedom in transgressing norms in the form of (temporarily) playing so-called girl games. This phenomenon is also found when it comes to homoerotic activities between heterosexual men. The more masculine capital one possesses, the more homoerotic activity they seem able to engage in without having their sexuality questioned. For example, Michael Robidoux's (2001) ethnographic research on semi-professional hockey players shows that they are permitted homosocial play that many would code as homoerotic. Both in Robidoux's and my research, this homoerotic play was expressed on a number of levels. For example, it was found in towel-snapping and wrestling, but it was also found in more homoerotic activities as well. Robidoux found that hockey players often grabbed each other's testicles, and I found this among water polo players as well. Additionally, I found that in my ethnography of heterosexual male cheerleaders, and in my own experience as a collegiate coach, there was a great deal of mock intercourse between heterosexual men. Kirby Schroeder has even found homoerotic expression to be compulsory among men in a military college.[17]

This phenomena illustrates why, when a popular and well-muscled volleyball player accepted my challenge and came to one of my classes dressed in drag, he was met with positive laughter and commendations of his bravery, but when an unknown 115-pound nonathletic male came to the same course in drag (a different quarter), he was received with cold stares and indifference. It is precisely this ironic juxtaposition, that football players are theorized to be able to slap each other on the butt and be thought straight despite it.

Although athleticism has little practical value for men once they disengage from the sporting arena (particularly as masculinity becomes more scripted in professional occupations in later stages of life), the jock identity may be maintained, or the individual may publicly recall his youthful sporting accomplishments in order to influence his level of masculine capital. In other words, masculine glory in one's youth can sometimes be tapped to influence one's perception among peers in the future. I call this the Al Bundy syndrome, after the television sitcom character who proclaims his middle-age masculinity not by virtue of his current athletic prowess, but rather because he once played high school football.

While the masculine hierarchy is mainly built via athleticism, consistent association with femininity or things considered to be consistent with gay males are important determinants in the downgrading of one's masculine capital, whether the association is real or perceived. Sociologist David Plummer points out that an accusation of homosexuality is the primary manner in which to verbally marginalize another male. He maintains that homophobic terms come into currency in elementary school, even though the words may not yet have sexual connotations. Still, he posits that these terms are far from indiscriminate as they tap a complex array of meanings that he says are precisely mapped in peer cultures (2001, 2).

Young boys who slip out of their bounded zones may be able to recoup some of their masculinity and be reabsorbed back into the masculine arena by deflecting the suspicion of homosexuality onto another boy. A higher status boy, for example, who transgresses gender boundaries, might call a lower status boy a fag in an attempt to displace suspicion.[18] By negatively talking about and excluding members who are presumed gay, boys are delineating their public heterosexuality, while collectively endorsing hegemonic masculinity (McGuffey and Rich 1999, 822). In such a manner, the marginalized attempt to gain power and control by marginalizing another, almost as if it were a game of "tag, you're it" with the "it" being the label of homosexuality. More so, in certain highly masculinized social locations, demonstrating one's heterosexuality is not sufficient enough to maintain an unambiguous heterosexual masculinity. In these locations, such as within football culture, it is also important to show opposition and intolerance toward homosexuality (Curry 1991).

Because homosexuality is equated with femininity, in order to avoid accusations of homosexuality, boys must vigilantly adhere to behaviors coded as the opposite of feminine at all times, something also described as fem-phobia (Bailey 2003). Should boys transgress these boundaries, they are quickly reminded of their transgression through a litany of homophobic and misogynistic scripts. Sociologists McGuffey and Rich show, for example, a case in which older boys observed a seven-year-old crying and said that he will "probably be gay when he grows up." To these young boys, being soft and/or emotional is a quality associated with females, and a boy possessing such characteristics must subsequently be gay (1999, 81).

In this manner homosexual accusation marginalizes boys, and their status as a marginalized boy is then naturalized through their association with other marginalized people. Olympic gold medalist Mark Tewksbury (who came out after retiring from swimming in 1998), says that at the age of fourteen, when a baseball flew by him, he elicited a characteristically feminine scream that prompted other boys to call him a fag. He said, "Within hours fag was written on my locker, and from then on out I was labeled the fag in school."

Highlighting the vicious nature of homophobic discourse and the use of stigma in the policing of masculine behavior, once a boy is labeled as gay, few other boys will associate with him. The stigma of homosexuality brings with it a guilt-by-association fear that the stigma will rub off onto those not already marginalized. In this aspect homosexuality is looked upon as a contaminant, similar to the childhood notion of cooties. For example, Tewksbury told me that once he was labeled a fag, his classmates turned against him, alienating him, for fear of association with a known deviant. Similarly, after I came out of the closet as an openly gay high school coach my athletes were frequently perceived as gay because they had a gay coach. Also illustrating the contaminant effect, McGuffey and Rich quote a nine-year-old boy yelling, "I don't care if I have to sit out the whole summer 'cause I'm not going to let that faggot touch me!" (1991, 81). Making boys contaminated in this way sends a strong warning to the other boys not to act like a girl, or they too will be isolated and ostracized by their male peers.

The homosocial patrolling may continue into adulthood, especially in the athletic arena. It has, for example, been discovered that in adult male figure skaters, "kind of feminine" is a phrase used to police the boundaries of acceptable heterosexual behavior (Adams 1993), and my research on collegiate heterosexual male cheerleaders finds both homosocial and institutional policing of men's behaviors designed to distance men from homosexuality. For example, in one cheerleading association, certain dance movements or stunts are considered too feminine and are therefore associated with the stigma of homosexuality (Anderson 2004).

Because homophobic and misogynistic discourse is used to police masculine behaviors, the terms that are most commonly employed are *faggot, fag, pussy,* and *wuss.*[19] None of this is to say, however, that these are the only derogatory terms males use in derision of each other. Certainly, they use a variety of terms related to sex and biology. Michael Messner maintains that these forms of homophobic discourse are also connected to misogyny.

> In short, though children obviously do not intend it, through this sort of banter they teach each other that sex, whether of the homosexual or heterosexual kind, is a relational act of domination and subordination. The "men" are the ones who are on top, in control, doing the penetrating and fucking. Women, or penetrated men, are subordinate, degraded, and dehumanized objects of sexual aggression. (2002, 33)

This is just one manner in which homophobia also serves as a form of sexism.[20]

Homophobic language is also used as a way to motivate males into increased performance. Openly gay (retired) professional baseball player Billy Bean first heard the word *faggot* used to "motivate" in the fourth grade.

> What, exactly was a faggot? How did faggots run? Clearly, it wasn't a good thing. It was probably the worst thing imaginable. It equaled weakness and timidity, everything a budding, insecure jock wanted to avoid.

Bean continued by saying that he has heard every coach he has ever had since the fourth grade use the term, even through the professional leagues. "As motivational strategy, it was effective. Coaches invoked the terms again and again. Players responded, almost reflexively raising their intensity level" (2003, 107). Similarly, a gay high school swimmer told me:

> I just grew up hearing the word fag all the time. I didn't really know what it meant, but I was damn sure that whatever it was I wasn't going to be one of them. I think I learned that it had to do with not acting like a girl and stuff early on, but by the time I was in maybe sixth grade, I knew that it meant that you weren't supposed to be attracted to guys; which was fine for me at the time, because I wasn't. Or at least I didn't know I was. But by the time I hit high school—it was a different story.

Homophobic discourse is used indiscriminately against any boy who acts in discord with masculine behaviors, whether he is gay or not. In fact, many straight athletes tell me that they questioned their sexuality because of the labeling of their feminine behavior. Matt, a heterosexual runner told me, "I used to think maybe I am gay. People called me gay all the time, so I really had to stop and question, am I?"

As a working hypothesis I maintain that while both homophobic and misogynistic discourse are used to establish dominance of men over women and men over other men, homophobic discourse is more effective in marginalizing other men because, unlike terms associated with femininity, a boy can actually *be* gay. While I frequently hear from heterosexual men that the litany of homophobic discourse led them to question their sexuality, I've yet to meet a male who questioned his sex as a result of being called a misogynistic term.

HEGEMONIC MASCULINITY IN SCHOOL CULTURE

The above section describes the use of athleticism and homophobic and sexist discourse in order to stratify men in a king-of-the-hill style competition for the upper rungs of a masculine hierarchy. Much like the game, where the most dominant male occupies the top of the hill and physically pushes weaker boys down it, the contestation for masculine stratification is played out on flat sporting fields and courts in the institutions of both sport and public education where sport, through physical education, is made compulsory and those on sporting teams have their associations glorified publicly. Jackson Katz calls this type of school environment a jock-ocracy, because the high school (and often university) culture is stratified around athletics, not academics.[21]

In a jock-ocracy boys that score the most touchdowns, goals, or baskets symbolically occupy the top of the hierarchy, and they often naturalize their status by marginalizing other males with homophobic and misogynistic discourse. Those who are softer, weaker, or more feminine are regarded as homosexual and are normally relegated to the bottom of the stratification, or cast out from masculine terrain altogether. Boys who reside atop the masculine hierarchy (that is, those with the most masculine capital) are required to maintain their social location through the continuous monitoring of masculine behaviors in order to assure complicity with masculine expectations at nearly all times. As mentioned before, a continuous process of homosocial patrolling occurs by both self and others, as boys who deviate are routinely chastised for their aberrant behavior through homophobic and misogynistic discourse. Michael Kimmel describes these processes by saying, "Masculinity must be proved, and no sooner is it proved than it is again questioned and must be proved again—constant, relentless, unachievable, and ultimately the quest for proof becomes so meaningless than it takes on the characteristics, as Weber said, of a sport" (1994, 122).

The system of using athleticism to stratify men along an access of power is described as hegemonic because it is maintained not only through the real and symbolic forces of those who occupy the upper tiers, but through the willing participation of those who are subordinated. A high school jock-ocracy provides a clear understanding of the process of masculinity as hegemonic oppression because ancillary players (those possessing subordinated forms of masculinity) keep this volatile framework in place by lauding social merits onto the kings of the hill, literally cheering them on. Women, adult men, and other marginalized boys pay tribute to them by supporting them in the very arena in which they struggle to maximize their influence—athletic competitions. The epitome of this is when women cheer for male athletes, relegating themselves to symbolic subservience, and when a student body votes a football player as homecoming king. The public celebration of masculine domination makes hegemonic masculinity a popular identity to adopt and therefore ensures compliance by other males seeking such admiration.

The praise of these kings by individuals and their institutions naturalizes and legitimates the power of those who control the jock-ocracy. However, as an operation of hegemonic oppression, the system is not necessarily understood in this context. Rather, hegemonic processes conceal the legitimating of power upon athletes via myths of school pride. Subordinated members of school culture do not view their cheering as praise for the so-called elite and powerful men who dominate and subordinate. Rather, they view it as cheering for "our school." Perhaps this system is also maintained because cheering for "our team" elicits hopes that the school's kings (in-group) will beat another school's kings (out-group). In this manner, even the marginalized can take solace in the fact that their institution is more masculine than the other's, gaining them symbolic masculine capital via association with dominance.

Even if the home team fails to win, men symbolically align themselves with the athletic prowess of their heroes by association as a spectator and are encouraged to equate their own masculinity with that which devalues femininity and homosexuality. This association can be seen in the common language spectators use to describe an imagined affiliation with the athletes of a team: "My team lost" or "our team was amazing tonight." This is a process similar to the one by which all men gain symbolic power over all women when *some* men beat all women at an athletic event or prevent women from competing against them in the first place. By associating with men, even men who cannot beat women gain power because their gender won. This, in essence, is one link between homophobia and sexism. Homophobia keeps all men in line, so that all men can benefit from the privileges of patriarchy.

The social processes that use homophobia and athletics to stratify boys—and marginalize women in school settings—are not the only troublesome results of the way we do sport in North American culture. The institution of sport serves as the creator and guardian of masculine production across many institutional settings and can be attributed to a number of societal-negative attributes. Varda Burstyn (1999) describes sport among the most culpable of institutions in modern society, almost a religion that regenerates individualist, competitive, and coercive values and behaviors.

PROBLEMATIZING SPORT CULTURE

The symbolic importance of sport to American society is made salient through examining the prominence of channels dedicated to sports on radio and television, the presence of newspaper sections devoted to the reporting of nonconsequential sports scores, and the identification with sports and sport metaphors in politics, the military, and sometimes even religion.

Varda Burstyn (1999) claims that sports have become a great masculine secular religion, which plays a profound and often invisible role in personal and public arenas of life. Sports, or at least the way Westerners do them, can be critically analyzed for the detriments they cause to both individuals and society on a number of social, political, and health related variables. We can, for example, examine the effect that sport has on public education and graduation rates, on violence against the self and others, or of the manner in which it distracts us from larger political and relevant social issues. This, however, is not a book examining the relationship between sport and society as a whole; rather it examines the relationship between sport and masculinity. With this in mind, many of the divisive and violent products of the way we do sport can be attributed to the fact that the way we structure sport necessitates that success be achieved only by another's loss (Pronger 1999). In this manner Lester Thurow (1985) describes sport as a zero-sum game because it is a social situation in which one person's success must come at the expense of others.

Coaches and athletes frequently express ill feelings toward one's competitor as they have been socialized into an in-group/out-group perspective that is predicated upon establishing the other team as the enemy. Rather than viewing competitors as agents in cooperation to bring out the best in individuals and groups, other teams are viewed as obstacles in the path of obtaining cultural and economic power. Recall Billy Bean's father saying to him, "It's just you and him, and you are better than him" (2003, 122). His statement explicitly recognizes Brian Pronger's assertion that sport is not premised on the idea of achieving one's personal best, but on taking a victory from another. In order for me to win, you must lose.

This makes sense when the distribution of goods is predicated upon one's social position among masculine stratification. If all men, regardless of athletic ability, were regarded as equally masculine, as equally heterosexual, or as equally worthy of public praise, there would be no need to marginalize or subordinate other men on grounds of their masculinity. Alas, this is not the case; sports are political because they are about the distribution of the power that comes with masculinity in a homophobic and misogynistic culture.

In order to tap into this power, sports, especially contact team sports, teach boys that it is okay to commit violence against another. Violence, in the name of victory, is acceptable because victory is the symbolic method by which masculinity is distributed in a postindustrial culture. Sport essentially institutionalizes, sanctions, and normalizes violence against other boys and men, something that is perhaps made more visible in the employment of so-called goons in hockey, or the brush-back pitch in baseball. Each is acceptable in the sport as it is naturalized as "just part of the game," even though one is tantamount to hiring a thug to commit a violent crime for you, and the other amounts to an intentional assault with a deadly weapon. Put into these contexts, we are more able to see the absurdity of the acceptance of brush-back pitches and our revelry for goons and team fights.

Institutional sanctioning of violent masculinity can be seen at all organized levels of sport. It is visible when two high school kids fight during a high school soccer match and are penalized with a red card, but when the same kids perform the same actions in the school's hallway they are suspended for five days or expelled from school. Similarly, legal sanctioning of violence in sport is made obvious when one considers that while two men who fight in a public place are subject to arrest, two baseball players who slug it out in front of tens of thousands of fans (including thousands of kids) are not. In this and many more ways, boys and men are socialized into the context that violence against other men is not only permissible but expected in sport. And because violence is naturalized as unproblematic as the way we do sport, boys and men are also taught to be receptive victims of violence. Alarmingly, this expectation does not seem to raise doubts about the value of sport to our selves or society. We are obsessed with sex and sexuality but not violence. For example, we were thrown into an uproar when Janet Jackson exposed part of her breast at the Super Bowl half-time show in 2004, but we do not critique the violence of the game itself. Parents were upset that children were exposed to a partial breast but unconcerned with the violence they willingly exposed their children to.

Just because we have naturalized violence as an outcome of sport, does not, however, mean that young men enjoy being splayed out by a linebacker twice his size, taking a pitch in the shoulder for the sake of a "free" base, or running through shin splints. Kids must be socialized into such sadistic acts. They are forced to ignore the warning system of the human nervous system that inflicts one with pain in order to deter potentially injurious behaviors. It is against their own stopgaps and bodily urges to cease an activity that boys must learn to repress their reflexes, suppress their fears, and oppress their peers. Even when the denial of protective instincts and physical damage manifests in the form of overuse or clonic injuries, boys and men are not allowed to criticize the system. They are discouraged from withdrawing out of fear of being stigmatized as a quitter or not being "man enough to take it." Instead, they are encouraged to get back on the horse, walk it off, or do whatever is necessary in order to get back in the game. In such manner, males are constructed to view aggression toward selves and others as not only part of the game but as a necessary component of masculinity. Michael Messner (1992) says that because participation in sports is nearly culturally compulsory and is made obligatory through its association with public education, the aggression in sport is naturalized, ubiquitous, and all-inclusive.

Furthermore, coaches exploit their athletes' fears of emasculation and overdedication to the system by pushing them too far and by knowingly having them play with injuries. Sacrifice becomes part of the game and athletes, particularly those with low self-esteem or poor social support networks, are willing to risk their health because they are so eager to be accepted by the team and their peers. Research shows that over 80 percent of the men and women in top-level intercollegiate sports in the United States sustain at least one serious injury while playing their sport, and nearly 70 percent are disabled for two or more weeks. The rate of disabling injuries in the NFL is over three times higher than the rate of men who work construction, as professional contact sports are the nation's most violent workplace (Coakley 2002).

In addition to the physical violence that sport both produces and naturalizes as part of masculinity, sport also provides a psychological violence against the self and others because it is a public activity. Along with verbal hazing, and the dehumanizing initiation rituals of many sporting programs, we also need to consider the way sport elicits schadenfreude, an ingrained concept because sport is played out publicly and is predicated upon the advancement of one player at the expense of another. Therefore, sports are more than just a zero-sum social arena, they are a public zero-sum arena. While this may have a boastful effect on the self-esteem of the winners, the nature of losing in public carries with it problematic circumstances.

For example, if a sixth-grade boy fails a test in his math class, the only other person to know his score (unless he elects to tell others) is his teacher. The teacher does not post the students' scores on the board for the class to take delight in the fact that they scored a higher grade. However, when a student fails to catch a football in physical education, his failure is visible for all to see, and his failure may upset his teammates who were depending on his performance for their needs. Thus, egos are built off the public humiliation of another, something William Pollack (1999) argues boys are not cognitively capable of dealing with.

Additionally, the social world created around men's power, physicality, and performance in sport subverts respect for women, who are not viewed as worthy participants in the sporting terrain. Rather, their social location frequently posits them as bodies to be pursued and conquered by the rightful participants of the sporting terrain. For these reasons, Mariah Burton-Nelson says, "It makes no more sense to celebrate male bonding than it makes sense to celebrate white bonding.

Exclusive gatherings of white people . . . are justifiably viewed with great suspicion." She maintains that sitting around the locker room talking about how much a player loves and respects his girlfriend does not score as many heterosexual points as graphically discussing the details of their sexual activity. Discussing the intellect of a female sports reporter does not cast off homosexual suspicion whereas objectifying her breasts does (1995, 122).

Hegemonic processes have enabled sport to reproduce all of these social-negative attributes because we have, as a culture, allowed sport to operate without critical examination. We believe so strongly in the myth of sport that 75 percent of American parents encourage their children to participate in sport while only 6 percent discourage participation in organized sporting programs (Miracle and Rees 1994). It is because of this powerful myth, the taken-for-granted assumption that sport is good (and it does do some good), that we rarely question the merit of sport and are blinded to the social realities of it. Sport largely escapes critical analysis, and empirical scrutiny goes unheard. This is a hegemonic process that reproduces the influence of sport on masculinity. It is the same process by which we do not question the assumption that heterosexuality and heterosexual relations are more healthful, natural, or desirable than homosexual ones.

For example, I argued for weeks with a number of functionalist graduate students in a coaching psychology course I taught. I heard, "Sport teaches kids to deal with loss," and "Learning to fail is good because kids need to learn to fail in life." So I decided to test their theory. Had sports taught them to deal with loss? Had it helped them learn to fail in public? Upon returning a midterm I wrote on the board, "High score 97%, low score 23%, mean 57%." I then wrote down the top three exam scores and the students' names who earned them on the blackboard under the heading *winners*. I next wrote the heading *losers* and proceeded as if I were going to reveal the names of the failed students. The class gawked. "You're not going to write the names of the three lowest scores are you?" "Sure I am," I responded. "Youth sports have taught you how to accept public failure."

Yet as athletes most of their lives and purveyors of functionalist ideology, this group of coaches and future coaches were *unable* to accept the exercise. They publicly protested the unfair nature of what I was about to do. One even proclaimed that it would be illegal for me to do such (he was right). After I pointed out my intent as an exercise, they began to get the message. If they couldn't handle the public humiliation of a low test score at twenty-five years of age, how could a nine-year-old handle the public humiliation of losing a game for an entire team?

The functionalist mentality of my students helps elaborate the cultural power that sports maintain. Sports exact social-negatives while wrapped in the cloak of providing near monolithic social-positives. They are wrapped in multiple and robust myths that overly generalize the potential for social-positive effects, and ignore the social-negative. Therefore, it is not surprising that my students had not actively challenged the myths of sport. They were previously merited by their sporting endeavors in youth and probably never experienced the harassment of repeated, public failure of those less gifted. As I will show in chapter 4, the fact that these coaches were former athletes has implications for the way they reproduce the system.

SPORTING HEGEMONY AND GAY ATHLETES

The hegemony of sport as a necessary good for boys and men is so pervasive that it has even escaped critical examination by those who have been traditionally oppressed by it. In fact, many times these groups of people attribute their marginalization in sport not as a product of a dysfunctional social system but as a lack of individual effort to excel within sport and they go on to espouse its virtues. Nowhere is this more obvious than with gay athletes.

Whereas one might suspect that gay athletes would maintain distaste for sport, this was not the case in those I interviewed. Both openly gay and closeted gay athletes almost unanimously espoused the virtues of sport. Athletes of all levels expressed their desire to compete and excel in sports, many couching their affinity with terms of endearment, such as, "I love water polo," or arranging their social identities around it, "I'm a soccer player." Still others attributed sport to be more than a recreational activity: "I'd rather be playing football than doing just about anything else. I'm all about football: it's like a way of life for me." They attributed sport with having gained them friendships, self-esteem, and recreational enjoyment. Almost all of the athletes studied aspired to assimilate and excel in the institution, and few suggested structural changes that could make sport a more hospitable place for gay men.

Gay athletes are not consciously aware of their blind acceptance of the virtues of sport, they have merely embraced the orthodox model of sport because the hegemonic underpinnings of sport have prevented them from critically examining the effect sport has on society and on the stigmatizing of homosexuality. For example, Marty, a gay football player, told me, "Yeah, I love football. It teaches you to be a team player. You really rely on others on the field, and the guys on the team have become like brothers to me." He continued to praise football, attributing to it the creation of many desirable social qualities, without once problematizing football for what seems to be some clear and highly problematic attributes, including the fact that the cohesion created on his team was structured in the antithesis of who he was—gay. Even after Marty experienced intense homophobic banter from several of the coaches on his team (he remained closeted), he talked of his desire to return someday to coach football, with the very same coaches who frequently used violent discourse against homosexuality. When I asked him why he desired to return to such a situation he responded, "Well it's not like I was the only one who's been called a fag. The coaches call everyone fags. Well, fags or butt buddies. If everyone who got called a fag was really gay, we'd have an all-gay team."

Marty illustrates that sport, and its use in the production of masculinity, is so heavily inscripted, protected, and promoted by metamyths that even those who are directly subjugated and marginalized by it ascribe to its values and maintain devotion to it. Hegemonic processes make sport one of the most cherished institutions within North American culture. But as a later chapter explores, the system of sport is also steadfast in its social operation because those who are merited by sport are also those who have engaged it as a near-total institution. They have, therefore, been subjected to the narrow worldview of the highly masculinized arena and are likely to reproduce conservative attitudes regarding sexual and gendered identities because of this. It is these very same, highly merited athletes, who then become coaches, who influence another generation of highly impressionable athletes into conservative masculinity.

3

The Relationship between Gay Athletes and Sport

Like many young Canadians, Aaron, who now plays for the National Hockey League (NHL), grew up in a culture obsessed with ice hockey. "I don't know a lot about hockey," I confessed at the beginning of the interview. "You are American," he laughed, "and you're from California. But if you're from Canada you just can't escape it," he tells me during our telephone interview from the lobby of a hotel. "I grew up in a town which was all about hockey, and my dad played hockey professionally, so I really don't remember a time when I couldn't skate." Aaron's early socialization (and natural talent) enabled him to excel at hockey as a youth. Hockey was Aaron's first love; boys became his second.

While most of the athletes I interviewed knew that they were gay before puberty, Aaron was different. He didn't figure out that he was gay until his early teens. It bothered him not because he liked guys but because he felt so alone in liking guys. "I couldn't go on-line to talk about it; there was no Internet back then, so . . . I told my priest. He encouraged me not to act on it, and to keep it silent. So I did."

In college the fear of exploring his sexuality began to erode, so while on a full scholarship to an American university, and with his first fake ID in hand, he was determined to find out where the gay district was. "I was successful. I found not one but two guys to go home with that night." He visited the gay district more frequently over the next few years, but because this time frame coincided with his ascendancy as a hockey player, he increasingly grew afraid of being recognized in gay clubs. His worry remained as he navigated the hierarchy of clubs and leagues before eventually skating for an NHL team. He has skated here for several years, even winning a Stanley Cup title.

As a hockey player, Aaron represents a paradox in relation to orthodox masculinity. He has survived the serious bodily risk that comes with this violent sport, but he fears another kind of damage—the loss of respect if he were to come out. "If people found out I was gay, it would ruin everything," he tells me. He was initially leery to give me this interview and revealed only parts of his identity to me at a time in order to build trust. He has more practical fears too. He fears coming out would cause him to lose ice time or to become "the bastard of the company unit."

"I'm not afraid of being selected out for punishment, my team would beat ass if anyone tried to mess with me, but I just don't think it would help my playing." He continued,

> I really love what I do. I'm like a racehorse on the track, eager to run. I want to skate. I want to play; it hurts me not to. I'm one of the luckiest guys, to be able to do what I want and get paid way too much for it, and I'm afraid that coming out would spoil that. I just wish people didn't care so much.

Aaron struggles to lead some semblance of a normal romantic and social life away from the prying eyes of his teammates. He has a boyfriend of several years, gay friends, and he permits himself to visit gay clubs when he is on the road—which is often. On rare occasions, he even runs into other professional hockey players when visiting gay establishments. "You know, hockey players have this sort of look to them. It just screams, 'I'm a hockey player', so when I go to the bars, I dress like a professional and tell people I work with computers." Still, on the few occasions when another professional hockey player enters the bar, he grows distressed. "It's like, holy shit. You can spot them from a mile away, and its just like, oh my god, what am I going to do?"

Most of the time the other player is equally willing to avoid discussing the situation. "A few times the guy has just said like, 'Aaron Barnes, huh?' Then I'll say, 'We will talk about this later.' But I never do." He informs me that he has seen about a dozen players in gay bars over the years. "One time, I ran into another player from my own team."

Despite being "absolutely terrified," he played the encounter off without candor. "What are you doing here?" his teammate asked. "Just checking the place out," he responded. "Me too," his teammate quipped. They have yet to talk about their encounter.

Managing a closeted gay identity is tricky for Aaron. Hockey necessitates that most all of his free time be spent with the team. "Even if you think that someone might be cool with it, you don't necessarily want to tell them because you might be shipped to another team, and you don't want them to have something to use against you." In order to pass as heterosexual, Aaron's public acts are in strict accord with masculine ideals. He conforms to the norms of masculinity exhibited in the sport, including having sex with women, because he is afraid of being perceived out of step with the masculine expectations of the sport. While he often feels he would like to disclose his sexuality to his teammates, he fears losing the competitive edge in acquiring ice time.

When I inquired as to the degree of homophobia in the NHL, Aaron informed me, "You know there was a lot of it in the lower ranks, especially in high school and college. But in the NHL we are professionals, and guys really aren't all that homophobic." He recounted a story about taking a long bus trip with his team after the Massachusetts State Supreme Court came out with their ruling that the state could not stop same-sex marriage in late 2003:

> We were on the bus not too long ago, and someone was talking about the Massachusetts marriage thing, and there were a few older guys that were closed-minded, and saying it was wrong. They were comparing it to marrying goats. I got pissed and said, "I really don't think marrying goats was the next logical step. You know, think about it," I said.

I asked him if others took his position. "A few players stood up and told them to settle down. Most were trying to sleep, and these guys were just annoying them." Aaron also reports that the use of homophobic language is surprisingly low. "I don't really hear *fag* in the locker room. In fact, I can't remember the last time I heard it at all. A lot of us just won't stand for that kind of stuff."

The secret he withholds from his teammates is a weighty matter. In our telephone interview (conducted from his cell phone in his hotel room) he stops several times or unrepentantly changes the subject in order to cast off suspicion as to the nature of his long conversation from his teammates who barge in and out. While Aaron truly loves the game he plays, like most of the closeted collegiate and professional athletes in my study, he finds the notion of team, and the time it takes to do all that is required of being part of a team, constraining. "You just can't escape the guys," he tells me. "I mean, they will just walk into your hotel room, and they always want to go out drinking with you," so it's hard to have much privacy. "One time I had my boyfriend visiting me in the hotel room, and the coach knocked on my door and wanted to talk. So my boyfriend went and hid in the bathroom while the coach talked to me for an hour and a half."

Where heterosexual athletes can incorporate their girlfriends or wives into certain team functions, Aaron has none of those freedoms. He sneaks guys into his hotel room when on the road (he is in an open relationship), and he cannot talk to his boyfriend at will. Although he has taken a few more risks as he has gotten older (he is an established and well-known player), including telling three of his teammates, he feels constrained from coming out any further. "I think about coming out to my team all the time. I think, 'Maybe today will be the day,' then it's not. I'd really like to. On the other hand I'm so used to being the way I am."

The Relationship between Gay Athletes and Sport

The near-total absence of openly gay athletes in the professional, collegiate, and even high school sporting system has led researchers to believe that sport is monolithically homophobic. Sport scholar Brian Pronger writes,

> I am aware of no scholarly research that shows mainstream sport to be a significantly welcome environment for sexual minorities. The fact is that mainstream sports continue to be overwhelmingly hostile to explicit lesbian and gay presence. (2000, 224)

This chapter investigates why Pronger maintains this. It looks at sport as a masculinizing institution and the circumstances in which gay athletes may be drawn to it or repelled. It asks whether athletes may be over or underrepresented in sport and, most importantly, examines the role that gay athletes play in challenging this masculinizing and homophobic institution.

Perhaps it shouldn't be a surprise that gay athletes like Aaron exist even at this level of professional, violent team sports. Nearly all boys (regardless of their sexual orientation) are socialized into sport (whether through networks of friends or compulsory participation in physical education) in early childhood. But Aaron's story does raise interesting questions as to whether boys who grow to realize that they are gay are more inclined to stay or disengage from sport.

Although the obvious answer seems to be that gay men would be repelled by the homophobia within athletics, some gay men might actually be desperate both to prove their masculinity (to self or others) and to hide their sexuality. They use the violent language and behaviors of masculinity found within athletics to do this. Supporting this contention, retired professional gay NFL player David Kopay told me that he was particularly intense on the field as a way of proving that he was in no way less of a man because he was gay (Kopay and Deanne-Young 1977). Kopay's nickname, Psych, highlighted his violent intensity on the field, as he overcomplied to the mandates of masculinity. Similarly, a closeted NFL player tells me that he has known of other gay NFL players who have been similarly "very intense on the field."

However, because gay men may be drawn to sport in order to prove their masculine worth or to cast off homosexual suspicion, this does not mean that they desire to come out. Coming out might defeat the purpose of why they seek the ironic shelter that sport provides them in the first place. Coming out, of course, is also a difficult thing to do in a highly homophobic environment. This is understandable, for coming out is not simply a matter of proclaiming one's sexual orientation. Coming out, in any social context, leads, as Judith Butler (1990) maintains, to a new type of identity entirely. And coming out is particularly antithetical to the ingrained language of heterosexual masculinity found within sport.

Coming out also conflicts with the standard language of orthodox masculinity, a language both gay and straight men have learned because all males grow up in the same homophobic and heterosexist environment. In this aspect, openly gay athletes represent a paradox to the masculine arena of sport. On the one hand, they are thought to be incompatible with masculinity, and on the other, they are often capable, violent athletes. Thus, Brian Pronger (1990) maintains that coming out in sport is to acknowledge an identity that challenges the nature of heterosexual masculinity and therefore challenges the masculinizing institution of sport as a whole.

If gay athletes can excel at the highest level of sport, they may threaten to expose the fallacy upon which heterosexual masculinity is built. Therefore, in an attempt to maintain sport as a site of orthodox masculine production, individuals within the institution are enabled to resist gay male participation through overt and covert homophobia. Ironically, sport becomes a safe space for those desiring to deeply conceal their same-sex desires. Athletes (particularly in team sports) are shrouded in a cloud of heterosexual assumption, while simultaneously engaging in a highly charged, homoerotic environment.

But while extreme homophobia provides athletes with a guise against homosexual suspicion, homophobia also serves to nullify the homoeroticism of sport. Pronger (1995) suggests that both gay and straight men find the locker room sexually stimulating and that this homoerotic atmosphere is sublimated through the aggressive, homophobic, and sexist humor and discourse found in sport. Sociologist Tim Curry (1991) maintains that simply being homophobic is not enough if one desires to be understood as heterosexual. He maintains that it is often not enough for heterosexuals to simply say that they are not gay; they must also behave in *vehemently* homophobic ways if they desire to cast off homosexual suspicion.

However, the same homophobia that draws some closeted gay men into the sporting arena subsequently hinders them from coming out when their emotional need for inclusivity and community compels them to. For example, in *Bloody Sundays* Mike Freeman (2003, 149) interviews an active but closeted professional gay football player who fears getting caught dating another NFL player. Freeman quotes him as saying, "In a strange way the homophobia of our society hurts and helps," he said. "It hurts because you deny who you are, but it helps you keep your secret because both partners are afraid of being discovered." In this manner, both victim and oppressor cooperate in a system of hegemony to silence the presence of gay athleticism in sport, nullifying the possibility of living openly and freely as a gay man in the athletic arena.

Although there are few openly gay athletes in sport, their existence (even if closeted) in the highly masculinized arena poses a serious challenge to business as usual for the institution of sport. For example, when I began formally collecting data on gay athletes in 1999, I had managed to contact only two dozen, but by 2004 I have heard from so many that I've had to limit myself to sixty for this study.[1] Similarly, where there were only two openly gay males in the 2000 Olympics, there were nine in the 2004 Olympics.

Essentially, our culture seems to be in the beginning of a surge in which gay athletes are increasingly coming out of the closet. This is not surprising because research shows that as cultural homophobia declines, people increasingly come out of the closet (Loftus 2001). This is perhaps due to a nexus of factors that include the increased networking of gay youth via the Internet, improved legislation for the protection of gay and lesbian citizens, and the dramatic reduction in cultural and institutional homophobia that has occurred in the United States since 1993 (Widmer et al. 2002; Loftus 2001). But these athletes are doing more than reversing stereotypes and myths about gay men being physically incompetent or not enjoying competitive sport. These athletes represent a challenge to the masculinizing nature of sport as a whole, and perhaps they also represent a challenge to gender segregation in sport.

GAY ATHLETES: CHALLENGING MASCULINE DOMINATION

Pronger maintains that homosexuality is not encouraged in our culture because it undermines, albeit in a positive way, the most important myth of our culture—the gender myth. Discussing the transformative potential of male homosexuality by illustrating the threat it poses to patriarchy, he writes,

> This is not so much a criticism of people as it is a criticism of the culture that has created an ugly gender order, which, through its myths of power, conceals the truth of our humanity by making us see each other always through the filter of gender. (1990, 1)

Pronger argues that if gay male athletes (who are stigmatized as feminine) can be as *strong* and *competitive* as heterosexual male athletes, they may threaten the perceived distinctions between men and women as a whole, something other sport scholars have discussed. Mariah Burton-Nelson (1995) has maintained that the more women have made advances in other institutions, men have relied more on sport in order to symbolically dominate women and Pierre Bourdieu (2001) maintains that the gay male is uniquely situated to undermine patriarchy. In *Masculine Domination*, he posited that gay men embody an ability to invisibly gain access to masculine privilege before coming out, as they are able to penetrate social spaces in a way that women cannot.[2]

If gay athletes, who are stigmatized as too effeminate to play sports, are shown to be as good or better than heterosexual athletes, then they threaten the perceived distinctions between gay men and straight men and the distinctions between men and women as a whole. Pronger argues that in this way a gay athlete is seen as a paradox because homosexuality and athletics express contradictory attitudes toward masculinity. Although gay athletes comply with the gendered script of being male (encompassing the physicality esteemed in sport), they violate another masculine script through the existence of their same-sex desires.

If a gay male can be as good in sport as a straight male, he necessarily challenges sport as a masculinizing agent and is therefore perceived "as a deviant and dangerous participant on the sporting turf"

(Clarke 1998, 145). Thus, the institution of sport resists gay male participation and the creation of a subculture of gay athleticism. Most researchers agree that these agents who comprise the institution of sport are highly intolerant of those who break from this dominant form of masculinity (see Griffin 1998; Hekma 1998; Woog 1998, Connell 1995; Messner 1992; and Pronger 1990). Accordingly, because gay male athletes do not fit the notion of what a masculine male is supposed to be—namely, heterosexual—gay athletes are often marginalized, and general intolerance toward gay athletes is exacted in both overt and covert ways.

Messner says, "The extent of homophobia in the sports world is staggering. Boys [in sports] learn early that to be gay, to be suspected of being gay, or even to be unable to prove one's heterosexual status is not acceptable" (1992, 34). Hekma states that, "Gay men who are seen as queer and effeminate are granted no space whatsoever in what is generally considered to be a masculine preserve and a macho enterprise" (1998, 2). And Pronger agrees, saying, "Many of the [gay] men I interviewed said they were uncomfortable with team sports. . . . Orthodox masculinity is usually an important subtext if not *the* leitmotif in team sports" (1990, 26).

Homophobia in all these forms presents itself as resistance against the intrusion of a gay subculture within sports and serves as a way of maintaining the rigidity of orthodox masculinity and patriarchy. Sport not only rejects homosexuality but also venerates hyperheterosexuality (see Hekma 1998; Griffin 1998; Pronger 1990; and Wolf et al. 2001). In this manner, the presence of homophobia and the assumption of heterosexuality both serve to nullify the *homoeroticism* of the locker room while esteeming hegemonic masculinity. Although my research does not fully answer the question as to the transgressive power gay athletes might have on eroding patriarchy, it does suggest that one way men might maintain patriarchal privilege would be to accept male homosexuality as being compatible with masculinity, something other research of mine (Anderson 2004) suggests may already be happening.

Some researchers think that the potential for gay liberationist ideas of undermining hegemonic masculinity, heterosexism, and ultimately patriarchy, has passed. They suggest that by the mid to late 1970s much of the radical impulse in gay liberation had been eclipsed by a more pragmatic approach that focused on individual rights and lifestyle alternatives. This model features gay men attempting to assimilate into the dominant culture rather than transform it. Indeed, throughout the 1990s and into the new millennium gay and lesbian leaders have positioned themselves (and their communities) for acceptance into mainstream culture by expressing themselves as "normal" people who endorsed social hegemony in every other way except in whom they love. Gay marriage serves as a perfect example for this model.

The issue of gay athleticism, in relation to the dominant sporting structure, reflects the relationship between homosexuality and the dominant heterosexual society as a whole. Since the modern gay liberation movement (roughly the 1950s to present) there has been tension between two working ideologies regarding the relationship between homosexuality and the dominant social structure. Simply stated, one frame of thought has been to open up the existing institutions for gay inclusivity, while the other has questioned the value of the way in which power is distributed in general. Assimilationists desire inclusion into the existing social structure and use identity politics as the tool to gain individual autonomy and civil rights. This ideology is sometimes referred to as gay liberation. Reformists, the leftist elements of the gay movement, however, have sought to transform dominant social structures, to challenge the nature of categorization and distribution of power.

Sociologist Peter Nardi (1999) says that gay men have largely settled upon the assimilationist approach. He maintains that the notion of a gay family has changed from one of kinship and a political family to the model of the heterosexual family.[4] Gay males began to lose the camp expressionism and liberating political overtones that characterized gay males of the late 1960s and early 1970s as they adopted every other attribute of masculinity, giving rise to what Connell (1995) calls a "very straight gay." A number of investigations of marginalized men support the contention that otherwise subordinate men attempt to approximate every other aspect of orthodox masculinity (Anderson 2002; Davis 1990; Majors 1990; Messner 1992; Williams 1995). Otherwise marginalized men cling to notions of hegemonic masculinity because it both begets rewards of patriarchy and stays off potential social criticism for performing further marginalized masculine identities. It should, therefore, be no surprise that today's gay youth largely value what they call *straight acting* and devalue what they call acting like a *flamer*. Thus, gay male stereotypes today define liberation in the ability to be thought equally masculine to heterosexuals.

In this respect, several interesting questions emerge regarding the relationship between the gay athlete and masculine domination. Do gay athletes maintain the ability to transform the nature of masculinity? Do they maintain the ability to help erode patriarchy? Or are gay athletes simply going to be accepted under the umbrella of orthodox masculinity, nullifying their transformative potential?

Gay and lesbian athletes have slightly queered the structure of sport in their own self-segregated space. Some pockets of gay athleticism do sport differently. Some clubs, leagues, and organizations attempt to downplay the competitiveness of sport and stress cooperation. But this queering only takes place in the context of their sporting space and does not challenge the dominant structure of heterosexual sports because gay athletes are removed from it. Essentially, marginalizing one's self makes it easier to be marginalized by the dominant structure. The best example of this comes with the creation of the Gay Games.

The Gay Games (founded in 1982) occur every four years and draw more participants than the Olympics. They represent the archetype of the inclusion model. A portion of the mission statement reads as follows:

> Based on the principles of inclusion and participation, the Gay Games welcomes all people without regard to their sexual orientation, gender, race, religion, nationality, ethnic origin, political belief, physical ability, athletic/artistic ability, age, or health status. There are no minimum standards to qualify for the Gay Games; the only requirement is the desire to support the ideals of the Games.

But while the games are premised upon the notion of inclusion, they still have retained the dominant structure of heterosexual sports. They *are* competitive and do pit people against each other. They produce a winning team and a whole bunch of losing teams rather than using people's coordinated efforts to gain equality. Indeed, world records have been set and ratified at the games, which serves to legitimatize both the games and gay athletes in the dominant structure.

Collectively, the Gay Games best represent our efforts in regard to the relationship between homosexuality and sport, but they are not alone. In the United States it is estimated that there has been a 50 percent increase in the number of gay and lesbian sports organizations since 1981, with between 11 and 13 million participants (Pitts 1990). The Gay and Lesbian Athletic Foundation held their first meeting in 2003, and the direction seems firmly entrenched upon the inclusion model.[5] Gays and lesbians have stressed that homosexuality is just another version of normal and are making headway in that goal. Just like heterosexuals, homosexuals have adopted, even embraced, most of the ugly attributes of sport. Their primary concern has been to remove the obstacles that have prevented full participation in the heterosexual sporting arena, not challenging the institution as a whole. For the most part gays have failed to critically analyze the larger purposes of sport in contemporary society. They have failed to challenge the use of sport to legitimate and reify male worth over women. Gays have failed to challenge the out-grouping process that teams produce and have failed to critique the manner in which *sport* (not recreation) teaches us that violence is a normal part of American masculinity. We have failed to disentangle nationalism from sport and have readily adopted the consumerism of American sport. Hargraves (1986) says:

> The struggle to redefine sport has ethical implications connected with the belief that male dominated and controlled sport has produced an excessive stress on competition, with ugly proliferations, and that macho models of sport that celebrate the male/female distinction are brutalizing and limiting, both for young males who are induced into them and for females who copy them. Probably the greatest practical threat to male hegemony in sport comes from both men and women who are involved in alternative sports which stress health, enjoyment and co-operation and de-emphasize destructive competition. (116)

Clearly, the path the gay community has chosen has *not* been to highlight differences, and in many ways the movement has been highly successful. Ultimately, this will lead to the erasure of their difference, making life easier for the gay or lesbian athlete but nullifying the transformative potential she or he once possessed. Brian Pronger (2000) states the situation succinctly and sarcastically when he said:

> Sport, I argue, has played a role, perhaps not the leading one, but a role nevertheless, in the appropriation, control, and perhaps ultimate erasure of the otherness of homosexuality and thus of its transformative power. From a legitimizing liberal perspective, this has been a good thing. The problem with homosexuality was its position as deviant, perverse, abnormal, and disturbingly invisible. Once it is no longer conceived as different from heterosexuality, once it no longer poses a threat, once it is respectably visible, the battle is over, and lesbians and gays can simply enjoy the privileges of normality. (253)

Pronger goes on to say that from a transformationist perspective the gay embrace of sport marks the end of a short period in which homosexuality once offered the possibility of a deeper transformation of society.

I stress that the platforms of the assimilationists and the revisionists are not that bifurcated. I argue that, indeed, the gay community as a whole and the gay community within athletics have made up their minds; we have fully supported the inclusion model. Data in this book clearly suggests that both gay and straight athletes are begrudgingly

working together for the slow but progressive assimilation of homosexuality into the sporting arena. It shows that heterosexual athletes
are increasingly willing to accept gay athletes as long as they adopt
the other aspects of orthodox masculinity, namely, that they are valuable to the overarching mantra of sport—victory. Heterosexual athletes increasingly say, "The sexual orientation of a teammate does not
matter as long as he can play ball." Heterosexual men are increasingly
willing to accept gay men into their terrain as long as gay athletes *do
not* play up their differentness, "as long as they don't make an issue
out it."

This research also finds that in an attempt to assimilate to the dominant structure, gay men are eager to adopt all other attributes of
orthodox masculinity. They attempt to manage their identities, to keep
pace with the construct of being masculine, by acting tough, competing well, and (often) partaking in sexist discourse alongside their heterosexual teammates—even partaking in discussions of the sexual
objectification of women. Gay men go to great lengths to downplay
their differentness by covering their sexual desires, assuring their
teammates that they are not checking them out in the locker rooms,
and self-silencing talk of their sexuality under a policy of don't ask,
don't tell.[6]

Still, this does not nullify the ability for gay athletes to challenge
the structure of sport. While the possibility for revolution is perhaps
over, once accepted into a dominant social structure (regardless of how
limited the membership is), homosexuals possess cultural agency
within the dominant structure. Gay athletes can continue to push sport
into a more favorable social location in a revolution through the evo-
lution model. They can begin to challenge the meanings of masculinity and heterosexual dominance from the inside. Of course, in order to
do this, there have to be gay athletes, and they must be represented in
sufficient numbers in order to make a change. This is the subject of the
next section.

REPRESENTATION OF GAY ATHLETES IN SPORT

Openly gay males are vastly underrepresented in sport. This is true of
most sports at all levels. For example, when examining the ranks of professional team sports (where tens of thousands have gone through the
system), there has *never* been an openly gay professional athlete to
emerge from the closets while playing in the United States. In fact,
David Kopay, Roy Simmons, Esera Tuaolo, Glenn Burke, and Billy Bean
are the only self-proclaimed out-of-the-closet professional athletes from

the top seven North American team sports,[7] and all of them came out after retirement. The question remains: Is this the product of there being *so few* gay men in professional team sports to begin with, or a result of the near-seamless heterosexual hegemony that prevents them from coming out? The only way to know the answer, of course, is to know what percentage of gay men are represented in the general population and what percent are in sport. This is a tricky proposition because the presence of cultural homophobia nullifies the possibility of knowing what percentage of the general population is gay (let alone what percentage of athletes are gay). It is impossible to survey the closet. The only accurate way to answer this question would be to ask once the last vestiges of homophobia and biphobia have long been erased from American culture. Only when homosexuality is esteemed equally with heterosexuality (once gays and lesbians have the same institutional, cultural, and spiritual merit as heterosexuals) might we begin to understand the numerical reality and the dynamic dimension of human sexuality. Until then, we can only theorize, and, in this theorizing, be relatively sure that whatever rates we come up with regarding homosexuality, they are underreported and heterosexuality is over estimated.

Crude estimates of the percentage of the general population that identifies as being gay have varied greatly. Alfred Kinsey (1948) widely popularized the 10% figure, while Laumann et al. (1994) showed that only 2.8% of American men identified as gay (although 9% admit to having engaged in same-sex sexual behavior). About 10% of the incoming freshmen in the UCLA dorms identify themselves as a sexual minority, but only 4.9% of the California electorate consider themselves gay or lesbian. These figures reflect the instability in assessing homosexuality and should remind us to be cautious about making assumptions about sexuality in general.

Further problematizing the demographic understanding of homosexuality is the fact that it is difficult to understand just what it means to be homosexual or heterosexual in the first place. Sexuality proves to be an extremely complicated affair that can be described by at least three separate dimensions: sexual behavior (what one does), sexual orientation (what one wants to do), and sexual identity (how one views his sexual identification). Therefore, the question of whether gay athletes are overrepresented or underrepresented in team sports is theoretically unanswerable because the question is too vague and definitions of sexuality are simply too fluid. If we can't even agree on what gay is, we certainly can't ascertain what percentage of the population is this thing we can't agree upon.

These complications aside, we can be readily assured that at the lowest level of sport (youth sports), the percentage of whatever it means to be a gay male is in statistical equality to whatever the percentage of gay males is in the culture at large. This is because the strength of association between sport and orthodox masculinity is so strong in North American culture that sporting participation has been nearly made a prerequisite for boyhood. Most boys are socialized into sport, and if they do not play for community teams, they are forced into sport through public education in the form of physical education.[8] Therefore, the important question for sport becomes: As athletes matriculate in the sporting realm, does their representation in sport change? In other words, we know that gays are being assimilated into the culture of athletics at the same age as heterosexuals, but as they mature, how might their sexuality influence whether they drop out of or remain within the institution?

The weight of empirical evidence *suggests* that they drop out, that gay athletes are exceedingly underrepresented in sport as adults. For example, since the gay liberation movement tens of thousands of men have played in and retired from professional sports. But in all that time, only five have come out of the closet after retiring. Leigh Steinberg, of *Jerry Maguire* movie fame, tells me that he has not heard one story of a professional gay athlete in twenty-nine years of representing clients in professional football, basketball, baseball, or boxing. "And I am telling you that players tell you stories about group sex, affairs, everything imaginable about sexual behavior. So if they are there, they are incredibly closeted." His belief is that gay athletes are underrepresented in professional sports because at an earlier point than college or the professional leagues, the hostility of men in groups is such that gay athletes in team sports drop out. "At an earlier stage gays find sport, at best, uncomfortable, and at worst, terrifying. They often drop out," he tells me. He contends that it is at the high school level where most males are defining their sexuality, and part of the rite of passage has been hostility toward gays:

> It must be so uncomfortable to someone who is gay to be in that culture, and men in groups sink to the lowest common denominator anyway. Male behavior in groups is much less sensitive than individual behavior. So any behavior that's not inherently rough and macho is ostracized, especially at that adolescent turning point. So, in a high school locker room the environment is so mocking and inhospitable toward the concept of gays that it must be terrifying for someone who is gay. To have to exist on a football team, I think—not being gay I can only surmise—that this would push someone who is gay off the team.

Steinberg is not alone in his views that the culture of sport forces gays out of the institution. Sociologist Gert Hekma (1998) found that once closeted gay men come out in team sports, they feel that they no longer need the façade of sport, dropping out of team sports in favor of individual sports or dropping out of sports entirely. He also reports that many gay youngsters believe that excelling in sport and being gay are incompatible. He found that only 36 percent of gay men rated themselves as high achievers in sport, compared to 56 percent of lesbians interviewed. Hekma theorizes that the heterosexual veneer that brings gays to sport may actually oppress them by simultaneously constructing homosexuality and athletics as being mutually exclusive.

Pronger believes that the mandates of orthodox masculinity found in sport create a sense of not being a part of the action for many gay athletes and of being an outsider. His interviews of gay athletes in Canada show that gay athletes feel what he calls an estrangement from sport. This alienation creates feelings of indifference and/or aversion for young gays regarding sports, which logically may lead them to avoid or drop out of them.

Without doubt, athletics are a symbolically (and potentially physically) hostile place for gay men. Athletics, particularly contact team sports, are constructed around the overarching doctrines of hegemonic masculinity, of which compulsory heterosexuality and dominance is the leitmotif. One study that examined NCAA Division 1 athletes about homosexuality concluded that the stigmatization of the gay athlete is so extreme that it is difficult for them to *even imagine* an out athlete (Wolf et al. 2001). These accounts suggest that the *obvious* answer to the question of whether gays are equally, overly, or underrepresented in sport is that they are not only underrepresented but they are *vastly* underrepresented. Sports writer Mike Freeman says:

> I am not swayed by the argument that because 3 to 10 percent of the general population is gay, according to experts, it automatically follows that 3 to 10 percent of the NFL is gay. If that were true, there would be somewhere between 50 and 169 gay men in the NFL, using an NFL 53-man roster multiplied by 32 teams. (2003, 150)

However, this and other research suggest the opposite. Gay athletes may actually be overrepresented in team sports in that gay males, who are highly motivated to conceal their gay identity from others, may actually be attracted to team sports or motivated to remain within them for longer periods of time. First, gay males, who recognized their same-sex attractions early, may have joined team sports with the hope that the masculinity embedded in sport would protect them from suspicion of their true orientation or that the masculine enterprise might actually change their sexual desires. Also, adolescent males who are not consciously aware of their same sex desires might find themselves drawn to team sports without consciously recognizing the homoeroticism of masculine arenas.

Pronger adds that adolescents who join team sports young (as most all professional team sport athletes have) may be deeply closeted or perhaps even in denial of their homosexuality simply *because* of the extreme degree of homophobia around them. If this is the case, kids who develop their identity and bolster their self-esteem around athleticism might be reluctant to give up sports and therefore less likely to come to emotional terms with their homosexuality. Essentially, competitive team sport might be an ironic safe space for homosexuality.

Pronger also maintains that rather than gay men *thinking* of themselves as being masculine, they come to think of themselves as *acting* masculine. Thus, if cultural homophobia alienates gay male youth from believing that they are *innately* masculine or that their homosexuality prevents them from becoming masculine, they may continually try to *act* masculine as a way to pass as heterosexual, so we might expect a lot of deeply closeted men to be drawn toward the arenas in which masculinity is exhibited the most—sport and the military.

Michael Robidoux attractively captures the entrapment of masculine bravado in the sporting arena in his examination of Canadian male hockey players, "The inevitable obedience that allows this process to take place reduces the player to a body—one that is bought, traded, drafted, and released—all of which has tremendous ramifications in an age controlled by the mind, not the body" (2001, 29). The fact that players willingly forsake their bodies to this corporal arena is perhaps not all that ironic; it is that same social space (that which desecrates homosexuality) that is also rich with homoeroticism. I argue that it is precisely the extreme homophobia (and possibly the extreme homoeroticism) that might initially draw closeted men to team sport athletics. Team sports provide the perfect space for athletes (who live in a homophobic society) to bond with other men, to engage with them on an emotional and a physical level, all of which occurs in a homoerotic and highly sexualized space.

The athletic body itself may also draw men with same-sex desires into the sporting arena. Athletes sexualize their bodies by building up their musculature and reducing their body fat. This occurs both as a by-product of physical exercise and also as a proactive measure to commit violence and prevent violence from being committed to oneself on and off the athletic field. Masculinity, expressed through muscles, is also a symbolic sign of the ability to commit harm to another man in all social arenas. It is, of course, the presence of muscles that makes gay men (whether athletes or not) *less likely* to chance injury by making sexual advances to another male. Ironically, it is the same deterrent to homosexual advances that many gay men find desirable. Lean and sculpted bodies therefore serve to both intimidate and arouse gay men.

Because the presence of muscle is considered incompatible with homosexuality, the more muscle-bound athletes are, the less likely they are suspected of being gay. Since football and basketball players are generally more muscular than cross-country runners, these athletes are less likely to have their sexuality come under suspicion than those in other sports or social arenas. Therefore, if a deeply closeted gay man is both attracted to muscle and also seeks a veneer from homosexual suspicion, team sports are specially attractive. Not only are team sports comprised of desirable phenotypes, the lack of homosexual suspicion allows for fraternal bonding and physical interaction that would make athletes of lesser sports suspected of being gay. Sports writer Mike Freeman says, "To play through pain, and to win, requires a bond that few outside of the sport can understand. NFL players tell me stories of how they become closer to the men in the locker room than they do to their own families" (2003, 143). It is for the erotic desire of muscles, the insurance those muscles provide against being thought gay, and the fraternal bonding that those muscles permit that leads me to believe that the most deeply closeted gay men are drawn to the sporting arena, although it may also repel closeted gay men less concerned with being thought heterosexual or masculine.

Before applying this theory to sport directly, it should be noted that it has been well documented that gay men have existed and continue to exist in great numbers, in other highly homophobic institutions, including the U.S. Armed Forces. In fact, of the nineteen countries that are members of the North Atlantic Treaty Organization, only two prevent gay soldiers from serving openly (the United States and Turkey). And although it is impossible to acquire an accurate figure as to the number of gay men who exist in the armed forces, the Center for the Study of Sexual Minorities in the Military at the University of California, Santa Barbara recognizes the obvious: The number of soldiers removed from service in the U.S. military for homosexuality is far smaller than the total number of gay, lesbian, and bisexual military personnel who serve.

The Office of the Secretary of Defense shows that since 1990, discharges for homosexuality have ranged anywhere from four to seven per ten thousand service members. They also report that 2 to 8 percent of military men acknowledge engaging in same-sex sexual behavior.

Furthermore, research on homosexual men indicates that they are at least as likely as heterosexual men to have served in the military.[9] In this respect evidence clearly suggests that the existence of gay men in the U.S. military at least mirrors their representation in the population at large.

More striking estimates of the percentage of gay men come from another highly homophobic arena, the Catholic Church. Estimates of the percentage of gay men in the Catholic Church are as high as 45%. For example, in the fall of 1999, the *Kansas City Star* sent a questionnaire to three thousand priests, of which only 27% responded. Of the responses, 15% identified as gay and 5% as bisexual. In 1990 a Franciscan priest in New Jersey mailed a survey to five hundred randomly selected priests; of the 398 responses, about 45% said that they were gay (Thomas 2000).

The most significant empirical evidence, however, for the overrepresentation of gay athletes in sport comes from a study of sport itself. The survey research on eighty-two team sport athletes, conducted in 1977 on collegiate athletes from three NCAA Division 1 colleges (over three separate occasions) found that 8% identified as gay, and that anywhere from 15% to 36% of the total population of athletes had at least a couple of homosexual orgasms within the last two years; 62% of the men even said that they would let another man give them oral sex.

The incredibly high rates of same-sex sexual encounters implies that the reason for so much homophobia in professional sports might, indeed, be at least partially related to the presence of so much homoerotic desire among male athletes, although I am not asserting that simply having gay sex makes one gay. Nor do I think these results would be replicated today, partially because heterosexual sex may be easier for men to obtain because there has been a lessening of the traditional double standard in sexual mores, so heterosexual men have more access to heterosexual sex, and same-sex sex among heterosexual teenagers seems to be decreasing.[10]

This might also explain why homoerotic hazing so often takes place in sporting programs. Athletes frequently report hazing rituals that involve nudity or sexuality.[11] One athlete told me, as part of his initiation ritual, an athlete on his team masturbated and ejaculated onto a cracker, which he had to eat. Athletes tell of all sorts of similar rituals. In 2003, three varsity football players were arrested after hazing junior varsity players by sodomizing them with broomsticks, golf balls, and (horrifically) pine cones, in at least three separate occurrences with a Pennsylvania high school football team. It is just one of forty-five appalling American hazing occurrences that Hank Nuwer has documented since 1995.[12]

One cannot ignore the homoerotic context of many of these hazing incidents. For example, the athlete who reported having consumed a teammate's ejaculate also reported that the boy masturbated and ejaculated onto the cracker in the presence of other boys. The notion of a highly masculinized boy masturbating in the presence of his peering teammates certainly carries with it homoerotic underpinnings. Because these incidents and rituals involve homoeroticism (and often illegal activity), they are often *unthinkable* to discuss publicly, thus a strong bond of silence develops around them. The nature of such rituals is that those who were victimized usually turn victimizer by partaking in the hazing for the next cohort.

Homoerotic hazing incidents like this highlight that while homophobic attitudes and behaviors have been assumed to be associated with rigid moralistic beliefs or sexual ignorance, several psychoanalytic explanations link homophobia to one's own anxiety-based sexual desires. These theories postulate that homophobia is at least a partial result of repressed homosexual urges or as a form of latent homosexuality in which the individual is unaware of or representing his homosexuality.

Psychoanalysts use the concept of latent homosexuality to explain the emotional malaise and irrational attitudes displayed by ostensibly heterosexual individuals who feel guilty about their occasional homoerotic interests. Individuals who struggle to deny or repress their impulses may overreact with panic or anger when placed in a situation that heightens their same-sex urges. Or homophobia can be viewed as an intentional response to displace homosexual suspicion, something Freudians call reaction formation. In this manner, if one does not want others to know that he is gay, he acts in opposition to homosexuality in order to avoid suspicion. Thus, in an attempt to seem heterosexual, the closeted gay man may act or be highly homophobic and act out against men he finds attractive in violent ways.

To test this theory, researchers at the University of Georgia conducted a study in which they selected heterosexual men, administered a standard questionnaire of homophobia, and later tested those at the tails of each group so that they only tested men who were either very gay friendly or those who were not. They attached erectometers to their penises and showed both groups same-sex male pornography. The men who identified as highly homophobic demonstrated significantly more sexual arousal than the other group. Interestingly, when the highly homophobic group was asked about their level of arousal, their ratings of erection and arousal to homosexual stimuli were not significantly different from nonhomophobic men, suggesting that they were consciously or unconsciously denying their arousal. From these results one can deduce that the presence of erections in the homophobic men is attributable to a physiological response to anxiety or sexual arousal. However, because both groups of men showed no statistical difference on a standardized aggression scale, it suggests that they harbor same-sex desires (Adams et al. 1996).

The theory of sporting arenas being occupied by an overrepresentation of gay men (albeit perhaps latently so) is also backed by a litany of stories that I have heard regarding homoerotic activity in athletics. One athlete tells me:

> It was unbelievable. We finished the race and we all went out to dinner. Later that night we came back to one of the guys' place to continue the celebration, and we got drunk. Tim put some porn [heterosexual] in the VCR, and we were just watching porn, drinking, and talking. Then one of the guys says, "I'm fucking horny, I'm going into the bedroom to jerk off. If anyone needs some lotion I got some in the bedroom." We sort of looked around at each other, and then one of the guys gets up and says, "Dude, me too." So these two guys start jerking off in their room, and before you know it guys in the living room are like, "Fuck I'm horny too," and they go in to get lube, and well, I went in too, and we all jerked off together.

Another athlete told me a similar story where four teammates were watching pornography and began masturbating. One athlete said, "Dude, I want a blow job" and the other athlete said, "I'll blow you if you blow me." The four athletes ended up swapping oral sex with each other. Furthermore, in my research on heterosexual collegiate male cheerleaders, I found a great deal of same-sex sexual interaction between men. In fact, I found that on one team five of ten heterosexual cheerleaders had engaged in same-sex behaviors. Interestingly, these cheerleaders did not view their same-sex sexual activities as being threatening to their status as heterosexuals.

These stories, taken with the 1977 research showing that 15% to 36% of team sport athletes have engaged in same-sex sex, highlights the complexity of understanding and categorizing human sexual behavior. Just because one engages in gay sex does not necessarily mean that he is gay. Similarly, just because one engages in heterosexual sex (even a lot of it) doesn't mean that he is heterosexual. The conflation of sexual identity, orientation, and behavior is a dynamic process that is not easily understood or explained. Even if one were to grossly oversimplify and reduce the understanding of sexuality to dualistic concepts of gay and straight, the arguments above make it clear that there is no easy answer to the question of representation of gay athletes in sport. Indeed, the more one examines the issue, the more complex it becomes.

The preceding discussion is also complicated by stratification and diversity of athletes in the institution of sport. There are a number of sports, at a number of levels, played at a number of institutions. Therefore, the only reasonable conclusion that one may draw is that the issue of how well gay athletes are represented in sport is very complex. And because it is impossible to study the closet, we may never know whether the extreme homophobia in combative team sport draws or deters more gays than are represented in the population at large.

4

Systems of Masculine Reproduction

ONE ATHLETE'S STORY:
TERRY, RETIRED CLOSETED NFL PLAYER

In his mid-fifties Terry's professional football days have been over for quite some time, but his body carries with it some remnants of his career. "My left knee doesn't work so well anymore," he tells me. "I had a few operations on it. And I might as well just sign my paychecks over to my chiropractor because my back is so jacked up." Terry, who played for two National Football League (NFL) teams in his career, left the sport when a tackle to his knee tore an anterior cruciate ligament. "I was forced out of the game before players made the kind of money that they do today," he tells me. "So I became a high school football coach and teacher." Eventually, Terry earned a master's degree and became an administrator. Terry has found that he makes an effective enforcer as a high school dean. "I'm really too nice a guy for the kids to be scared of me," he tells me. "But if they haven't met me before, and I point at them to come with me, you can bet that I get full compliance." Terry learned that his physical stature could get desired results early in life.

> My dad encouraged me to play football in, oh, I don't know, must have been like fifth grade, and I was bigger than most kids, so I became his

little superstar. It was just something I did on the weekends for a while, or maybe we'd practice one night out of the week, but the older I got, the more time it took.

In high school, Terry found his time, and identity, totally consumed with football. He practiced with the team, stayed in the weight room late, and hung out with his teammate in the evenings. "It's really all I did," he tells me. "It was all about football. Football. Football. Football."

Terry's success on the field brought him respect and fear among his classmates. "Its funny, you know, I'm a real nice guy, and I always was, but my size just intimidates people. It always has." Terry walked the school hallways atop the masculine stratification. He was honored at pep rallies and written about in newspapers. "Everybody knew who I was, but because I only knew the guys on the team, I really felt lonely a lot of the time. Even though I was never alone. In fact, even though it might seem that the team was all about me, I never really felt part of it."

Terry, who has been with his life-partner for over a decade, didn't figure out that he was gay until he was in high school. "I had a girlfriend, and I became best friends with her younger brother Steve," he chuckled:

> Steve and I shared nothing in common. He wasn't an athlete, wasn't known around school, and he never came to the games. But one night after a party Tiffany and I were both so drunk that we called Steve to give us a ride back to her house. Her parents weren't too happy about this, but decided that I could spend the night—just not in her room. . . . I had a horrible headache so Steve started to massage my temples for me. It freaked me out at first, but I relaxed and he continued to massage me. It was something like two or three hours later, I was lying on my back with my head in his lap, and he leaned down and kissed me on the forehead and said, "Is that enough or do you want me to keep going?" It was amazing. It was just a kiss on the forehead, but I was so relaxed and it felt so warm and smooth and tender. It was the most tender thing I had ever experienced, my whole body was numbed, like I was paralyzed. I didn't answer for a second, then said, "Keep going." And boy, did he.

Terry describes the event as the process of unlocking his homoerotic desires. He found himself intentionally coming over to his girlfriend's house earlier than expected, in hopes that he could have some unsuspicious alone time with Steve. "I just kept putting myself into these situations where I could be alone with him. . . . We'd flirt you know, make joking comments about gay stuff, without acknowledging that either of us was gay. We never talked about that night, but I'd say we slowly fell in love with each other."

I really liked being around Steve, and when we knew Tiffany was going to be gone a long time, we'd do much more than just hang around each other. But we never talked about it, and I always felt guilty after. With Steve I was the most mellow, and silly, and cuddly. It was a total different side of me. Then at practice I'd tell the guys on the team that I was fucking Tiffany. I wasn't; I hadn't even had sex with a girl, but you know you can't say that. So I struggled, I mean, I really liked being around Steve, but I didn't want to be gay. The thing is, I wasn't feeling guilty about cheating on Tiffany at all. In fact, I sort of knew that I was only dating her because she wouldn't have sex with me, and I could use her to get to Steve. I was having tremendous guilt, however, over having gay sex. I'd feel horrible right after, but then I was always drawn back for more. It wasn't healthy.

Terry stopped talking to Steve a few months before he left for college. He left his town, his girlfriend, and his lover behind. For Terry, college was the next round of what he described as, "an escalator of slavery," because he says football became increasingly more consuming as you advance levels. He related the feeling to as if the outside world was being closed off to him, and football became his only world, saying, "It's hard not to, when ten thousand fans are cheering for you." Terry roomed with teammates throughout college, they took classes together, and their social lives were intertwined.

I don't think I spent a day away from my teammates in college. Really, it's like we'd lift in the morning, go eat together, then we were in the same classes, and then we'd eat lunch together, and then go to afternoon practice, and then after we'd go home and crash. We'd party together, take road trips together; it was as if college was football.

While Terry enjoyed many of the friendships he made among his teammates, he avoided dating women, and even though he wanted to be with guys, he felt he couldn't escape the gravity of his teammates. He participated in all of the required masculine bravado. "Oh, yeah, I talked about women like all the other guys, and a couple of times I had to have sex with them. You know, to prove I was straight and all. But I never dated."

It really wasn't until I started playing professional that I began to branch out a bit to explore the gay community. You know, when you are traveling from city to city, the guys talk, disparagingly, about where the gay parts of town are. You know, like someone will say, "Hey, Coach, pull over on Dupont Circle. Ronnie wants to get out." So I went to a few gay bars, when I could escape the guys.

I asked Terry how he managed to escape.

> I'd come up with creative ways. Like one time my teammates and I were at a club, and I found a girl and asked her if she wanted to, "blow this joint," and then I'd tell my teammates I was going back to her place. But I'd take her for a drink then say I wasn't feeling well and needed to take a cab back to my hotel. Of course, you know that's not where I took the cab.

Terry reported a good deal of fear in these acts. "Oh, yeah, I was scared shitless that my teammates would see me leaving her, or that I'd not have a good enough excuse as to where I was. But what really scared me was thinking someone would recognize me in a bar. That made me really uneasy."

Over a decade later, Terry maintains much of that fear. "I'm not afraid of being recognized anymore, sometimes people will ask me if I played ball, but it's not because they think they recognize me, it's because I'm big." Terry, does, however, maintain a solid fear of being outed at his current job. "I'm working with kids, you know. And I don't need to do anything to jeopardize that." Apparently, the fear he developed of being outed in college and professional football has largely remained with him today. He avoids the gay places in town, has told none of his colleagues that he is gay, and maintains a very limited gay social network.

Terry indicates that his current social situation is, at least partially, a product of his socialization into football.

> I just learned to hide and pretend in football. There was absolutely no way I was coming out. I certainly thought about it. A lot. I still do actually. But in high school I told myself that I'd come out in college. And then in college, there was no way I was going to come out to my teammates, so I thought maybe I'd just find the gay community when I played in the NFL, since I would be making enough money to live on my own. But when I got to the NFL, I was too scared that someone would recognize me in a bar, so I told myself that I would come out after retiring. But then I was coaching, and I don't need to tell you anything about that. I heard what happened to you when you came out of the closet [as a coach]. So now I'm thinking maybe I'll come out after retiring from this job. Who knows? I feel like I'm getting too old now anyhow.

I asked Terry if he regrets having played football.

> I don't know. Who is to say what might have happened to me? I mean, now that I'm older I see how football was good for me. I got a college

scholarship out of it and did something that every kid dreams of. But on the other hand, my body is a wreck; there are gay kids at my high school who are braver than I am, and I'm still afraid that people will find out that "my friend" is not my friend. . . . I heard that Steve came out of the closet in college, I've always wondered what might have happened had I come out. But you know, you just can't do that when you're on a team. Even today, how many gay football players are there? None. I mean there is Kopay and that Tuaolo guy, and that's great that they came out and all, but that's not for me.

"I know you don't have kids, but let's say you had a young boy. Would you put him into football?" I asked. "Oh boy," he responded,

That's a tough one. I think sports have something to teach kids, I really do. But, you know, nothing has changed. I've gone out to watch my nephew's games a few times, and it's just like it was when I was there. Parents are screaming; people sit on opposite sides of the field like it's a friggin' war, and then when it's over there's dad to be the armchair quarterback and to tell his kid what he needs to do because his old man did- n't do it. Nothing has changed. It's a tough question, but I think if he was just average I might want him to play, but if he was good, that brings with it a whole new set of pressures and ideals. I don't think I'd want my kid to be subjected to that.

THE STRUCTURE OF SPORT

In a time in which social institutions have radically reinvented and improved upon the understanding and treatment of gay and lesbian people, both closeted and openly gay athletes tell me that sport remains steadfast in its production of conservative gender orthodoxy. For example, whereas big business in North America has increasingly offered domestic partnership benefits, established antidiscrimination policies, and even provided for gay and lesbian support groups, the business of professional sports has made no such progress.[1] Whereas public education has been reformed in terms of providing protection to homosexual students, there has been a real disconnect between aca- demics and athletics in both the high school and university settings.[2]

This chapter investigates how sport has remained behind the times. It asks how, in a time of greatly decreasing cultural and institu- tional homophobia, institutions of sport have remained steadfast in their production of a homophobic and conservative gender ideology. It shows that there are three interwoven factors. The first is that sports are a near-total institution in which athletes find it difficult to escape a single-minded way of viewing sex and gender. The second is that sports are a segregated institution that prevents heterosexual men from hearing the narratives of women and gay men. The third is that the institution of sport is a closed-loop system in that it lacks critical self-examination. When taken together, these factors enable sport to near-seamlessly reproduce itself as an institution of orthodox masculine expression.

Sport as a Near-Total Institution

Athletes who rise through the ranks of sport report an increasing consumption of their time and a narrowing of their masculine identity in order to be competitive with others. Collegiate and professional team sport athletes interviewed for this research express that that the requirements for high-caliber performance in sport necessitates increasing devotion of time and uniformity of thought with other athletes. Essentially, they support Michael Messner's theory that athletes maintain less elbow room the higher they move up the athletic hierarchy (2002). This research shows that athletes sacrifice other parts of their identity, friendships, and nonathletic social networks in order to devote themselves to the increasing demands of high-caliber performance. In this aspect higher-level sports can be described as a *near-total institution*.

A total institution is an isolated, enclosed social system (such as a prison or mental hospital). The primary purpose of a total institution is to control most all aspects of a person's life (Goffman 1961). While I do not maintain that sports are a total institution (athletes do have the agency to quit sport), the myth of homogeneity of thought and action required to produce desirable athletic results is so strong that athletes willingly subject themselves to severe restrictions in their social lives.

The process, I argue, is similar to the argument Foucault made concerning the ability of a military to transform peasants into soldiers. Foucault suggested that through intense regimentation and implementation of a standard ideal of behavior, men can be taught to become more docile in their identity because their growing identity as a soldier is also one of subordination of agency. He said that the longer a soldier remains in the institution of soldiering, the less agency he maintains to contest it (1977, 136).

Much like the military, sport structures men into ranks and divisions. Athletes are obliged to dress in uniform, to follow the orders of coaches without question, and to think in alignment with their team-mates, putting team expectations first. I maintain that a subtle but pro-gressive ideology is imposed upon athletes that, like the soldier, in time, deconstructs their individual agency and restructures them as highly masculinized conformists in thought and action. The longer an athlete remains in the field of sport, the less agency he might have to come out.

Terry's recollections of trying to escape his teammate's social group reflects the operation of the near-total institution that he navi-gates. This type of environment effectively secludes the athlete from the rest of culture. Andrew, a closeted collegiate swimmer, reported to me that he couldn't escape the gaze of his teammates.

> It's bad enough that I have to spend all day with them in the pool, but our university policies require that all freshmen live in the dorms, and wouldn't you know it, they force athletes to live with athletes. If I lived in another dorm I would at least be able to meet some other gay guys. You can imagine how many are out in our dorms. None.

He continued to tell me that he had a hard time escaping the social avenues of his teammates too.

> After practice or dinner I might want to go out, you know with other friends, or to the gay part of town. But my teammates are always like, "Where you going man, why can't we come?" It gets annoying, it's like I'm being monitored.

The emergence into the total institution can begin in early child-hood. Athletes are indoctrinated into the thinking of team sports at a very young age, influencing their identity to grow and center on their athleticism. But this also limits their social networks to mainly other athletes. Athletes befriend each other off the field, and their social lives are routinely dictated by their rigid schedule of practices and compe-titions and other team functions. In doing so, they have to shut out other cultural options, limit whom they befriend, particularly those who do not fit the notion of orthodox masculinity.

Furthermore, athletes must publicly acknowledge the same goals and team commitment as other athletes if they are to retain their mas-culine and social status among peers. This involves adopting a collec-tive worldview that tends to be narrow and restrictive, one that they maintain until adulthood. One athlete told Michael Robidoux that he calls the social environment of professional hockey a "cocoon" because the social pressure to adhere to a rigid masculine code frequently sus-tains all walks of an athlete's life (2001, 129).

The effect of uniform thinking and willing subjection to the masculinized ideals of orthodox thinking was made clear in a classroom project when my sociology of masculinities course was analyzing same-sex male erotica. I informed the four hundred students that participation in the screening was not mandatory and that they could leave. Only three walked out. Interestingly, all three were athletes sitting adjacent to each other. I later asked one of the athletes why he left, "No offense," he said. "But when Don left, and then Tom, I didn't want the guys to think I was into the porn."

One can understand how ingrained the shame of homosexuality must be to a male who has been socialized and promoted up the masculine hierarchy in the athletic realm. Understanding this can better explain why Terry, or other gay athletes who have predicated their identity upon highly masculinized athleticism, have such a hard time coming out in the sporting terrain. Because of this, one might even expect that professional team sport athletes would be the *last* to come out of the closet, as their agency has been almost willed out of them.

The fears that Terry maintains regarding coming out is, by his understanding, largely a product of the institutional structure and its masculinizing influence upon which he graduated from youth to the professional ranks. From the moment his talent was identified as a football player in the fifth grade, he was pushed toward making the next level of an ever-increasing structure without being given the opportunity to look around to see what other interests he might want to pursue.

Gay Olympic gold medalist Mark Tewksbury reflected this structure in competitive swimming. "From the moment you win you're first race you enter a system aimed at making the Olympics." Tewksbury maintains that the devotion required to meet the ever-increasing demands yields a myopic and conservative gender perspective.

> Olympic athletes are underdeveloped human beings. They lack life outside of sport and are emotionally underdeveloped. By the time they retire from sport they are well into their adult years and it's harder to break out of the masculine model.

Similarly, a professional hockey player told sport sociologist Michael Robidoux that professional hockey players maintain a stunted development because, "You're playing a game for a living. You are never serious and you're playing with a bunch of guys who think exactly the same as you do. You never really have to grow up. So I think it makes you regress instead of progress" (2001, 137).

The consequences of coming out in this near-total institution is made worse when one considers that advancement is not solely determined by the physical ability of the athlete to perform his sport. Athletes who reflect the institution's creed are deemed as "team players," and they are selected over other athletes who may be equally or physically superior. Conversely, if they do not reflect team norms, they can be labeled as loose cannons. In this regard, any variance from orthodox masculinity is viewed as subversive and is therefore likely to result in decreased opportunity for promotion to the next level. This virtually necessitates that those who aspire to the next level (or even the next game) must disengage with any public notion of a gay identity.

This protracted disengagement from one's homosexual identity must be difficult to challenge after retiring from decades of living within this rigid institution. Just because one is removed from the athletic arena physically does not necessarily mean that one has disengaged from his athletic identity emotionally. Recall the lack of agency Dale (from chapter 2) exercised in face of his involvement with both sport and the military and the fear of coming out. Although he loathed both institutions, he was unwilling to disengaged from them. In this context it is easier to understand the habit of fear Terry maintains, even though he finished his NFL career decades ago. The prospect of being stigmatized and marginalized as gay is more terrifying to him than the daily torment of the homonegative environment he endures.

Perhaps some closeted athletes view the near-total institution of sport as beneficial because of the way it deflects suspicion away from their homosexuality? For example, the incredible consumption of time that an athlete invests into sport enables him to avoid having a heterosexual dating life without arising homosexual suspicion. A college runner told me,

> I consciously used my devotion to sport as an excuse for not having a girlfriend in high school. I avoided school dances because I was resting for the following day's race, or was too tired from the previous. I mean, I dated, but only very occasionally. And when I did date, I was sure to bring her to a party with all my friends so that they could see I was heterosexual.

Dale told me that he didn't date much in high school either, "because I was too busy. Well, at least that's why I said I wasn't dating." Athletics are deemed a worthy masculine enterprise, so men are given permission to avoid heterosexual coupling as a matter of conserving time or energy. In fact, athletic pursuits are so valued, that myths persist that ejaculation robs an athlete of his energy, which permits heterosexual men to vow (at least temporary) chastity.

But gay athletes, who like heterosexual athletes, spend most of their free time in the near-total institution, report that they also feel alienated from mainstream *gay* culture. This can occur because they do not have the time to escape their athletic network, or because they are too young or live too far away from an urban arena in order to seek out gay life in the bars and clubs. Jeff, a university swimmer, told me that in addition to not coming out to his teammates, he was virtually kept from having a gay social life.

> I live with three of my teammates, and between practice, school, and social life with them, I just can't get away. They always have something planned for us to do. And when I do want to go somewhere gay, I totally have to make up some excuse. I can't do it often. People would just get suspicious.

Like most gay athletes I talked to, Jeff links into gay culture through the Internet. But despite the fact that he maintains a host of gay friends in his online cyber community, he feels isolated both in the gay community and on his team.

> I never really feel like I belong. The guys are my friends and all. But I just feel like I am missing something. I'm not sure what would happen if I came out of the closet. I'm afraid I'd then be isolated on my team too.

Similarly, a track athlete said: .

> My team and I went to San Francisco for a race one time. I had never been to a place that's known for gays, and we were traveling all throughout the city as a team. I kept thinking, out here is gay life, but I just couldn't touch it. Then we went to tour Alcatraz, and we were in the dining room, and the tour guide said that the prisoners could often hear the sounds of music, and even smell cooked food floating across the bay to them, and when the wind was right they could hear people's conversations from across the water. I was struck at how similar their experience must have been to mine. All around me I know there is gay life, I can see it, but I just can't touch it.

These interviews make it clear that the near-total institution of team sports provide a mixed bag for gay athletes. On one hand, they provide them with an excuse for not dating and a homoerotic venue for befriending other men. However, the compulsory homophobia required to remain (or advance) in the institution shelters them from the gay community and withers away at their agency to fight homophobia within the system.

SPORT AS A GENDER-SEGREGATED INSTITUTION

Other than jails and mental hospitals, few other institutions segregate men and women so perfectly. Highlighting the hegemony of this segregation people largely support this segregation, sometimes framing their support in analysis of its benefit to women. It is easy to understand why feminists value segregated women's sporting programs. It was not until the passage of Title IX in 1972 that women were really given a start in the institution of sport. Todd Crosset (1990) shows that sports were produced as a masculine preserve in order to deter boys from becoming effeminate in an emerging industrial culture. The exclusion of women from sports was at once deemed necessary because of perceived frailty. As women overcame this perception and began to partake in sports in larger numbers, they were segregated away from men's sports because of the myth of male physical superiority. Therefore, sports are segregated under the guise of providing equality of competition, even in sports where there is no physical danger to men and women competing together and there is no gendered advantage (like golf or bowling). Therefore, sports and the way we do them remain largely segregated because people fear that desegregating sports will lead to women being excluded or injured by masculine violence. Sex segregation allows men to exist in a homogenous, highly masculinized, homophobic, and sexist arena without the voices of women to contrast their conservative understandings.

While women's sporting programs certainly have been shown to be beneficial to women (see Sabo et al. 2004), the near-total segregation has a great number of deleterious effects for women as well. First, there is a disparity in the allocation of sporting resources, as women's athletics have consistently been shown to fare worse than men's (Messner 2002). Specific to the reproduction of orthodox masculinity, however, is that structural segregation removes men from the narratives of female athletes who might otherwise enlighten them about their athleticism. For these reasons Mariah Burton-Nelson (1995) maintains that sport unites men across the spectrum of class (and one can assume race) but renders women invisible.

When I interviewed ex-football players who, for a variety of social and structural reasons, turned collegiate cheerleaders (which is desegregated) about their attitudes regarding female athleticism and women in general, men credited the sport of cheerleading as having highly impacted their views regarding women. "Oh, we totally learn to respect women, I mean they are like our sisters," one athlete told me. Another confirmed, "Yeah, I never really understood women too much before, but my teammates are a family to me. I have grown real close to them, and now I can often see things from their perspective."

I asked several dozen cheerleaders and a number of cheerleading coaches about their interaction between men and women and conducted several group interviews on the subject. The responses unanimously indicated the development of a cohesive group and learned or enhanced respect for women. One coach said: "Oh, yeah, they become like family. I mean they spend so much time together, they change in the same locker rooms sometimes, and they just get real comfortable with bodily issues."

In cheerleading, men are able to partake in conversations with and about sex and gender—the kind of conversations they were unable to have in a homosocial, ostensibly heterosexual (and homophobic) culture such as football. In this environment they are able to socialize with and develop team cohesion with women as participants of equal agency and responsibility for the outcome of a game. They are often able to experience women as leaders (as women are most generally the team captains in cheerleading), and to even see gay men do what they do, but frequently better (because gay men often cheered in high school too). Therefore, by entering the coed division of cheerleading in college, these men hear the narratives of women's sexual and gender identities. My research suggests that in desegregating sport men develop a form of masculinity that is based less on misogyny and homophobia.

Sport as a Closed-Loop Institution

Not every boy who dreams of making it to the NFL will succeed. Boys, who are less physically adept at sport, either self-segregate out, are selected out, graduate out, drop out, or are forced out through injury. Boys who are less willing to put up with the highly masculinized attitudes are deselected for the next round of competition or labeled as loose cannons. Being told that one is not a team player is a mark of shame that is likely to drive nonconformists away from the sporting terrain. Therefore, athletes who withstand the selection process do so because of their outstanding athletic ability *and* willingness to conform to orthodox masculinity.

Athletes who excel in sport are merited in the form of social prestige; they are given cultural power and they are publicly lauded. From their perception sport is a socially positive vessel. But for every athlete who has excelled in sport, there are scores who did not make the cut. Others have had horrifying experiences in sport.

Success stories like Terry's fail to recognize the statistical reality of sports. Not every kid can play professional football. But books aren't published, sponsorships aren't given, and movies aren't made about those who didn't make it. In this manner only certain stories are being told, stories (including my own autobiography) that glamorize the struggle and romance of the sporting hero genre. These stories make for great entertainment but falsely lead us to bestow upon sport qualities that may not actually exist or that only exist for those born with the talent and social circumstances to excel at sport.

As discussed earlier, athletes who pursue sport find that the farther they advance, the more time and emotional investment they must devote in order to remain competitive. This serves to further narrow their social life to the point in which everything revolves around their sport. They grow so wrapped up in their status as an athlete that it often becomes their master identity. But centering one's identity on athleticism carries with it great risk in such a volatile field. At any time an injury can end a career, or the athlete can be cut from the team on a moment's notice. And whether they suddenly lose their association with their athletic identity or their body slowly ages out of competitive form, eventually athletes are forced to disengage from the social location of that master identity.

Men who drop out, are forced out, or otherwise do not make the next level often find themselves detached from much of the cultural masculine power they once enjoyed—something sport psychologists call the disengagement effect (Greendorfer 1992). Retired professional football player Marvin Upshaw stated:

> You find yourself just scrambled. You don't know which way to go. Your light, as far as you're concerned, has been turned out. You miss the roar of the crowd. Once you've heard it, you can't get away from it. There's an empty feeling—you feel everything you wanted is gone. All of a sudden you wake up and you find yourself 29, 35 years old, you know, and the one thing that has been the major part of your life is gone. It's gone. (cited in Messner 1987, 203)

Under such conditions, most athletes report a desire to be part of a team again, so that they can recoup some of their masculine worth. Michael Messner says, "Many retired athletes retain a powerful drive to reestablish the important relationship with the crowd that served as the primary basis for their identity for so long" (1987, 204). It makes sense that athletes who rode atop the masculine hierarchy would also feel the greatest loss upon disengaging from that status. Coaching often becomes the avenue to get back in the game.

Sport almost always draws leaders from those who ascribed to the previous cohort's ideals. Conversely, the vast majority of those who were marginalized by sport do not go on to coach and tell their stories so their ideas about how sport ought to operate are not heard in the athletic arena. When athletes leave the sporting arena, their perceptions of how sport ought to operate go with them. Sport, therefore, is a closed-loop system.

Much like the military, those who survive are promoted to leadership positions, where they reproduce hero genres to inspire a new generation. Complacency and overconformity get one promoted. Only highly devoted athletes (who usually were rewarded by sport) return to coach, denying sporting experiences and narratives of those whose experiences were not so wonderful. This closed-loop system serves elite athletes. It is held in place by the hero myth that so thrills Americans, particularly the underdog genre. We listen to those who have made it through the abusive system tout the wonders of sport but are not privy to the stories of those whose experience was poor.

If we were to examine the institution of sport from a medical perspective, however, sport would fail to gain the mass approval it now has. It would likely appear inefficient in producing significant positive results for the majority of those who experience it. Sport, undoubtedly, does *some* people some good, but as Miracle and Rees have shown in their book *Lessons of the Locker Room* (1995), the cultural myth that sport is good for everybody is wholly misguided.

Knowing that the few who gain merit in sport go into coaching, we should next note that most American coaching positions, public or private, require no training in pedagogy, sport psychology, or even physical education. In fact, coaching youth sport requires no degree at all in most states. Whereas one needs a license to cut hair or run a day care, anyone can hang a whistle around his neck and call himself a coach.

Coaches largely learn their trade by modeling what their coach did. In other words, coaches tend to reproduce themselves because they both value the system they have progressed through and they are not required to critically analyze the institution. Without such intervention, there is little input to evaluate or change the system.

When taken together with the near-total gender segregation and the near-total institutional atmosphere in athletics, sport manages to maintain and reproduce orthodox notions of masculinity that are based on homophobia and misogyny. Male athletes are removed from the presence of women and (openly) gay men; they are influenced by the top-down modeling of the total institution, and the institution itself excludes input from those not within its network. Therefore, although sport is a century removed from its origins as an institution to promote men's interest over women and other marginalized men, it should be no surprise that the effects of the second generation of feminism and gay liberation of the later part of the twenty-first century have yielded little.

5

Coming Out in Sport

ONE ATHLETE'S STORY:
BLAKE, HIGH SCHOOL BASKETBALL PLAYER

The wooden floor of the high school gym squeaks a bit as Blake shuffles his six-foot, four-inch body up and down the court. Only a sophomore, Blake is already one of the best players in his midwestern state, drawing coverage from local media and praise from his community. Despite the fact that the rest of the team has gone home, Blake remains late into the evening, shooting basket after basket in order to better himself as an athlete. Blake had no dreams of superstardom when he began playing ball, but today he hopes that putting a ball through a hoop will not only provide him with the image of being heterosexual but that it will provide him with a college scholarship too. "Basketball is my ticket out of here," he said. Like athletes from the inner cities and reservations, Blake uses sport as a possible escape from a challenging environment. He hopes to escape the immense homophobia from his midwestern home and community by relocating to a metropolitan area for college.[1]

Blake grudgingly picked up basketball in the fourth grade because he had already perceived that popularity among boys was based primarily on athleticism, and he desired to raise his social standing. "I was actually more interested in reading," Blake tells me over the phone at three o'clock in the morning so his parents could not hear our conversation, "but that's not really cool. I mean I really hated basketball. I'd much rather read a book, but other boys didn't do that. Everybody played basketball, and I wanted to fit in, so I did too."

Blake was sufficiently talented at basketball, and his height and hard work enabled him to become better than other players, and he quickly learned that as a top player he was socially merited for his athletic accomplishments. He found himself respected by his peers. "Oh, yeah, I am the man all right," he comments sarcastically. "Even back in sixth grade I was. I would score twenty-five points a game as a sixth grader."

It was also during the sixth grade that Blake began to worry about feelings he increasingly recognized as gay, and by the eighth grade Blake knew with certainty that he was what he feared. "It's not easy to be the thing that all the boys use as a put-down. It's what you call someone when you're trying to dis them, and I certainly did not want to be that!" So Blake learned both to play the game of basketball and the game of heterosexual passing. On the court he learned that when you are the best "everyone wants a piece of you," and that every victory brings an added pressure of yet another. Off the court, he was able to shed the heterosexual façade he displayed publicly, and the Internet became what he describes as his cyber-home. He met and talked with other gay boys from around the state and nation. Near the end of his eighth-grade year, he even ventured out to meet other gay boys, and eventually found a boyfriend.

Having a boyfriend as a freshman in high school helped Blake immensely. "Actually meeting gay people was so amazing," he said. His boyfriend helped him realize that he was not alone, and that loving another boy was nothing to feel guilty about. "We dated for a few months, which at fourteen seemed like forever, and then one day he just stopped calling. I couldn't figure out why he wasn't returning my calls or my e-mails." Blake began dealing with a harsh rejection. Being closeted however, Blake had no adult to turn to, nobody to lament his anguish. So he returned to vent online. "I was talking to a friend, asking him if he had heard from Chris." His friend responded, "Didn't you hear? Chris was killed in a car accident."

"I started to cry. Hard," he said. "So I ran to the bathroom and turned the radio up as loud as it went so nobody could hear me." Alone, Blake had nobody to turn to, nobody to hug him and hold him. He would have to mourn in secret.

> I tried to tell myself that it didn't matter to me. But it did. I loved Chris.
> He was my first love, and I was young, and it hit me twice as hard. I only
> wished I could have told others, but I didn't have anyone I could talk to

about it. I made a reference to him in a paper my freshmen year but I couldn't tell my teacher or my parents why he died, or who he was, or why I was upset. Hell, I couldn't even tell them that someone had died at all.

Blake's story makes salient some of the hardships of concealing one's sexual identity. Blake repeated to me, "I just wish I could have talked to someone." His voice began to crack, and through muffled tears he angrily said, "If it had been a straight friend it would have been easy, but no, it was my boyfriend, and nobody wants to know about that." His tears subsided, "I was all alone."

Today, Blake walks the hallways of his rural high school popular publicly but emotionally alienated. He describes his high school as "a typical jock high school." By definition Blake's ironic position atop the pyramid should be a great location for him, as those on top receive public praise and social privilege. But from where he stands, towering above the others literally and physically, he feels alienated. There are no openly gay students at his school, and Blake isn't even sure if there are any in his community at all. "If there are, I certainly don't know of them," he says with discord.

Blake is also daunted by the insistent fear of being discovered:

I fear all the time that others will find out. That people's opinions of me will change if they find out that I'm gay. Like my teachers, they won't think the same of me; they make gay comments and say them in a derogatory manner. Even my own bro will say stuff about gay people. It makes it hard, I'm always thinking in the back of my mind, would you feel this way about me if you knew I was gay?

He adds, "My friends, it's the same thing with them. I have a lot of good friends, but a lot of them are religious, which strikes quite a bit of fear with me." Compounding matters, Blake fears that his parents may have an inclination that he is gay. "They don't want to think about it. Mom says, 'Blake you need to get a girlfriend.' 'Mom I don't want to,' I tell her. 'I don't have time. I'm too busy. I have to get my workout in.'"

Basketball becomes the all-purpose excuse for Blake. It not only provides him with a veneer of heterosexuality (as there is a near-total assumption that all team sport athletes are heterosexual in his town), but it gives him something to do other than dating women. Spending his free time shooting hoops for several hours a day provides Blake with an acceptable excuse for not dating, as it is socially permissible for him to spend less time in the pursuit of women when pursuing the noble and masculine goal of basketball stardom.

Blake tells me about his brother's expectations, his parents' desire to see him succeed in basketball (over academics), and the social drama created when everybody is trying to live vicariously through him. "My parents really care about my basketball. They acknowledge it a lot more than my academics," he said. "They are much more concerned that I represent the family in basketball than in academics because they can go to a game and point and say, 'That's our son.'"

Shooting baskets also provides Blake with a sense of solitude and self-esteem. It helps him deal with the stresses and fears continuously swirling around him, even though the pressure to succeed is the genesis of much of that stress. Still, Blake feels that physical exercise and "taking it out on the courts" helps him to deal with the stresses of being closeted in a homophobic community. The amount of time basketball takes helps Blake mitigate some of his loneliness, his longing for love, and the alienation he feels from those who share his identity. "When I'm in the gym by myself, it calms my nerves. If I'm upset, I'll go shoot by myself."

Coming out is certainly something Blake ponders—daily—but he just has not been able to bring himself to do it yet. I asked him how he thought he would be treated if he were to come out to everyone in his town today.

> In all honesty, there will be some people who are not okay with it. But at the same time, I think it might open a lot of people's eyes. Like the people at my school; they don't have any gay friends. They don't know any gay people at all. They might just look at me and say Blake has been my best friend since I was little, and he's gay, and he's cool. I just hope they see me as the same goofy Blake.

His response is pleasantly absent of fears of being victimized by homophobic violence, partially because he embodies the ability to commit violence himself—he is tall and muscular.

Blake's decision to postpone his coming out is complicated. Gay or straight, out-of-state tuition is expensive, and a scholarship for playing ball would help; Blake fears that coming out would hurt his chances, something hard to refute. "I definitely plan on coming out when I'm in college; there is no question about that. The question is, will I come out during my junior or senior year of high school?" Bravery is not so easy. Coming out in a small homophobic town and battling homophobic parents, teachers, and teammates is more pressure than any million-dollar athlete would like to handle. It is, without doubt, as tough a decision as any sixteen-year-old should have to make.

FEAR OF COMING OUT

This chapter examines the experiences of gay athletes in the coming out process. It examines the fears that gay athletes maintain before coming out, and then documents the ease of those fears, as they do not materialize after coming out. It finds that gay athletes who come out to their teams feel a sense of elation about their coming out that may blind them to some negative aspects of their coming out. It also turns to a discussion of homophobic discourse and the complexity such language poses to understanding the nature of homophobia in sport.

Fear is the hallmark of closeted gay athletes. One swimmer told me, "Every action has an equal and opposite reaction, coming out is a big deal, so one can expect a big backlash." Virtually all gay athletes fear losing face, losing friends, or losing the support of teammates and the coach. Others fear losing starting positions, college scholarships, or as in the case of professional athletes, sponsorships and contracts. I asked a professional figure skater why he did not come out of the closet. "Are you kidding me?" he sharply responded. "I'll be a target for judges looking to knock my score. On top of that, I can just kiss my sponsorship goodbye."

Still, others fear violence. "Hell no, I am not coming out," one football player told me. "I'd get my ass kicked, if not on the field, then off it." These fears of violence are intensified when stories of ill treatment toward gay men (and gay athletes particularly) make news. For example, in 1998 ESPN broadcasted "Outside the Lines" on gay athletes, featuring the story of Greg Congdon. Greg, an average football player, was suicidal over his sexual identity and was outed against his will after a suicide attempt. The word soon got back to his high school football teammates, and despite the fact that Greg had been their close friend, he was shunned. Teammates even threatened him with physical violence if he were to try to come back to the team. Greg told me:

> I walked into the school and I started getting shoved around, and pushed around. My friends wouldn't talk to me, so that kind of made me really hate myself more. Like I was told that if I played any sports that they'd make my life a living hell. My teammates felt betrayed. They felt that they had known me their whole life and that I had lied to them. They couldn't believe that I had slipped right under their eyes. They thought they could always tell a gay guy from a mile away. And I believe it made them question themselves a little bit. One of them tried to say that I was hitting on him because I used to sit with him at lunch. After that, nobody would sit with me at lunch. I just sat alone. And then they would drive by my house in the middle of the day and yell obscenities at me.

Although not an athlete, in 1998, a young gay male was beaten, then strung to a fence and left to die in the frigid air of Laramie, Wyoming. The vicious murder of an attractive, white, educated youth shocked America. News of the homicide and the trial of his assailants dominated headlines in a way that previous gay killings had not. My partner and I received two phone calls that day, one from my mother, and one from his. Each vicariously identified with the mother of Matthew Shepard. Each had worried about such brutality happening to their own children. Each implored us to be more careful.

Statistically speaking, however, there is little reason to be more careful, as hate crimes against gays are actually quite rare. For example, in 2002 there were 140 violent crimes reported against gays and lesbians among the 9.6 million people in Los Angeles County.[2] And while 140 hate crimes is certainly 140 too many, it is also important to know that if a hate crime were to occur in the athletic arena, like most gay bashings on the street, it would not be anonymous. Therefore, statistically speaking, Matthew Shepard's killing, as horrific as it was, was a statistical anomaly. But the fact that it *did* occur is hard to let go of for those who fear such reprisal against their stigmatized sexuality.

Gay athletes also fear because athletics are intrinsically violent. This is especially true of contact sports. Pronger (1999) stresses that athletics, at least the way Westerners do them, are about the violent acquisition of territory, taking, and hurting of other men's space and bodies. Making matters worse, representation of hypermasculine athletes in the media, on television, screen and print, often portrays athletes as being inclined to solve social issues through violence, covertly (and often overtly) suggesting that gay men should fear homophobic athletes who are trained in violence and who use homophobic language to indicate their potential violence. It is this language that athletes use to judge their sport as being highly homophobic. It is the unbridled use of homophobic discourse that leads them to fear violence should their sexuality be revealed. In this respect homophobic discourse is *symbolic violence*. While it does not leave bruises on the skin, it imprints fear on the mind, particularly if you are harboring a gay identity. This is particularly true in sport, where there is a pervasive use of the word *fag* as a general, specific, or nonspecific insult. Athletes, gay and straight, tell me that their teammates use the word prolifically, as do many of their coaches, even though one study shows that only about 50 percent of men mean it in a derisive manner (Burn 2000). One athlete said:

> Are you kidding me? Of course I hear *fag* all the time. Yeah, like *all* the time. If you pass the ball to one guy when some other guy wants

it, he calls you a fag. If you are messin' with some guy and he does-n't like it, he says, "Knock it off, fag." If you want to get in some guy's face you call him a fag.

The fear of retribution for coming out in sport may also be heightened because athletes are often the unofficial rule enforcers of hegemonic masculinity in school settings.

Jason, a high school cross-country and track runner, feared that coming out to his teammates would be a difficult, and perhaps dangerous, event.

> One of the things that was holding me back from coming out was like my own fear of locker-room situations. Because in my mind I didn't want to make other people uncomfortable around me in the locker room, and I didn't want them to make it an issue. I'd heard some horror stories from some of my friends. One of my friend's friends was beaten to a bloody pulp because they thought he was gay.

Steve, another high school cross-country and track runner, also feared coming out. "I didn't know how they would react, even though they seemed to be cool with it, you know. It's like the fear of rejection, I guess." Chris, a college hockey player, expressed why he feared coming out:

> I thought about it a lot, especially when coming out at first. I figured a lot of people would just sort of freak out. It's just sort of the culture. In the locker rooms you know, there's always joking. Guys talking funny things about other guys, grabbing their butts and stuff. But the minute you enter or add a tone of realism like, "Hey, that actually does it for me" or tell them about my boyfriend or something then it would totally shatter a lot of trust that's there. At least that's what I figured from playing hockey for the past six years. And I haven't read much about other guys doing that, and I don't know what the reaction would be in other sports, but hockey is a very only-tough-guys-play-it kind of sport, and who knows how violent some of these guys might get.

The fear of negative responses by athletes may limit the number of gay athletes who might otherwise come out of the closet (Pronger 1990). For example, Dale, the closeted high school and now college football player from chapter 2, avoided talking about his fear specifically, but it was easy to see the trepidation he felt about the issue of homophobia and football players when I asked him if he perceived his team as being homophobic.

Oh my god, let's just say you have never met a group of more homophobic guys in one sport. They would talk to no end about "you faggot," "fucking faggots should all be shot," shit like that. I think it
comes with the territory. Football players are supposed to be the most
macho guys on campus, and we have to live up to that stereotype. So
I guess gay bashing made the guys feel like they're more of a man
and tougher and stuff. It made me sick, but if I wanted to play the
sport I grew to love, I would have to put up with it.

Eric, a college bowler in Texas, expressed similar concern about
homophobic attitudes in his town. "I was afraid of the athletes, yes.
But I was also afraid of everybody else. I mean, this is Texas, and it's
not like I live in Houston or Dallas either." A Pennsylvanian high
school cross-country and track runner also describes his team as being
incredibly homophobic.

There was no way in hell I was going to come out. . . . This is a very
uptight, very strange town; it's pretty much 99 percent white Chris-
tians. It kind of amused me how a town with so little diversity could
be so prejudiced and biased toward certain groups of people. Actually you will find this interesting, because of the homophobia, when
we would go on overnight trips, there would be four guys in a room,
but only one person in each bed. Two guys had to sleep on the floor.
And these were standard queen-size beds.

However, this research suggests that athletes' fears of physical
reprisal, of being beaten up for coming out publicly to their teammates, may actually be unfounded. In fact, Greg's story exemplifies, by
far, the worst experience of all the subjects I have interviewed, casually
spoken with, or even heard about since I began collecting data for this
book in 1998.[3] Indeed, the beating of my athlete in 1995 is the last physical attack on a gay (or suspected gay) athlete that I know of in the
United States. While my sample is too small to make the claim that
physical aggression and verbal harassment toward openly gay males
in high school and college sports does not happen, it does show that
sport is not *always* overtly homophobic. Almost all of the athletes in
my study were free from overt discrimination in the form of verbal or
physical violence. Still, the fear of potential violence remains.

While these results seem not only different from what athletes fear,
and from what researchers might predict, athletes still fear; whether
being victimized by homophobic violence is statistically reasonable or
not, athletes fear it. This fear comes through myths and stories embedded within their social networks or from fictional accounts in the

media. In this respect, the types of fear that gay athletes report can be compared to Barry Glassner's work on American fears. Glassner (1999) posits that frequently our fears are grossly exaggerated given the actual frequency of such events. He maintains that fears are spawned and reproduced by the constant bombardment of extraordinarily rare events that are made to seem ordinary when they are portrayed repeatedly in the media. The Matthew Shepard case is such a case.

Such events impress the fear of selective violence, even if it is a statistical improbability, on gays and lesbians because it is as if the perpetrators were saying, "We're out hunting, and we're hunting your type." Herek and Berrill (1992) call these types of events hate crimes because they send a message to the entire gay community to "watch out, this can happen to you," effectively terrorizing an entire community even if the statistical reality is contrary. In this manner, targeted hate crimes seem to send a message of fear that random events are unable to. These fears help to relegate gays to a second-class social status by their self-silencing, preventing sexual minorities from having the same sense of social freedom as heterosexuals. Yet some athletes brave these fears and come out anyhow.

COMING OUT IN SPORT

The most celebrated openly gay high school or collegiate athlete to come out of the closet was Corey Johnson, the cocaptain of a Massachusetts high school football team in 1999.[4] His story received tremendous publicity in 1999 when it ran in the *New York Times* because it defied what both the public and those who examined the issue of gays in sport largely thought about sports—that it remained a physical, hostile terrain toward gays, making it nearly impossible and certainly inhospitable to come out. Corey's story, however, which is largely that of acceptance, actually fits the mold of most of the narratives in my research.

Like most athletes, Corey examined the terrain before coming out. Indeed, his acceptance was made possible by several factors. First, Corey had met with faculty members before coming out to his team, and even though the majority advised him to stay closeted, he told them he felt he needed to come out now. He then came out to his best friend and teammate, also acquiring his support. He next told his football coach, who was supportive and agreed to create a meeting for Corey to come out to his teammates.

With the cooperation of the administration and his coaches, Corey pulled together his team in a postcompetition meeting where Corey stood before them and publicly declared:

> Guys, I called this meeting because I have something I really want to
> tell all of you. And I hope you'll be supportive. The reason I'm telling
> you all is because I don't want you hearing it from somebody else.
> I'm coming out as an openly gay man. I'm still the same person I've
> always have been. I hope this won't change anything.

Corey next told them: "I didn't come on to you in the locker room last
year. I'm not going to do it this year. Who says you guys are good
enough anyway?" a remark that he says broke the tension.

Corey's teammates seemed to take his sexuality in stride. In the
locker room, they, unlike most teams, asked about what kind of guys
he likes and where the nearest gay bar was, and then joked about
wanting shirts from the establishment. Corey tells another endearing
story, on the bus ride home from a game, somebody said, "Let's sing a
song for Corey." They started singing the Village People's "YMCA"
and, later, the Weather Girls' "It's Raining Men."

Steve, a cross-country runner, had anxiety about coming out to his
team. "Oh my god, I was so nervous. But I just had to do it; people
were starting to talk as it was, and I just wanted to set the record
straight." When I asked him why he was nervous he replied, "Well,
you just really never know how people are going to take it. But once I
came out, oh my god, it was awesome! Like the guys were totally cool
with it, and I'm so glad I came out." Ryan, a college skier shared a similar experience, telling me that his teammates were very supportive of
him, and that he had, "no problems at all."

These stories contradict fears that athletes largely maintain about
the possibility of physical violence. In fact, of the forty openly gay athletes studied, not one encountered overt intolerance or physical harm,
and only one athlete (Greg) classified his experience as "awful."

These results seem not only different from what researchers have
predicted, but also different than what many of the athletes expected.
In fact, most of the athletes I interviewed were very pleased with their
coming out experience. When I asked them, "If you could do it all over
again, what, if anything, would you do differently?" Most said that
they would have come out earlier because it was not as difficult as they
had thought it would be. Ryan told me, "It was nothing like I thought
it would be. The guys were great and I can't believe I worried about it."

These results parallel some of what Hekma found in his research on
gay athletes in the Netherlands. Hekma, who examined the experiences
of gay men and lesbians in organized sport by surveying 203 gay male
athletes and 116 lesbian athletes found that most of the athletes he studied were not out to their teams (although he fails to say how many
were). He found that closeted gay men and lesbians in the Netherlands

do not experience *much* overt discrimination in organized, nonprofessional (or nonacademic) sporting teams. "Discrimination does exist in organized sports, but because most gay men and many lesbians conceal their sexual identities, it does not—as far as we could ascertain—take on extreme forms" (1998, 7).

Hekma's results may be explained by several factors. First, the overall level of acceptance of homosexuality in the Netherlands is much higher than in other industrialized nations (Widmer et al. 2002). Second, and most obvious, the lack of overt homophobia reported may simply be due to the fact that most all of his subjects were closeted to their teams! Nonetheless, it is striking to see how many gay men favored individual sports over team sports.

Of twenty-six gay athletes who used to play soccer, Hekma found that all but five abandoned soccer for an individual sport. He found the same with sixteen gay hockey players, of which only one still played. He therefore suggests that gay athletes, who desire to continue participating in sport, may no longer feel comfortable, safe, or welcome on their teams, and they drop them for individual sports. His findings, however, should be taken with skepticism, as they were not compared to attrition rates of heterosexual athletes. Consequently, his results might simply be a function of decreased team sport opportunities with increased age, thereby highlighting yet another difficulty in obtaining a significant sample size from this population.

FEELINGS OF LIBERATION

Because the coming out process allows one to embrace words that were once used to marginalize them, most athletes felt an immense sense of liberation after coming out. In essence, coming out changes the course of defense from silence to defiance, and it is often so intoxicatingly powerful that each successful coming out creates a psychological desire for another. One athlete said:

> I came out to my best friend, who happened to be on the team. He was like stoked that I came out to him. He thought it was great that I was gay, and he encouraged me to come out to another guy on the team. So, I told him, and like, he hugged me! I was so stoked I just wanted to tell everybody. It felt so good to tell people. It still does.

Another athlete told me:

> Coming out was by far the best thing I had ever done. I can't believe how good it felt. It was like I was locked in a dungeon, and then all

of a sudden the door was open and I could see the light. I started telling people, and the more people I told, the more people I wanted to tell.

Still another athlete said:

> I compare it to going on a roller coaster. At first you're scared shitless, and the closer you get to going up that hill, you know, toward the top of the ride, well, that's like the night before you've decided to tell your team. And then that roller coaster drops, and you're scared shitless but at the same time you're totally excited. Finally, the ride ends, and you just can't wait to get back on and do it again. That was me. After I told everyone on my team, I just wanted to tell more and more people.

Knowing that coming out elicits an elevated state of power and confidence, the pattern of these athletes being in such high spirits about their coming out experience made me wonder if there might not also be something occurring that they were not reporting, or not able to recognize. Essentially, I wondered if their exuberance was also preventing them from seeing the negative, which was often revealed much later in their narratives. For example, as clean as Corey's story sounds, and as wonderful as the press made it out to be, like most other narratives in this research, it was not free from overt discrimination. For example, even though Corey's teammates weren't too upset, a few of the team parents were. One even suggested revoting for captain, and if this suggestion was vocalized, one can only imagine what went on behind Corey's back. Fortunately, regarding the revote, the coach stood by Corey, and said that a revote was not an option.

One of the subjects who spoke of his experience in the most glowing terms was Grant, a high school runner who came out after two of his other teammates did. Grant talked in glowing prose about his coming out experience, describing all as being "very good" and praising his coach and teammates for their wonderful support.

> The first people I came out to were actually runners, and my coach. I went to a private Christian school in Ohio, and one day we were sitting around talking and a runner came out to us so I did too. From then, I was able to open up to other runners. And no one really had a problem or an issue with the fact that we were gay.

Grant's experience seemed truly positive to him (and indeed, much of it was), but he later went on to tell me that he had lost a friend after coming out.

We were at camp, and we had been around these guys for years, and someone had found out that we were gay and had a fit over it. I was kind of hurt by it. Certain things that were said were out of place. This individual completely left the camp and did not run that year because of what his friends would think because he was running with us. I'd say he was one of our good friends, he no longer spoke to me.

Jason, a high school runner, was outed against his will. He was more fortunate than Grant, in that he didn't lose any friends in the coming out process.

I've heard stories of people who've come up to them [his friends] and ask them why they were hanging out with me, because I was gay. Or "why do you hang out with gay people? Gay people are disgusting." And luckily, enough of my friends didn't back down, and they were supportive about it, and they were like, "It doesn't matter that he's gay; he's still my friend." I'm so lucky to have friends who are so supportive; I haven't lost a single one.

However, while Jason didn't lose any friends, he did have problems with teammates, who, as part of practice, are required to stretch with the assistance of a teammate.

A lot of them [teammates] stopped talking to me. And you know sometimes in workouts when you have to have a partner? That became kind of difficult. Nobody wanted to do stretches with me. Everybody was like standoffish. It ended up that the people doing [stretches] with me were either people who didn't know yet, or like friends of mine.

Derek, a college speed skater in Canada, also had positive stories to report. After he came out to his teammates, they expressed interest in homosexuality and asked him a lot of questions in order to help understand and accept him. Derek said, "They even come to the local gay club with me regularly; they have fun and they dance. So they have no problems." However, when I questioned further, I discovered that not all of his teammates were this comfortable with him. Derek told me that one teammate was particularly uncomfortable with him, especially when it came to sleeping in the same bed on overnight trips. "Well he would just say, 'Oh, you're not going do anything are you?' One time he volunteered to sleep on the cot because he didn't want to sleep with me, and then one time I volunteered because I didn't want to make him uncomfortable." And when I questioned Derek more, he remembered that one time this same individual had insulted him. "We got to the hotel, and we ended up being in the same room, and I remember he said, 'I don't want to sleep with a faggot.'"

REVERSE RELATIVE DEPRIVATION

Perhaps these athletes were so relieved to not have physical altercations or blatantly mean-spirited acts of intimidation against them that they were unaware of the homophobia they actually did encounter. It seems that in the absence of severe expected intolerance, their sense of how well things went may have been artificially boosted. In this manner we may have a type of reverse relative deprivation occurring with openly gay athletes. Whereas sociologists usually discuss people who compare themselves to those who have it better, these athletes seemed to compare themselves to those who had it worse. They are similar to some older African Americans seeing things better than younger African Americans because they compare today to yesteryear. Things seemed "good" to the athletes in light of what "might have been." When one expects to be treated hostilely, a little prejudice, or a few mean-spirited gay jokes, doesn't seem so bad.

Other athletes also report coming out experiences as positive compared to what might have been. Yhon, a Texas high school football player who was outed to his teammates, reports his outing as "positive," even "a relief," despite the fact that a few of his teammates decided they could no longer talk to him.

> Well, at first I didn't want to go to practice, 'cause I was scared about what was gonna happen. But my coaches came to me and said, "Don't worry it's gonna be OK; they [teammates] like you a lot." So I went out there, and I was kinda scared, but everyone kept being the same. You know, they kept being my friends, and there were like only two or three that stopped talking to me . . . and one of them, I used to be best friends with him . . . and as soon as he found out he stopped talking to me.

Having only "two or three" players stop talking to Yhon because of his sexual orientation was defined as a good result. Yhon expected things to be much worse.

Yhon and Grant were not the only ones to lose friends. Chris, a Canadian hockey player, described his coming out experience as being "pretty good actually," despite the fact that Chris also lost a friend.

It took about four or five weeks for it to sink in. Even when I was introducing them to my boyfriend they were like, "This is a joke." So it took a while and the guys were a little different. At first there was this, "Oh." They weren't shocked, but they were surprised. And then it kinda sunk in, and with one of them it was "OK, that's cool," and with the other it was "OK, that's neat, but we can't do certain things anymore." He never really said that, but that's what has worked out. So the one on the one hand was really quite good, and the other was all right. It could have been worse from what I've heard.

Homophobic Discourse

If attitudes toward homosexuality can be changed, then it may be reasonable to expect to see a change in homophobic discourse as well. However, this greatly varied. Many athletes reported that their teammates continued to use homophobic discourse, even after they came out. The reverse relative deprivation influenced these athletes to maintain that everything "went very well." Still, not all athletes continued to use homophobic discourse after their gay teammates came out. This research, therefore, found no definite conclusions about the use of homophobic discourse. It simply found that when exposed to gay male athletes, some heterosexual athletes' attitudes and language *might* change.

For those who did continue to use homophobic language, sorting out intent from effect proves complicated. First, homonegative discourse is a habit for most team sport athletes, whether they intend to cause harm through this discourse or not. In fact, research on college men shows that while most men use the word in a derisive manner, only about 50 percent of men mean it as a specifically homophobic insult (Burn 2000). Because of this, many gay athletes mitigate the damage caused by this discourse, dismissing it by saying, "They don't mean it that way." Finally, other athletes attempt to empower homonegative discourse through usurping them and redefining the words as homopositive.

Athletes in my study were almost unanimously called a fag directly *before coming out* of the closet, as the word is used to stratify men in athletic culture. For many of the athletes in this study, however, this direct labeling all but ceased *after* they came out to their teams. This was even true of those who came out without directly saying it. These athletes commonly heard heterosexual teammates say to one another, "Knock it off, fag" as a form of either venting frustration, or in a supposed jocular manner, but they did not report hearing it used at them directly.

One football player told me, "Oh yeah, I hear fag all the time. But not directly. I mean they don't say, 'You are a fag.'" Indeed, only Greg and Derek reported being called a fag in a harassing or violent manner, but all athletes reported hearing it in a nonspecific or general manner, such as saying, "Hurry up, fag." In fact, most of the athletes reported that their heterosexual teammates tried not to use the word *fag* in association with them at all, even if they did continue to use it as an insult among each other.

Frank, an openly gay football player, told me that he was surprised at how well he was received on his team because his teammates had used such a high degree of homophobic discourse before he came out.

> I couldn't believe how cool the guys were with me. I mean I expected them to be really unaccepting of me because they'd called me a fag for so long. I mean, they call everyone a fag, so it's not like they thought I was gay or anything, but still I thought that when they found out I really was, you know, gay, that they'd hate me.

When I asked him if they still call him a fag now that he came out he responded, "No. Not really. I mean, every now and then they might say it, but they usually apologize and say that they didn't mean it that way. But they still call each other fags and athletes from other teams at our school do too."

Not all of the heterosexual teammates used the word *fag* in general ways. Many athletes vowed to cease using the word in casual or purposeful ways altogether. This was also the case with other ethnographic research I have conducted on ex-football players who move from a disposition of homophobia to acceptance of homosexuality as male cheerleaders (Anderson 2004). Here I found that when exposed to the narratives of gay men, once highly homophobic men can quickly deconstruct their homophobia and remove homophobic discourse from their language.

But despite the attempts of some of their teammates to reduce homophobic discourse by eliminating the use of the word *fag*, most informants reported much less sensitivity toward their teammates' use of the word *gay*. Frank said, "Oh yeah, they say everything is gay if they don't like it. I mean, if you're being dumb, they say, 'don't be gay,' and if your team was given a penalty unfairly they say, 'That's so gay.'" Ken said, "They say this is gay and that's gay, but they don't mean it like that," even though Ken reports not using the word in such manner himself. In fact, few of the informants strongly objected to their teammates using the word *gay* when describing things distasteful, even though they didn't use the word in such a manner themselves.

These findings are consistent with what other researchers have found regarding the frequency in which gay athletes hear antigay language spoken by their heterosexual teammates and opponents. Ironically, these studies found that the gay athletes themselves do not necessarily view this language as being homophobic.[5] Some explain this by saying that homophobic language takes on a significantly different meaning as it appears to be an accepted element of the game. Gert Hekma (1998) also found that antigay verbal harassment was reported so frequently (even in the Netherlands) that gay athletes treated it casually, dismissing it by saying, "They didn't really mean anything by it."

Indeed, many of the openly gay athletes I interviewed did not seem to take offense to the use of the words *fag* or *gay*, either. They too justified their use of the words by saying, "Oh, they didn't mean it that way," perhaps as a survival mechanism of mitigation. But the use of homophobic language in sport proves to be a complex issue. Just because one does not "mean it that way" does not nullify the possibility of harm arising from the casual use of the discourse.

Unlike other research, my study reveals that not all athletes dismissed the hostile capacity of such discourse. Specifically, many of the closeted, and/or lower-level athletes, felt that it created a hostile environment for gay athletes. These athletes used such discourse as a way to gauge the level of comfort their teams maintained toward homosexuality in making choices to come out of the closet or not. Their perception of the stigma of such discourse is made obvious by their refusal to use such discourse themselves. Indeed, most of the closeted athletes I interviewed reported to me that one of the reasons they had *not* come out was because they perceived their teammates as being highly homophobic. When I asked them why they thought their teammates were so homophobic they often answered, "They say fag all the time."

I argue that in order to understand the power of the word *fag* we must first consider the context and intent of the user, but even when "no harm is meant by the word," we must also analyze the word's meaning and how it is codified in cultural homophobia. We must, as David Plummer suggests, understand that homophobic discourse is clearly mapped in peer cultures as a way to subordinate men. It has a specific purpose, which cannot be idly dismissed. Judith Butler says that homonegative discourse changes the perceptual frameworks of gay identities, so that the gay identity itself includes notions of deviance. So even if we do not consider the use of the word *fag* to be homophobic (by intent) it is still injurious homonegative speech because it is understood from a framework of homophobic cultural meanings. Butler says that in this way symbolic violence is made possible, "because the action echoes prior actions, and accumulates the force of authority through the repetition or citation of a prior and authoritative set of practices" (1990, 205).

A final strategy is that some gay male athletes attempt to use the word *fag* in order to empower themselves. A high school runner told me, "I call myself a fag all the time. Like every now and then, a new guy will be doing a hard workout, and I'll all be, 'Don't let the gay guy beat you,' or I'm like, 'The fag is in the house.'" The strategy of reversing discourse, not only enables victims to reclaim agency (by inverting the tools of oppression), but it may also be more practical. When faced with the alternative of taking on the pervasive use of homophobic discourse in youth culture, usurpation seems an easier option.

Overall, homophobic discourse in athletics proves to be pervasive, even when heterosexual athletes avoid aggressively calling their gay teammates fags directly. My research shed some light onto the possibility of attitudinal changes among heterosexual athletes; some of whom can be seen in the strategies and manner in which they use homophobic discourse. What my research does not answer is just why some gay athletes felt that homophobic discourse created an air of hostility toward them, while others did not. Perhaps it is because athletes who come out, or were outed, discovered unexpected acceptance levels that blinded them to the homophobic discourse. Or perhaps it is because most of the openly gay athletes in my study were so rich in masculine capital (almost all were the best on their teams) that they did not perceive the discourse as pertaining to them.

THE EVOLVING COMING OUT STORY

Since 1998 there has been a subtle but tangible manner in which gay athletes tell their coming out narratives. The amount of support gay athletes' teammates provide to them seems to be increasing, so that today's stories reflect more support than yesterday's. Ryan, for example, who is a nineteen-year-old freshman at a university in California, came out to his team in a rather public manner. He tried out for the crew team while wearing gay pride jewelry. His petite frame and leadership skills made him perfect for the position he occupies as a coxswain where his job is to order eight 200-pound athletes to row "faster" or "harder." He yells at them, "Get you're fucking oar in sync damnit!" Yet Ryan reports never hearing a negative comment from them. This despite the fact that crew, "is a typical macho sport," he says. "As macho as football?" I asked. "Almost," he replied.

I asked Ryan how these buff and masculine athletes react to being ordered around by a 125-pound gay guy? "Nobody cares," he said. "The whole school knows about me, so from the first day of practice the team also knew about me." His comment gives credence to the argument that athletes on teams in schools that already have a strong support structure for gays and lesbians will have an easier time than those who aren't (Griffin 1998). I asked Ryan how comfortable his teammates were with him when it came to overnight trips. That, after all, seemed to be where other athletes encountered discrimination.

> I was a bit nervous at first. I mean these are buff and good-looking guys. I thought the real test would be when we were out on the road, when we had to share a bed. That was when it would come down to it. But it wasn't a problem. I walked into the hotel room, threw my bag on a bed and said, "I call that bed," and some other guy did too. It wasn't an issue. We didn't even talk about it.

Another time the bedding situation worked out to where only three athletes needed to share a room. With two beds per room, one person could have their own bed. But the rowers didn't want that bed to go to Ryan. They expressed to Ryan that they feared that not sharing a bed with him would send a message that they were homophobic. So they decided that one of them would sleep with Ryan. But they then feared that Ryan would think he was sleeping with the *less* homophobic of the two. "We talked about it for a while, and we just pushed the two beds together and made one big one. That way nobody felt bad," Ryan said.

Brian, who used to play football as a freshman in high school, quit the team to join swim instead. As a sophomore he came out to the swim team and allowed a few key people to tell the rest of the team (and school) for him. Brian, who was good-looking and popular on campus, had remained friends with the football team all along, and after coming out he remained an integral part of the team, cooking at their pregame meals, and remaining good friends with several of the players. As a senior, he joined the cheer squad, and was making an announcement at a rally. During his announcement a student yelled, "Get the fag off the microphone." Brian continued, "Let's just say that a few of my friends on the football team taught him a lesson after the rally," as a way of indicating the strong support he had from most of the guys on the football team.

These coming out stories illustrate homogeneity in narratives before coming out of the closet; primarily that gay athletes were highly fearful of social and physical repercussions. However, once gay athletes did come out of the closet, most of their fears were not realized. In fact, the lack of overt homophobia (particularly the lack of physical hostility) combined with the strong support of some teammates lead to a reverse relative deprivation in which they overinflated their experience.

Interestingly, coming out may also lead a gay athlete to quit sport for reasons not based in homophobia. Many athletes feel that after coming out they no longer need the representation of heterosexuality that team sports provide. This parallels Gert Hekma's findings of gay athletes as well (1998). Many of the athletes I studied realized that they had been devoted to sport (in part) out of avoidance of gay social desires. No longer needing the veneer of heterosexuality after coming out, they predictably drop out of sport in order to pursue romantic and social interests to which they have previously denied themselves access.

These narratives also tell us that while there is no one universal experience when coming out of the closet, the average narrative is couched within the realm of being positive. So much so that athletes almost unanimously wish they had come out sooner. However, these relatively positive experiences may not necessarily predict the experience of just any athlete who comes out of the closet. There are a number of mitigating factors that influenced their experience, factors that are flushed out in the next few chapters.

6

Mitigating Gay Stigma

ONE ATHLETE'S STORY:
BOB, COLLEGIATE TRACK STAR

A leanly built distance runner, Bob was indoctrinated into the masculine arena of sport at the age of five, participating in both baseball and soccer. However, as he grew older he became increasingly disillusioned with what he called the "overly macho" genre of team sports. He expressed discomfort with such attitudes and thought that running might provide him shelter from such bravado. In the process he also discovered that he had swift feet, and after training for only two years, he was good enough to be recruited by a local junior college.

Although his first two years of junior college athletics had been publicly successful, internally Bob reported having trouble ignoring his burgeoning sexuality. He felt marginalized by the endemic use of homophobic discourse on his old team, and he relayed to me that he felt adverse toward everything about them. "I didn't feel close to anyone," he said. Making matters worse, "I was attracted to some of them too; one in particular. But it was pointless to say anything to him. I saw everything in a different light than my teammates did."

The conservative attitudes of those around him kept him closeted and silent about the homophobia on his team. The turmoil weighed heavy on his emotional health, and he chose to remain closeted during his second year of college where he had accumulated enough accolades as a collegiate distance runner to receive a full scholarship to a Division 1 program. But the geographical change did little to help his angst.

> I remember feeling sort of lost, and not really accepted by anyone. Here I was on a new team, with a good scholarship, and new friends, but I just felt more depressed than before. On top of it all, I continued to use homophobic language with my new teammates, just as I had with my old ones.

As a Division 1 runner there was much more pressure to perform than in junior college. His renewable scholarship depended on performance, and his running slowly moved from the realm of play to that of work. Fortunately, his talent enabled him to outperform his teammates, giving him a tenuous but substantial amount of capital on his team; a power that he hoped to call upon if he were to come out to them someday. "I just kept thinking that if I became better than everyone else on the team, they would have to respect me, and it would be easier for me to come out."

Eventually, Bob worked his way up to be the most valuable distance runner on his team, *and* he was elected team captain. With this status he began to permit himself to let go of his insecurities regarding his sexuality, and he began to come out. He began by telling his roommates, who were also on his team. They pledged their support to him, and the positive experience led Bob to tell others on the team. Soon the whole team knew.

His teammates embraced him privately, but publicly they continued to use homophobic discourse. "Eventually, the constant barbs of homophobic discourse started to eat at me, I felt like I was being slapped every time I heard someone say *fag*. Even my coach was calling us fags."

> I thought that maybe by outing myself to my close friends I would develop allies. I mean I was hoping that once they knew that I was gay they would just stop saying *fag* out of courtesy. But they didn't, and sometimes it would frustrate me so much that I would hide from the team during workouts.

The pain of this social isolation manifested in habitual binge-drinking and an excessive workout regime. Bob was out of the closet but also out of control. He knew he needed to do things differently.

> One day I sat down and just constructed a plan to fight the homophobia. I decided I was going to say something to someone every time they

said something homophobic, no matter who it was. My teammates were irritated with me, claiming that they didn't mean things the way I was taking them, but I continued to put them in their place when they used homophobia, and eventually it faded.

Bob turned the tables on his homophobic teammates and coach. Over the course of a year the atmosphere of the team shifted from overtly homophobic to one that was gay-friendly. He no longer felt alienated.

Whenever a kid would start using homophobic language, I would casually run up alongside him. I would start a conversation about racism, and ask them whether or not they would ever use the *n*-word. They always said no, and when they did I would continue my lesson by explaining that the *n*-word has the same meaning as fag. People started to agree with me because they respected me as a runner.

With their enlightened attitude, teammates began to shed some of the baggage of hypermasculine posturing. Bob says that guys began to hug each other more frequently, and they ceased to make homophobic comments when stretching each other out. New athletes were indoctrinated into a fresh way of thinking—shunning homophobic discourse and supporting gay rights became empowering for all.

Using Masculine Capital to Mitigate the Stigma of Being Gay

Bob's story highlights the value of being a valuable athlete to a team when coming out in sport. That change is most easily made when the athlete who comes out is otherwise highly valuable to the team. As the fastest athlete on his team he was bestowed with a capital that others weren't. That is to say, if an athlete is vital to the success of his team, his heterosexual teammates might be willing to overlook a gay athlete's stigmatized sexuality.

This chapter examines the use of masculine capital in order to mitigate the stigma of being gay. Although it is recognized that gay athletes do not fit the definition of hegemonic masculinity because of their sexuality, they may still raise their masculine capital by acting in accord with the other tenets of orthodox masculinity. In other words, by being good and giving it his all he can potentially mitigate some of the stigma of his sexuality.

The first way gay athletes can raise their capital is by being good. Being the big wheel is highly valuable in a system predicated upon dominance over other men. In other words, how much he directly contributes to the point-scoring process is likely to raise his masculine worth among peers. The other way that he can raise his masculine capital is more symbolic in nature and reflects how much a gay athlete attempts to adopt all other aspects of orthodox masculinity. For example, by being emotionally stoic, and participating in macho bravado, a gay athlete will raise his masculine capital. Essentially, acting like one of the boys helps a gay athlete be perceived *as* one of the boys.

Being "good" mitigates all types of stigmatized behaviors or attributes in sport. It has, for example, certainly mitigated the stigma of being black in a racist American sporting culture. While Jackie Robinson was the first to break the gentlemen's agreement in baseball when he was signed to the Brooklyn Dodgers in 1945, it would be hard to say that he, or any other trailblazing black athlete, was permitted to play because society demanded racial equality on the playing field or because club owners came to their senses on racial issues. A more appropriate analysis is that black athletes were levied into sport *against* the overwhelming desire of a racist population because franchise owners perceived a profit to be made from their inclusion if their teams could perform better because of them. Arthur Ashe maintains that Jackie Robinson, Joe Louis, and Jesse Owens were such athletes.[1] He says that each was substantially better than his white counterparts, thus the stigma of being black (which was largely viewed as a detriment to team cohesion and spectator support) was nullified by the fact that their sheer athleticism would help the club win meets.[2]

Similarly, in contemporary professional team sports the symbolic challenge an openly gay athlete represents to the hypermasculinized arena of sport (the supposed "distraction" a gay athlete might have on his ostensibly heterosexual team) might only be tolerated by owners, players, and coaches if those detriments were negated by the potential superstardom and the resultant financial gain that athlete might make for the club. Famed sports agent Leigh Steinberg is frequently quoted as saying that it would take a gay athlete who was better than all the others to withstand the blast and resultant media fury, and possible hostility that would come to a gay professional team sport athlete after coming out of the closet.[3] While we have no examples of this in American professional team sports (because nobody has come out), we find when examining just who has come out in the world of professional individual sports that the trailblazers were most often athletes who were unbeatable. In fact, of the few openly gay athletes who have come out in professional American sport while actively competing, all have been national or world champions.[4]

INCREASING MASCULINE CAPITAL THROUGH PERFORMANCE

Data from my informants clearly shows that, at present, only athletes who have something valuable to offer their teams come out of the closet. In other words, the better an athlete is, the more social currency he may have to purchase social acceptance, and (perhaps) change homophobic attitudes on his team. This is something that previous research has also found. Gert Hekma's (1998, 10) study on gay male athletes in the Netherlands found that gay athletes who had higher abilities reported having fewer problems than gay athletes with less ability. "Coming out is easiest for those who excel in sports or have otherwise served their clubs well," he says.

Gold medalist Mark Tewksbury says that he was accepted in swimming, whereas he was not in school, because he was good. "Excellence is a great deterrent in prejudice. The only way for me to be safe was for me to be good. As long as I was faster than everybody else, I was protected, even though everyone suspected I was gay."[5] Bob too was more equipped to change attitudes on his track team because he had previously earned his teammates respect as the fastest runner.

The notion of permitting more social transgression for quality athletes is common, even if unspoken, in sport. I asked my coaching psychology graduate students, "Do you treat each athlete equally on the teams you coach?" They unanimously agreed that they do. But later, when talking about problem situations, it was readily discovered that when it came to disciplining their most valued athletes, justice wasn't handed out evenly. The coaches, much like our American legal system, took past contributions to the team into account, justifying unequal or privileged treatment. For example, one student said, "Well the top athlete on my team has contributed to the team all season long, while the benchwarmer hasn't, so it makes sense that I give him an extra chance or a bit more leeway." Essentially, the athlete's capital has mitigated his transgressions against formal rules.

A soccer player who is publicly out at his high school provides an example of the effect high masculine capital may have on nullifying the stigma attached to homosexuality. Between seasons, he watched boys playing a pick-up game of basketball in the gym. "I really wanted to play . . . so I asked the guys if I could join them, and they said no, and I was like why not? And they said it was because I was gay." Frustrated and determined to prove his merit, he went to the adjacent court and began shooting free throws. When the boys saw him sink baskets repeatedly, they invited him to join their game.

Dan, an openly gay national collegiate champion in track and field, was aware that his status as a star athlete made his acceptance by his college teammates easier. "If I had never achieved the status that I did, I would have had it tough," he said. He told me that his ex-boyfriend, who was a closeted gay athlete on the same team, used to tell Dan that he didn't come out publicly because he wasn't as good as Dan. "He thought he had to be good to make it as an openly gay athlete in the sport."

Sotia, a cross-country runner and soccer player, told me that on his junior varsity soccer team, where he possesses high capital, he has been widely accepted by his teammates. However, when he attends the varsity matches (to cheer them on), the varsity players treat him differently than they did his heterosexual junior varsity teammates. "I can just tell that there is something about me being there. . . . There are snickers . . . and I know they are talking about me. I just know it. I can sense something."

Therefore, when examining the issue of sexual (gender) transgression in athletics, one can assume that the experience an athlete would have with his team after coming out would have an entirely different outcome if he were not an elite member. Exemplifying this phenomenon, Bob said:

> I know that had I been less important to the team at the time I came out, Coach would have forced me to leave. I have no doubt that he would have disregarded my concerns and simply ignored me, just like everyone else he didn't like. But because I was the best, and the team captain, he had no choice but to keep me on the team for the sake of winning.

THE EFFECT OF MASCULINE CAPITAL ON COMING OUT

To determine the effect of capital on the experience of the gay athletes in this study, I divided informants into three categories: high, average, and low. An athlete was determined to have high capital if he was essential to the team (meaning that without him, the team's performance would suffer). In order for an athlete to be judged as possessing high capital, he must also be irreplaceable (in other words, without him the team would surely suffer a loss). An athlete was determined to have average capital if he was valuable to the team in that he helped score points or wins, but was replaceable by an athlete of equal ability. Finally, an athlete described as having low capital did not contribute to the team's success and was therefore easily replaceable.

I determined an athlete's level of capital using the following criteria. First, I asked the athlete to rank himself on the team. Realizing that self-rankings can be problematic in that athletes may either inflate or deflate their own abilities, I also questioned them about their athletic statistics. One of the advantages to studying sport is that ability, in most sports, is easily quantifiable. Using a combination of self-evaluation and my calculations, I assigned each athlete to the high, average, or low capital category, without telling them which category I had assigned them.

I only used this technique with thirty openly gay athletes from my study, as I removed the ten openly gay cheerleaders from this statistical evaluation because cheerleading is less quantifiable than other sports. Strikingly, of the thirty openly gay athletes whom I analyzed using this method, twenty-four were judged to be highly valuable to their teams. Astoundingly, six of the thirty were so good that I call them superstars. These six athletes owned state championship (or equivalent) titles. Three of these six athletes were ranked in the nation's top ten among their sport. One athlete was a three-time All-American and a national collegiate record holder at the NCAA Division I level in track and field.

Of the thirty openly gay athletes I evaluated, only five had average abilities, and just one was classified as below average. To fully appreciate these numbers, one must realize that the numbers of athletes that potentially lie in the high capital category are considerably fewer than the number who can occupy the lower capital category. There can only be one most valuable player on a team, but many who classify as below average. It is also important to note that my sampling technique should not be held accountable for the large number of high-capital, openly gay athletes in the study, as an athlete's level of ability was not part of the selection criteria, nor was I aware of these athletes' abilities before I conducted the interviews.

One could argue that lower caliber gay athletes may have dropped out of sport, leaving only higher caliber athletes to be interviewed. However, the data from my surveys of closeted athletes refutes this argument; of the twenty closeted athletes studied four maintained high capital and five were average capital, while eleven were low capital. Therefore, this study distinctly shows that possessing high capital influences who comes out of the closet voluntarily and who does not. These results were verified by unpublished independent research conducted by a graduate student at Harvard. In 2003 Brad Rathgeber studied the changing nature of acceptance of openly gay athletes and the importance of human capital in oral histories of five gay men. He concluded that all five athletes maintained high human capital, which they viewed as helping their teammates accept them more fully.

Still, it is important to recognize that the effect high human capital has on athletes coming out may only be specific to this point in time and may be difficult to reproduce with each passing moment. After all, the athletes who come out in athletics today are trailblazers for those who follow. Therefore, we might expect to find middle and low capital athletes coming out in greater numbers in the future.

ADOPTING ALL OTHER TENETS OF ORTHODOX MASCULINITY

Similar to possessing high ability in the form of scoring points, an athlete's bravery, fortitude, toughness, independence, willingness to commit violence against others, and willingness to sacrifice himself for the sake of victory is also esteemed in athletics because these traits are associated with heightened performance and loyalty to a sporting ethic. Thus, independent of the actual ability of the athlete, masculine bravado is also valued in sport.

We can imagine that if a gay athlete was not only a team's top runner but also exhibited the aforementioned traits, he would be an easier sell to a homophobic team than a gay athlete who was the team's top runner but also denounced masculinity and embraced feminine thinking and mannerisms. In other words, the stigma of being gay would be reduced if the athlete subscribed to all the other traits of orthodox masculinity, with the sole exception of his homosexuality.

Theoretically, greater masculine capital also allows one to possess enhanced social agency in shaping social thinking than those lacking masculine capital. Therefore, when regarding gender norms, the acquisition of high masculine capital may allow the athlete certain exemptions from the policing of sexual and gender roles within the context of the athletic institution. For example, McGuffey and Rich (1999), in their study of preteen boys, found that those at the top of the masculine hierarchy were provided more leeway in transgressing narrowly defined gender boundaries than the marginalized boys. Essentially, transgressing gender norms for a marginalized boy only served to reify his status as a lower class or effeminized boy, while the highest ranked boy was capable of making the exact same transgression without threat to his masculine status because his high masculine capital had bought him insurance against such a threat. This is ironic because high capital boys also have the most to lose with regard to homosexual suspicion.

Athletes seem to know that in order to make their homosexuality less affronting to their teammates, they need to adhere to as many of the other mandates of orthodox masculinity as possible. Indeed, it is possible that an athlete's level of masculine capital may be highly influential in determining the type and intensity of discrimination that an openly gay athlete experiences in sport. This relationship is affirmed by the manner in which Bob was able to deter his coaches and teammates from using homophobic language on his squad once he came out. Not only was he the fastest runner, but he was also elected team captain (before coming out), and he was also an upperclassman. Bob reflected on this by saying:

> I think that being good, being outgoing, and being relentless in my pursuit of victory forced people to listen to what I had to say. I mean, how are you going to ignore the team captain, especially if he is faster than you? Being a higher valued member of the team made me feel like I could say what I wanted, and that was very empowering.

Indeed, one aspect of masculinity is that it is partially reproduced because of the willingness of younger boys to look toward older boys for a modeling of expected masculine behavior. It is the "because I am older than you" phenomenon that allows new ideas to pass quickly around a team, but it can also be used by older orthodox boys to cease otherwise liberal notions of gender variance when propagated by younger men. Acting as a role model, Bob used his status to change the team environment and to portray a new way of doing masculinity.

Further evidence comes from a study of a gay men's rugby team in Britain, where gay rugby players found themselves increasingly accepted into mainstream rugby culture.[6] However, in order to facilitate this acceptance, the gay rugby team went through exhaustive measures to present an image of "normality" for everything except for their sexual orientation by implementing a don't ask, don't tell policy. In this manner, the researcher suggests that rugby players subscribed to the same Faustian deal of silence or conformity that many of the athletes in my study do (see chapter 7). On the one hand, their sexual variance(s) were tolerated, but they compromised their agency and identities in the process.

The influence of high masculine capital through both being good and through acting in otherwise macho ways raises interesting questions as to which tenets of masculine capital might give the gay athletes more social influence. Does being better than others carry more social currency than acting in otherwise orthodox tenets? In other words, would a flamboyant national champion be less stigmatized and maintain more social currency than an average gay athlete who acts in highly masculinized and heterosexualized ways?

My study does not contain enough athletes to draw this type of comparison. The athletes I interviewed almost unanimously managed their identities by adopting every other aspect of hegemonic masculinity. In essence, the athletes in my study often acted in very straight ways. Openly gay athletes tried to be tough, macho, and competitive in order to prove their masculine worth. It seems to be a strategy that works.

I asked Ryan why he thought there was so little homophobia directed against him on his crew team, and he responded, "I guess it helped that I'm pretty straight-acting. Because if I were a big old screaming queen, I'd probably get a lot more trouble. I could fit in with the guys, but I could also be myself." Similarly, Yhon, a high school football player who found some nonathletes physically aggressive with him said, "He started to say stuff to me . . . , 'Oh, you're so gay,' . . . so I went up to his face and I was like, 'You're gonna get big and tough right here?' He just walked away . . . just got scared."

Some of the athletes purposely went into sport to prove that they were tough to themselves and to others. Jason, the high school cross-country runner, for example, said that he went into running because he got picked on for being gay in elementary school (before he came out). Dan, a national collegiate record holder, says that he went into track because, "The more powerful I got as an athlete the less I would get teased about being gay," even though he had not publicly acknowledged that he was. Both Jason and Dan expressed that they displayed feminine qualities early in childhood, and that they were picked on because of them. Both thought that sport might change their feminine display.

Grant, the high school runner who came out with two others on his team, left his supportive team environment for a highly homophobic Christian college. He mistakenly thought that because his Christian high school accepted him, so would a Christian college. In his new environment, however, Grant found he had to act tough: "I held myself up. Don't mess with me just because I'm gay because I will defend myself if you try to do anything stupid. . . . People would joke around, but they knew where not to take it."

While it is difficult for me to quantify the effect that being a big wheel has versus acting in all other aspects of orthodox masculinity, two examples suggest that acting in hypermacho ways might maintain more currency for acceptance than simply being good. One striking example came from Zach, an ex-football player turned swimmer. Zach tells me that he didn't get along too well with the members of his high school's gay-straight alliance. "Well, they didn't like me too much, but it's really because I was friends with the football players, and they all hated the football players and stuff. In fact, two gay guys got beat up at my school by football players, but it's not because they were gay. It's because they were so damn queeny!"

Zach's story epitomizes the most affective strategy in dealing with homophobia in sport. He attempted to assimilate into the power structure by identifying with those who maintain the power. In the process he even willingly marginalized other gay men. "I don't know why they have to act all queeny and stuff, and they shouldn't be talking about gay stuff or kissing other guys in public! I'm not down with that." By maintaining a masculine guise, Zach attempts to nullify the stigma of being gay. He recognizes that he is accepted by his teammates only because he is not "queeny." By assimilating into the dominant power structure, Zach was able to avoid violence and gain acceptance by those he previously described as having committed violence.

Similarly, the following year that Bob came out, CJ, an openly gay freshman, joined his team. He possessed a moderate degree of human capital through his ability to make the traveling squad, but unlike Bob, CJ was not willing to partake in the masculine bravado of running through pain or "taking one for the team." Furthermore CJ was stereotypically flamboyant. Predictably, CJ was not treated as well as Bob.

In fact, Bob often came to the aid of CJ. "Yeah," Bob said,

> I used to defend him, especially when the coach began one of his macho tirades against the team, chastising them for being too soft, too weak, or for giving up too easily. But it was clear that the coach was just couching his comments against the team; he was really talking about CJ.

CJ told me:

> I'm doing the same workout, at the same speed, as all the other people in my group, but when he yells at us for not having hit our splits or something, he often uses my name, and not other people's. Like he will say, "CJ, what is it with you and your group?"

In this manner, the coach not only used CJ's sexuality as a stigma against him, but he attempted to "motivate" those around him who did not want to be associated with homosexuality. Bob realized the problem:

> I think that he wasn't really excited about going through another year of having things blamed on him. It's as if the coach thought that CJ was weak because he was gay, and that somehow he made others weak around him. I think not having the status I did [as the star athlete] made him feel helpless in an environment that was still volatile.

Both Bob and CJ violated the traditional masculine script of heterosexuality, but since Bob adhered to all other attributes of orthodox masculinity, his experience in the same social space as CJ was vastly better. While CJ likely experienced less overt homophobia than he would have if Bob had not paved the way the previous year, his lack of masculine capital eventually drove him from the team, as he simply felt too marginalized to continue. Clearly then, the experiences of these athletes, on the same team, with the same coach, were drastically different because of the varying degrees of masculine capital each possessed.

These two narratives indicate that the stigma of homosexuality may be refuted in the athletic arena, as long as gay athletes do not bring with them an overtly homonormative gay identity. Most openly gay athletes studied adhered to all the other mandates of hegemonic masculinity, including the devaluing of femininity. This is highly problematic because it denies the transformative potential of gay athleticism to undermine patriarchy and it does not represent a genuine reversal of thinking on homosexuality. By requiring gay men to act consistently with straight men, not only is masculinity continuing to be esteemed over femininity, but gay identity and culture are effectively silenced.

7 | *Don't Ask, Don't Tell: Resisting a Culture of Gay Athleticism*

ONE ATHLETE'S STORY:
JOHN, HIGH SCHOOL BASKETBALL PLAYER

Like almost every Navajo boy, John grew up with a basketball in his hand. John takes me to see the hogan he grew up in and points to the basketball hoop off to the side next to a pile of firewood to burn for heat in the winter. "That's it. That's what I grew up practicing on," he said. It looked no different than the others I'd seen, there was no concrete below the hoop (just dirt), but it had a noticeable tilt to the pole that held the rim and unpainted backboard. Despite the lack of facilities, John worked hard at his sport, largely because he wanted to earn a scholarship to attend a school outside the reservation but also because he was successful at basketball, and as John attests, basketball is what it's all about in Navajo high school culture.

The obsession his community has with sport, particularly basketball, places a great strain on John. "I'm representing more than my school," he tells me, "when I'm out there playing white teams, I'm representing the Navajo people as a whole. It's not about me, it's about our culture." This makes coming out to his community all the more difficult because homosexuality is also shunned. Not because of Judeo-Christian morality, he informs me, but because it highlights one's difference. Therefore, being a gay athlete is really a difficult identity to navigate as a Navajo. The pressure to excel is intense, but so is the pressure to conform. "Being gay," he tells me, "is not like being like everyone else."

John traces his sexuality back to early childhood, "I just remember thinking that I liked this guy or something. But while being gay is okay in Navajo culture, it's not talked about, so I didn't talk about it." John's socially enforced silence on the subject however did not prevent him from acting out his desire. En route to a far away game one day he played around with a teammate in the back of a car, even though a third teammate was in the back seat.

John and Tim didn't speak about the incident in the car, but in the hotel room that night, Tim choose to share a bed with John. For the next two years Tim came over to John's hogan, where they frequently engaged in sex without ever talking about it. Tim dropped out of basketball his junior year, and John became the team's leading scorer.

On another overnight competition as a senior John was sharing a bed with the teammate that had seen him and Tim jacking each other off in the back seat of the car. "He never said anything about it, and I know he saw. So because he said he'd share a bed with me that night, I just sort of thought. . . ." Late that night John made an unwelcome sexual advancement. "He jumped up and was like, 'What the hell are you doing?'" alerting the other two boys in the other bed as to what had happened. John replied, "I'm sorry. I'm sorry. Oh shit, I'm so sorry," as he buried his head into his hands and began to cry. "I just wanted to take it back, to make it go away."

His teammate calmed down, "Look. It's cool," he said. "Just don't do that again," while the other teammates sat in shocked silence. John volunteered to sleep on the floor, "And that was it. We never talked about it. It was just done. I asked him if the other guys on the team found out. "Oh yeah, of course. But they don't talk about it." "So do they think you are gay?" I asked. "Yeah, they know. I mean, they avoided me for a while, especially that next day. Nobody wanted to sit near me, and there were some initial comments about me not wanting girls and stuff."

At the time of this interview, John was in the prime of his high school career. A year had passed since the incident, and John grew a bit more courageous in presenting his sexuality as "not heterosexual" but without saying that he was gay. "I don't take girls to the dances, and I've been seen hanging out with an openly gay guy at our school. I don't care what people think of me, but I'm not going to tell them that I'm gay." I asked, "Do you tell them that you are straight?" "No," he replied. "I let them think what they want. I just don't talk about it."

Not talking about it is something common on John's team. "They all know it, but they are not going to say it. They just pretty much go about ignoring that part of my life." He added, "Like when the guys are talking about girls, they don't ask me what I think of them. They know I'm not into girls, so they just leave me out of the conversation. And they knew I was seeing Tim, but they never asked about that either."

"Do they ask you about guys at all?" I asked.

"Of course not. No. We don't talk about my being the way I am. Besides, it's none of their business. It has no impact on how well I play or anything."

John's assertion that nobody wants to talk about his sexuality is made clear in my interviews with some of his teammates [as part of another academic project]. Not once did they ever mention that that one of their teammates was gay—they didn't even allude to it. So I asked, "How would you guys treat an openly gay teammate?" One athlete answered, "We wouldn't care," but John's name continued to be evaded. As we left, I asked them if they had any other teammates that they thought I should interview. One looked at the other two before saying, "John."

Don't Ask, Don't Tell

John's experience parallels that of other gay athletes throughout North America. Athletes who came out of the closet willingly, and even those who were outed against their will (although these numbers are fewer), found that they were free from many of the fears of losing friendships, being kicked off their teams or being victimized by overt physical aggression. This is not to say, however, that openly gay athletes are treated equally in peer culture. Oppositely, a pervasive system of hegemonic heterosexuality serves to deny their sexuality publicly and to relegate gay athletes to second-class citizenship. This unquestioned hegemonic system influences gay athletes to rationalize that they *rightfully* should not discuss their sexuality publicly, despite the fact that discussions of heterosexuality are commonplace.

This chapter clearly shows that the transformative potential of gay athletes in sport is somewhat neutralized through the silencing of gay discourse, identity, and behaviors and through the normalization of homophobic discourse. For example, Jason, a high school cross-country and track athlete illustrates the implications of covert mechanisms that deny gay athletes the creation of a gay subculture. "The general rule was, 'I won't talk to you if you don't talk to me.' Sort of like a don't ask, don't tell policy."

Don't ask, don't tell is an expression popularized by the U.S. military to reflect a policy of not asking soldiers about their homosexuality—and not allowing them to express it for fear of discharge (Britton and Williams 1995). This attitude posits, "We know it exists, but we're not going to recognize it or talk about it," while also enforcing the rule through criminalizing discourse about one's homosexuality. Although gay male athletes do not encounter the same threat of institutionalized legislation, they do encounter a great deal of covert institutional and cultural heterosexual hegemony that curbs them from speaking as freely about their homosexuality as heterosexuals do. This, Gayle Rubin (1984) argues, serves to maintain heterosexuality as charmed and homosexuality as deviant.[2]

Illustrating the power of hegemony in this application, Sotia described his coming out as a success, telling me about the acceptance of his teammates. He went on to tell me, however, that even though his teammates accepted him, he still didn't discuss his sexuality with them after the initial coming out. "The gay thing was never talked about after that because we ran together, we enjoyed running cross-country, and that was the extent of it." I asked, "Did they ever talk about your sexuality? Did your sexuality ever come up?" "No," he responded. "Why would it?"

Yet, when I asked Sotia if his teammates talked about girls in the locker room, he said, "Yeah. They'd be like 'she's kind of pretty' and would be talking about a female runner. And I would be like, 'Yeah, she's pretty.'" In doing so, Sotia is not so much denying his sexuality but engaging in a conversation that fails to explicitly recognize it. It seems that because heterosexuality is the dominant social script, it is okay for Sotia to talk about girls but not okay for him to talk about boys, even though everyone knows he's gay.

Yhon, a high school football player, reported having great support and good experiences playing high school football. "I'm out to like a lot of people around here. And I guess some of the people on the team know, but they just don't ask me anything, I guess. But they are cool with me." I asked Yhon what he does when the guys talk about girls at the lockers. "I just go along with them. I don't like going along with it, but if anybody asks me, 'Is this girl pretty,' I'm like, 'Yeah, she's pretty.'" "And what if they ask you if you're interested in a certain girl?"

> They did once and I said no. They asked, "Do you like this girl?" and I said, "No, I don't like her." And they were like, "Why?" And I said, "Think about it" . . . and they were like, "Okay, we'll think about it." They know, but they don't want to ask.

Brian dated another athlete on campus who was publicly out of the closet, making his sexuality also visible. But despite his public visibility he never talked about his sexuality to his teammates, and neither he nor his teammates addressed it. At times Brian said that his teammates even prodded him to come out, but they could not bring themselves to say it directly:

> And people would say, "You guys act like a married couple. You act like a gay couple." People would say that all the time . . . we thought, "This is amazing, maybe we should tell everyone?" But then we were like, "no way."

It took the emotional pain of a difficult breakup before Brian finally opened up to his teammates and began to talk openly to them about his sexuality. Yet, even after he did, there was still resistance to such open dialogue:

> And even to this day, people know, but people just won't say it. . . . It's like they just can't talk about it. It makes me so uncomfortable knowing that some people know but then they still ask me about girls. . . . It's really frustrating. . . . Not one time on the team did anyone ask me, "Brian, are you gay?"

Rob, a crew athlete who came out implicitly to his team by snuggling with another guy in the boathouse, illustrated a public coming out that lacked discourse. I asked him why he was willing to display it but not speak about it. "I just didn't feel it was necessary; it never really came up. I mean I didn't jump out of the closet at them or was forcing my homosexuality on them." Rob's use of the phrase *forcing my homosexuality* to describe a simple affirmation of his sexuality, and Sotia's phrase *the gay thing*, illustrates the power inherent in stigmatizing an identity. In this case, the verbal recognition of heterosexuality is considered "just" and "right" and never scrutinized, but the mere mention of homosexuality is perceived as being inappropriate.

Publicly discussing homosexuality is an act or script that is more acknowledging than simply witnessing public displays. People who witnessed affection between Brian and his boyfriend can choose to ignore them, pretend they never saw them, or dismiss their actions as a product of close friendship or other association. But dialogue about homosexuality cannot be mistaken; it cannot be so easily deflected, and it often requires one to proclaim a position on homosexuality.

John illustrated the difficulty in discussing the matter with his teammates, "I'm not sure if I would want to talk about it anyhow. I might find out that they aren't as over it as I think they are, and I don't want to know if they talk about me behind my back." Heterosexual athletes often discuss talking about it as "being in your face," something that helps keep gay athletes silenced. One heterosexual cheerleader told me, for example, that he didn't have a problem with gay cheerleaders as long as they "don't make an issue out of it." He equated public displays or discussions of homosexuality as "acting unprofessional."

These athletes highlight that much of the locus of control on the issue of silence is domain to gay athletes, as the hegemonic process and the desire to reflect cultural norms frequently influences them to be willing participants in their subordination. These attitudes are reflected in statements like "Sport is not the appropriate place for such discussions" or "Well, it's none of their business." Such silence not only removes agency from the gay athlete, but it insures heterosexual men that their discomfort at discussing the issue is justified. It enables all involved to continue to examine heterosexuality as a public sexuality and homosexuality as a private matter.

Not all gay athletes were subject to don't ask, don't tell, however. Ryan, the college crew member whose heterosexual teammates pushed their bed together to sleep with him, expressed that his teammates frequently asked him about his sexual orientation. Similarly, Bob reported that his teammates (mostly in private) would talk to him about not only what it is like being gay but about the sex he had too. Clearly then, there is no dominant pattern for the public recognition of gay athletes, and there are likely a host of variables that influence the manner in which an athlete's sexuality is expressed. Much of this locus seems to be in the hands of the gay athlete, for when an athlete desires silence, even heterosexual athletes who would like to discuss their teammates' homosexuality cooperate in the silence. For example, one athlete's teammates clearly illustrated this when they tried to prod him to come out of the closet. Similarly, I frequently hear from heterosexual athletes who believe that one of their teammates is gay but are too afraid of being perceived as trespassing onto personal matters to ask. This is similar to parents who tell me, "If my kid wants me to know he's gay, he will tell me," while the kid tells me, "If my mom wants to know if I'm gay, she will ask." By mutual consent don't ask, don't tell is reproduced and enforced.

Taken in this light, we can better understand that rather than homosexuality being a nonissue, it is such an issue that people are fearful of making mistakes in discourse about it. The fear of speaking about the subject has led homosexuality to be thought of as a private sexuality, while heterosexuality is so public that it is assumed to be the default sexuality. Athletes are afraid to broach the subject of homosexuality for fear of not only trespassing social norms of silence but also of misspeaking—something made easier because of the lack of vocabulary friendly to homosexuality.

Still, part of the reason gay athletes may reproduce the don't ask, don't tell culture of athletics is that they may still be trapped in the amazement of not having been flatly rejected, beaten up, or otherwise driven out of their sport. In large part, gay athletes seem elated to have been "accepted" so much so that that their status as publicly gay is willingly compromised, viewed as a small (or even proper) sacrifice. Effectively, their silence is bartered for their sexuality being treated as a nonissue. It is, of course, a Faustian wager because they sacrifice their voice in exchange for surface level acceptance. Since the policing myth of violence is so imminent, once the athlete feels he has escaped it, he may not attempt to go further, or push the boundaries of the unspoken bargain.

Whatever the reason, the don't ask, don't tell settlement not only exists between gay athletes and their straight teammates but also between gay athletes themselves. Mike, for example, was an openly gay high school and (now) collegiate diver who described diving meets as being a "gay Mecca," but with an unusual twist. "Everyone knows about everyone else, but no one talks about it. . . . It's not a big gay thing; you go, you dive, and you leave." I asked him why he thought this might be, "I'd describe it as fear, and you think that every-one else is. But what if they're not? So you don't say anything."

Coaches also seem to be in on the deal. One athlete's coach calmed his fears of violence (even if he relegated homosexuality as unworthy of conversation), "Even though he never talked about it . . . he made me feel like some of my fears were based on nothing. . . . He'd wink at me sometimes, and he'd make those jokes [about him taking a girl to a dance]." And when I asked him specifically if the same don't ask, don't tell attitude existed with the coach, he responded, "We never had conversations about it."

While Rob's coach showed acceptance in some manner, his coach never could bring himself to address it publicly, avoiding explicitly using the words *gay* or *homosexual*. Rob said, "I mean like the coaches make references like, 'Oh, if you're bringing your girlfriends or *what-ever* out to the meets.' . . . They seem really open-minded to the fact that maybe not all the guys have girlfriends and might have boyfriends." Yet, his coach is not able to say the word *boyfriend* publicly.

Rob's coach may also be partially responsible for his team's don't ask, don't tell policy. His coach was supportive of him when Rob told him of his sexuality, but didn't talk publicly about it. Although Rob told me that, "He had a big talk with me . . . and he told me that I was one of his favorites, and that I had special talents and that he relates to me a lot. . . . After the talk we both cried, and he embraced me in the middle of the track." Rob also reported that this was the only time he ever talked about Rob's sexuality. In fact, when other teammates use the term *fag* (frequently) at practice, his coach says nothing about it at all.

THE PRICE OF DON'T ASK, DON'T TELL

The silence that these athletes endure is not always an easy compromise. Many athletes find that the position, while acceptable at first, grows wearisome, as they desire full equality with their teammates. I talked to Dave, an openly gay tennis player, and asked him if he was treated any different after coming out. "No," he said. "They didn't really treat me as gay, if that's what you mean. In fact, they didn't even mention it really. They just treated me like one of the guys . . . like nothing had changed or anything." I then asked him if this included verbal sexualizing of women. "Yeah, they ask me like who I think is hot and stuff." But when I asked Dave if they ever asked him what guys he thought were hot he replied, "Hell no. They'd never do that. They don't want to hear that kind of stuff. It didn't bother me at first, but it kind of bugs me now. Like I can't tell them whom I'm dating, and I don't feel comfortable introducing him to them. It's like we are all walking on eggshells."

Dave's social existence in don't ask, don't tell requires him to manage a compartmentalized identity. His teammates know he is gay but don't treat him as if he were. They are willing to recognize his athletic accomplishments but unwilling to talk of his social and sexual life as they do with the heterosexual athletes. The Faustian contract he agreed to carried with it several benefits. First and foremost, gay athletes report that by not making an issue out of it, they believe they are promoting their connectivity and quality of experience on their teams. Their semi-invisibility also provides virtual assurance of physical safety, and this is quite a relief compared to how bad most athletes thought coming out would be. Perhaps these benefits enable both Dave and his teammates to truly believe that don't ask, don't tell is the best approach, but the compromise comes with costs.

The contract denies these gay athletes a gay identity; and in a heterosexist culture being denied a gay identity is the same as being given a straight identity. This provides protection but also nullifies the gay voice in the athletic arena and helps stunt the growth of gay athlete networks. The stress of self-silencing not only retards the growth of a gay subculture within sport, but remaining silent reminds some athletes of being closeted, causing them to return to a state of stress about their status. Keeping gay athleticism silenced also helps these athletes retain patriarchal power because, to many, gay athletes (like gay men in general) are publicly constructed as feminine. Silencing their supposedly feminine voice helps prevent their impacting social attitudes regarding the myth of feminine frailty.

Not talking about it helps insure that the athlete is not berated, but it does not enable the athlete to feel secure that his teammates have no problem with him either. Essentially, it keeps them guessing as to whether their teammates are accepting of their sexuality or merely tolerating it. But more significant is the fact that teams who do not acknowledge the presence of gay athletes within their ranks feel less reason to police their use of homophobic discourse. Collectively, this mutes the gay athletes' difference in the arena, virtually nullifying the chance of creating an accepting culture for gay athleticism.

Collectively, the maintenance of a don't ask, don't tell culture serves heterosexual masculinity well. First, silencing the existence of their gay teammates helps nullify the possibility of their stigma affecting others. In other words, don't ask, don't tell helps prevent heterosexuals from being contaminated by homosexual stigma. Furthermore, the maintenance of a don't ask, don't tell policy allows heterosexual athletes to avoid potentially politically sensitive subjects regarding homosexuality. Essentially, it gives the heterosexual teammates a ticket out of discussing the implications of homosexuality in society. Don't ask, don't tell, however, also plays a role in the maintenance of patriarchy. Because cultural stereotypes of homosexuality maintain that it is equated with femininity, these gay athletes (willingly or not) represent femininity at some level. In this aspect, their athletic performance is measured against heterosexual performance in a contestation of masculinity versus femininity. Silencing their homosexuality enables heterosexuals to deny the feminized nature of their gay teammates and helps avoid risking the symbolic power of masculinity should they be outperformed by gay men.

8

Factors That Influence Acceptance

ONE TEAM'S STORY:
THE TROUBADOURS CHEERLEADING TEAM

The cheers echo from several thousand cheerleaders at a national collegiate cheerleading championship competition where I prearranged to
meet with the Troubadours, a coed cheerleading team, in order to conduct
participant observation. I saw hundreds of men among the thousands of
women, most with arms folded across their chests, doing their best to act
every bit the masculine football player that most used to be.[1] Energy was
high in the arena. Pop music blared, as mostly women performed parts of
their routine and danced in the aisles. The majority of men in the arena
seemed disengaged from the energy. But I heard male voices from one
corner of the stadium—a long protracted cheering, "Go orange, go blue,"
the colors of the Troubadours. I focused to see three guys standing high
atop a rail, men from the team I was to study, swaying their hips and dancing with team spirit placards high above their heads.

I knew there were three openly gay members on the squad, and just
as I was secure in the fact that I had found my three gay subjects, I
noticed another Troubadour giving a deep, long, and slow back massage
to another male teammate. Still, to the right of me are two more Troubadours, one sitting in front of the other, slightly elevated from the stadium

seating, with his hands slumped over the shoulders of the boy in front of him. I have been told that of the twelve men on this team, only three are gay, but there are, according to dominant notions of what it means to act heterosexual, seven "acting gay," and I can't figure out who is who.

The men dancing seem oblivious to the fact that none of the other men in the arena allow their bodies to move as fluidly, or are as relaxed as they are. And, as the reading of the results begins, a hush draws over the Troubadours, as they anxiously wait to see if they have (yet again) won a national championship title. As the results were counted backwards from the top twenty teams, there was as yet no mention of the Troubadours. And when the second-place team was announced, and it was not them, they instantly knew that they had won another title. A wave of joy hit them, and they celebrated with uproarious hugs and cheers.

Unlike the rigid masculinity I witnessed on many cheerleading teams from throughout the United States, in this cheerleading association, the Troubadours did not display the tough-guy attitude commonly thought to pervade the sport. "Oh, I say to hell with all that macho stuff," one heterosexual athlete tells me. "We are just here to have fun, and if others don't like us for who we are, to hell with them." Another added, "Everyone here is like a family, and no matter what the problem is the other guys are here for you." I asked Eddie, a gay cheerleader how accepted he felt on his team, "Oh, totally, I mean, we bring our boyfriends to meets and stuff; it's totally cool."

Interviews with the Troubadours clearly indicate that they were aware of the uniqueness of their masculine identity. They report that much of their progressiveness stems as a result of having two openly gay male coaches and three openly gay men on their team. They also report being able to be emotionally expressive, sensitive, and nurturing with one another. The heterosexual athletes on the team were clearly aware that their attitudes and behaviors are coded as either gay or effeminate, but they verbally acknowledge that they do not care.

I interviewed the athletes for a few hours before heading over to partake in a celebratory dinner with them. We arrived at the restaurant, and moments after sitting, I heard a ruckus from the end of the table. I looked to see one of the heterosexual boys on the ground, holding a leg cramp; he was in pain. Two of his male teammates (one gay and one straight) came to aid him. One held his leg while the other supported the hurt boy's head in his lap. His teammates tenderly reassured him until the painful cramp subsided. They slowly helped him back to his chair, and then one of the boys hugged him from behind and asked, "Are you sure you are okay?"

The Troubadour's coaches have succeeded in creating an atmosphere in which men are free of the baggage of hypermasculinity. They are free to open up with each other and express their love and affection for one another—even across sexualities. I heard one heterosexual boy tell his coach, "Thank you, Mike; you are the best coach I've ever had," as he hugged and kissed his coach on the cheek.

FACTORS THAT INFLUENCE HOMOSEXUAL ACCEPTANCE

This chapter examines many of the micro and macro variables that are also likely to influence the homonegative or homopositive attitudes on any given team. For example, much of the credit for the Troubadours' softer version of masculinity may be attributed to the outspoken attitudes of their coaches. Troubadour athletes attribute the attitudes of their coaches toward shaping not only their individual perspectives on homophobia, but on masculinity as well. The coaches do not require or encourage hypermasculine posturing and foster a feminist perspective on coaching that is concerned with the development of friendships and unity.

But while interviews with the coaches and athletes squarely place merit on the attitudes and abilities of the Troubadours' coaches for the reconstruction of gender and acceptance of homosexuality, it might also have to do with the metropolitan area they hail from, the institutionalized notions of gender within the sport, and the act of individuals and organizations. In other words, there are multiple variables that influence the pervasiveness of homonegative attitudes on any given team, in any given sport.

THE COACH

This research shows that the coach is a decisive element in shaping social attitudes on his team. Athletes desiring to excel in their sport generally look to their coach as a vessel to achieve their athletic dreams and are therefore likely to open themselves to suggestion from the coach in order to achieve preferable treatment. This might mean that athletes are willing to actively (in attempting to assimilate) or passively (in viewing the coach as a role model) interpret the social world in the same manner as the coach.

Furthermore, the coach represents the man with the most masculine capital on athletic teams. The coach is inundated with legitimate, authoritative, expert, and often referent power, making him a highly influential factor in the lives of young athletes who desire to be promoted within the masculine hierarchy. Finally, to some degree a coach is also able to structurally shape a team closer to his social desires. He is able to drop and promote athletes at will, to assign ideologically similar kids to be team captain, and to provide those with whom he is more aligned with other avenues to empower them in peer culture.

For example, one athlete told me that he was out to some of the athletes on his team, but because his coach was "old school" he and his teammates decided not to tell the coach. They feared that the coach might, somehow, try to prevent him from starting. The athlete (who was valuable to the team) maintained that this proved the solidarity of his teammates in his support. When one takes all these variables into consideration, it is easy to see the tremendous influence a coach has on all matters among those he coaches. A homophobic coach will likely impede the mitigation of homophobic behavior, and a gay-friendly coach will promote the fostering of acceptance among the men he coaches. For example, Bob's coach was highly homophobic and expressed his views (blatantly against school policies) by prolifically using the word *fag*, both around and directed at his athletes. These actions made it harder for Bob to create a safe space on his track team. "If Coach had been an accepting person, or even neutral toward gays, I think things would have been a lot better, particularly for CJ," he said.

Regarding her research on lesbian athletes, Pat Griffin (1998) also suggests that there may be a link between the amount of emphasis a coach places on winning and the degree of homosexual acceptance a team offers. According to this principal, the more emphasis a team has on winning, the less tolerant it will be of difference, as deviance is likely to be perceived as detracting from the goal of winning. What this model fails to account for, however, is that the more pressure there is on a team to win, the more likely they may be in accepting a gay player if that player is highly valued in the pursuit of victory.

While my research was not able to isolate the particular effect that the desire for victory had on the level of homophobia a coach might express, my study did reveal that many successful coaches were highly tolerant or downright supportive of their gay athletes. Certainly Corey Johnson received a high degree of support from his coaches. Rob (the crew athlete who came out by snuggling in the boat house) accredited his coaches for helping make the team more tolerant, as did Ryan the other crew member who slept with two beds pushed together. Furthermore, recall Yhon the high school football player whose coaches expressed a desire to help protect him off the track. In fact, Yhon's coaches talked to him, saying, "Everything will be okay" and reassuring him, "Your teammates like you." And when I asked Yhon what his best, most affirming experience as a gay athlete was, he said:

Well, one of my coaches said, "I want to talk to you," . . . and he said, "I don't want you to ever be afraid about being gay. And if you ever have any problems, just come and talk to me, to *us* [meaning he had the support of all the coaches]. We will be there for you."

Grant's coach was also very supportive:

He's also a counselor and a psychologist; he knew where to take it and where not to take it. But he was very protective of his kids; of his runners. . . . If they had problems, or something was going on, . . . he'd handle it and take care of it. . . . After graduation [the coach] just gave me a smile and a pat on the back and told me to enjoy college and have fun. He said, "You are who you are," and that I don't have to be what everyone else wants me to be.

Since then his coach has even asked Grant back to help out as an assistant coach.

This research makes it clear that the social attitude the coach displays toward homosexuality is crucial in the athletes' analysis (testing the waters) of what life might be like as an openly gay athlete on the team. In fact, all but two of the athletes in this study reported having coaches that ranged from somewhat gay-friendly to proactively supportive of gays and gay rights. Only two informants had coaches who were not supportive: Greg, whose coach never spoke to him again, and Bob.

While I do not have enough data to analyze attitudes on homosexuality among athletic coaches in general, not one of the *closeted* athletes in this study reported that their coach was highly supportive of homosexuality. Most reported their coach as being either homophobic or unreadable as to their attitude toward homosexuality. From this analysis it can be safely argued that the coach's attitude regarding homophobia not only influences whether a gay athlete will come out of the closet, but it also has a heavy hand in determining the experience that the athlete will have after coming out.

SOCIAL SUPPORT NETWORKS

The fraternity between members of sports teams bridges many relational aspects. Teammates often spend the better part of their day together, practicing, attending school, and (in the case of collegiate and professional athletes) living together, in a near-total institution. This creates a rigid and tightly policed bond between team members in accordance with the mandates of orthodox masculinity. In the hyper-heterosexual world of athletics, the presence of an openly gay athlete creates dissonance where there was once masculine homogeneity.

Gay athletes remind their teams that athleticism does not necessarily imply heterosexuality. This often results in an immediate, but usually temporary, backlash against the athlete's social desirability on the team. Recall that John's teammates refused to sit with him the day after he made an unwanted pass at a teammate in bed. Although closeted gay athletes may not understand the reasoning for their fear, or be able to articulate the reasons why they suspect they will be ill-treated, they nonetheless know that once they come out of the closet their social relations will be altered. Therefore, most athletes test the waters and gain social support by first covertly asking for opinions on homosexuality among their teammates.

The first manner in which athletes do this is to judge the frequency and intensity of homophobic discourse. The previous chapter found that almost all closeted athletes used this type of discourse in order to gauge homophobia. But in addition to gauging their teammates' use of homophobic discourse, they might say something like, "My dad has this gay friend . . ." in order to test the waters and see what type of reaction they elicit from their teammates. Once they find less homophobic heterosexual teammates, they often work at that relationship.

The significance of support by teammates was a central issue to all the athletes I interviewed. They told me that they had the strong support from at least one friend on their team before coming out, and even after coming out, friendship was clearly very important to them. The athletes I studied frequently talked about who supported them with praise and who didn't with disdain. The openly gay athletes in my study felt a certain reverence for the friends that steadfastly stood by their side. Yhon, for example, relayed an amusing and affirming story about acceptance.

> One time during the football game, we had like two minutes on the clock and we were losing, and I went out to kick the field goal, and I made it, and you know how they always slap your butt? And they said, "Good job," and one of my friends was gonna do it, and he looked at me and started laughing, and I started laughing too, and he was like, "Ahhhhh, forget it," and he did it anyways.

Dave also found strong verbal support from his tennis teammates. "I've only told two of my teammates [out of three] because the other one seems a bit homophobic. But the two that know are very supportive, and when the other one makes antigay comments, they are all over him." Derek attributes his positive experience to the length of time he has spent with his teammates, making the point that friendship is largely (but not wholly) determined by duration of the relationship.

> I think it's good because we've played together for a long time. So they got to know me before. Like I'm sure if I was on a new team . . . things would be different. I think it's been fine because they've known me for a long time.

Grant had phenomenal support from his friends. For example, Grant, another gay runner, and two heterosexual athletes were getting ready to run the final race of their high school career. After warming up for the 1600-meter relay race the two heterosexual runners approached Grant and the other gay runner. "We have a present for you," they said, as one of the athletes reached into his bag and pulled out two pairs of gay pride (rainbow) socks, handing them to each of the gay runners. In symbolic defiance of the gag-order placed on them by the homophobia of their private high school, the heterosexual athlete said, "There's more." He reached inside his bag and pulled out two more pairs. "We're going to wear them too," he said. Together, two heterosexual allies and two gay runners ran and won the state championship race.

Conversely, when gay athletes lack strong support from their teammates, mixed responses and constantly contested terrain are more predictable. Bob recalls that privately many teammates supported his sexuality, but that they also felt he was "overstepping his bounds" by "making an issue out of his sexuality." Others labeled him a rebel who was trying to disturb the sanctity of the team. "They would say things like 'Bob is making an issue out of things' when I wasn't there, but then in private, like when it was just me and the same person, they agreed with my challenging the homophobic attitudes of our coach and team. It was awkward and uncomfortable," Bob said. "I had to be careful. My teammates pretended to be indifferent around the team, and even supportive to my face, but I knew when push came to shove that I stood alone against my coaches and the administration."

The indifference of Bob's teammates, and the manner in which they attempted to marginalize him because of his sexuality, was partially the product of the fear of "guilt by association." In associating with Bob, many of his teammates feared that their own masculine capital might diminish if others thought that they too were gay. Bob said:

> Sometimes I would feel so ostracized from the team. I mean, the only thing that the guys would talk to me about were girls, or school, in other words, things that weren't related to being gay. I stopped getting

invited to their houses as much, and I started to feel lonely. It sort of seemed like everyone tolerated what I was doing, but that no one really wanted to be seen closely connected to me.

Without the support of teammates and the coach, Bob had very little on his side. Marginalizing fringe members among athletic teams is a way to out-group undesirables, and like with his teammate CJ, this often produces a social climate so uncomfortable that athletes self-segregate out. However, with the support of teammates and coaches, athletes stand a much better chance of surviving the pressures that they will undoubtedly face from those not associated with their team (as well as other teams) and homophobic members of the school in general.

Already one can see how the perfect balance of situations and temperaments must exist for a closeted gay athlete to consider emerging from the closet. If the athlete is good enough, and if his coach is either neutral or supportive of homosexuality, if he can befriend at least one solid, pro-gay friend, and if he can gain that friend's support for his coming out, then the athlete may consider coming out. These findings confirm the research conducted on lesbian athletes as well. In her book *Strong Women, Deep Closets* (1998), Pat Griffin also shows that it is easier for lesbians to come out if their schools do not provide scholarships or receive a lot of media attention. Essentially, this shows that the more a team has at stake, the less difference is tolerated. Griffin also shows that it is easier to come out at schools with institutionalized support systems for gays and lesbians.

INSTITUTIONAL ATTITUDES

The closed-loop system of sport described in chapter 4 is largely responsible for what seems to be a plethora of homophobic coaches in men's athletics, at all levels, and across all institutionalized sports. Indeed, overt displays of homophobia and the unbridled use of homophobic discourse pervades even university athletics, despite the fact that most university policies prohibit discrimination based on sexual orientation. Administrators rarely intervene on matters of homophobia, partially because they too have also emerged from the same social milieu of antigay, antiwomen attitudes that mobilized organized American athletics in the first place.

For example, I recently spoke with a closeted assistant football coach who filed a complaint because the other coaches on his team were using homophobic discourse during practice. The coach quit and reported the situation to the district administration because such language violates a California educational code designed to protect gay and lesbian students from an abusive environment. Two weeks later, the school's internal investigation determined that there was no corroboration for the story, so no action was taken against the coaches.

Similarly, another athlete reports telling me that after hearing of a blatant case of homophobic discourse by a coach at his university, he approached his school's gay and lesbian center for help. When the center talked to the athletics department, a high-ranking athletic administrator proclaimed her outrage at the homophobia but refused to take immediate action against the coach because the athlete was not willing to confront the coach. In negotiations with the school's gay and lesbian center it was determined there would be a sensitivity training program for the coaches. Four meetings later, the athletics department continued to spin reasons why the program had to meet a litany of specifics, making it painfully obvious that they were intentionally filibustering. The athlete told me that by the time he graduated four years later no sensitivity training had taken place. Similarly, after publishing my autobiography about my experience as an openly gay coach, I was invited to about a dozen Division 1 universities to discuss the issue of gays in sport. Normally, the university's gay and lesbian center brought me in but they also extended an invitation to the staff of the entire athletics department. At one major university an assistant athletic director showed up to thank me for coming, before telling me that he couldn't stay. He was the only member of any athletic department to even make that much of an appearance at any of the schools I visited. In fact, it took a lawsuit before the University of Florida instituted some training against homophobia in 2004. Helen Carroll, coordinator of the Homophobia in Sports program for the *National Center for Lesbian Rights* said, "It was groundbreaking because this was the first time a top-ten institution has gone out of its way to do such training for coaches and administrators" (Buzinski 2004).

The existence of covert homophobia within an athletic department that claims to be gay-friendly highlights an important contradiction; while a publicly funded institution must accept all regardless of class, religion, ability status, or gender, little has been done to create or enforce an environment free of covert discrimination based on sexuality. Bob, during the time of his coming out, remembers the empty posturing of his athletic department:

> They would promise me that they were setting up meetings to teach sensitivity. Several times they asked me to speak to a panel of coaches to help eliminate homophobia within the department. Well none of it ever happened, and it still hasn't happened to this day. I just remember feeling frustrated, sad, and hopeless because no one was helping me.

The National Collegiate Athletic Association (NCAA) has done very little to help in matters. The NCAA hides behind the claim that they are driven by the desires of the universities that it is comprised of, and because they have not heard from the universities on this issue, they have taken no action. While the NCAA has recently adopted a nondiscrimination policy for its own members regarding sexual orientation, they have not implemented a policy for the athletes with whom they oversee.

The institutional attitude toward homosexuality outside the athletic department may also play a factor in choosing whether an athlete comes out or not, as well as how he will be treated once he does. When an institution promotes homophobia, as was the case with Grant's school, it forces the athlete to remain closeted out of fear of institutional punishment. The best example of this comes from a nonsporting institution, the U.S. military. The official policy requires that gays and lesbians maintain second-class citizenship by not revealing that they are gay, or engaging in homosexuality. If they fail to do so, the U.S. military will not only discharge the soldier but may also sue for the cost of his or her training. One can easily see why soldiers choose not to come out in such an institution. Essentially, the dominant social norms surrounding the institution can have a powerful effect on the decision as to whether a gay athlete comes out or not, and the manner in which he is treated once he does.

THE INTERSECTIONALITY OF RACE AND COMING OUT

It is my belief that race, class, gender, sexual orientation, and other categories of identity that are based on a social stratification model should be viewed as a system of interlocking categories of experience. However, research about these categories has historically examined each as unique and independent of each other. Even within identity categories researchers have historically compared dualisms. For example, studies of blacks have been compared to that of whites[2] and studies of women have dominantly examined the experience of white women in relations to white men.[3] The same can be said about the comparison of white gay men to white heterosexual men.[4] Thus, the experiences of gay minorities can be nullified: as if the experience of a black gay male was the same as the experience of a white gay male. Unfortunately, this research does little to improve upon this. The respondents in this research are overwhelmingly white.

This does not reflect an intentional bias however. Quite the opposite, I looked very diligently to find openly gay athletes of color. In the end I was only able to locate two black cheerleaders, a black football player, an Asian runner, an Asian tennis player, a Mexican soccer player, and a Navajo basketball player; the remaining thirty-three athletes all identified as white. The difficulty in locating gay athletes of color is explained by a number of variables. First off, with so few gay athletes coming out of the closet in sport, and if all other social variables were equal, one would expect that the numbers of athletes of color to be equated according to population demographics. Essentially, since I was only able to locate forty gay athletes to study, one would expect only four black athletes and, perhaps, one Asian athlete to be represented. Thus, finding three black athletes is slightly underrepresentative of the population at large, while finding two Asian athletes is overrepresented. Of particular note, however, is that both the Asian athletes were closeted to their parents, even though they were out to their teams. The underrepresentation of black athletes, and the fact that two black cheerleaders came from privileged backgrounds, suggests there may be other variables at play that make coming out of the closet more difficult for athletes of color than for white athletes.

Perhaps this is no surprise: Gay culture, gay support systems, and much of what can be described as gay male identity has been established in the essence of whiteness in America. For example, in his (2004) book *On the Down Low,* J. L. King describes the manner in which notions of homosexuality and gay identity do not seem to apply to urban blacks. He suggests that blacks view homosexuality as a problem domain only to white men and that black men who have sex with other men do their best to keep it hidden from their community. Thus the language of my advertisement alone might help explain the difficulty in finding black gay athletes, for I advertised on list-serves and on the website www.outsports.com that I was looking for *gay* athletes.

Another significant variable regarding teammate support comes in the analysis of support toward homosexuality by black athletes. While my study does not contain enough members of any racial category other than white in which to draw conclusions or comparisons, a study of professional black athletes shows that black athletes are considerably more homophobic than white athletes. Of 175 NFL players interviewed, 91.7% of white players say they feel comfortable playing with a gay teammate, with just 60% of black players feeling comfortable. Similarly, 52.9% of the Caucasian players said they would be comfortable sharing a hotel room with a known gay player, while only 29% of African Americans were. Perhaps of most interest, it was found that among players who indicated that they would react with a "physical assault" if a gay player were to proposition them, 29.4% of African Americans indicated such while only 5.3% of Caucasian respondents said they would react with a physical assault.[5]

Thus, fewer athletes of color are likely to come out of the closet not only because of the threat of intersecting marginalized identities in a racist and homophobic society, but gay athletes of color might also have to deal with elevated levels of homophobia within their own racial category as well. When one considers the difficulty of dealing with a racist society, and the notion that he might lose his social support system if he comes out to his own community that may exhibit elevated levels of homophobia, it quickly grows understandable that these intersecting identities would make it extraordinarily difficult for a gay athlete of color to come out in athletics. Essentially, he might find himself trapped between communities of support.

Furthermore, in her research on lesbian athletes Pat Griffin shows that lesbian athletes of color might feel they have to choose their social justice battles, and determine that the intersectionality of their race with their sexual orientation is beyond the margins of manageability: "For lesbians of color the triple-threat identities of women, person of color, and lesbian present issues of identity and community that make becoming visible as a lesbian a complex decision" (1998, 164). My research supports her findings because the athletes of color that I did interview were not reliant upon social support systems of color. The black football player, for example, lived within a white community and had no social support system of African Americans. The same can be said of both Asian athletes, one of which (as the result of having been adopted) even had white parents. Oppositely, when John, the Navajo basketball player, came out in his community, he found himself isolated not so much because he was gay but rather because his sexuality reflected poorly upon his community. Thus all of the athletes of color who came out did not face the intersection of managing their stigma in a community of color, with John being the notable exception.

As if the intersectionality of race with homosexuality wasn't enough, Griffin suggests that because people of color are more likely to hail from lower socioeconomic areas, gay athletes of color might also have to add a third category of marginalized identity into the mix. Poorer athletes might view remaining closeted as a higher necessity if they desire a college scholarship as an avenue out of poverty. Similarly, it might make coming out of the closet as a collegiate athlete more difficult if they rely upon a scholarship to pay for college tuition. Essentially, coming out of the closet and risking one's position or scholarship to a homophobic coach might be considered too large a gamble for a poorer athlete. On the other hand, athletes of wealth (which is highly correlated with whiteness) may not need the scholarship to remain in school should things go awry after coming out of the closet. This research therefore suggests that, at present, gay athletes of color are more likely to emerge from the closet and identify as gay only if they live within white communities, are not dependent upon financial assistance from an athletic scholarship, are not dependent on a social support system of other people of color, maintain high capital on their teams, and possess the support of coach and institution—a tall order to fill.

NATURE AND ORIGIN OF THE SPORT

A number of particulars about specific sports are likely to affect the presence of homonegative or homofriendly sentimentality that have less to do with individuals or organizations and more to do with the sport itself. For example, Pat Griffin, author of *Strong Women, Deep Closets* (1998), suggests that homophobia most widely varies depending on whether the setting is a team or individual sport. She hypothesizes that the hypermasculine atmosphere surrounding team sports is more likely to permit gays to come out in individual sports where the attitudes are not so macho.

Griffin explains that the cohesion required in team sports leaves less room for individual variance on a number of determinants than for individual sports; team sports require that athletes adhere to narrow boundaries on many traits, not just sexuality. Athletes in team sports have really made a commitment to other men, an esteemed masculine trait that is also found in fraternities and the military. Although athletes in individual sports may also make such a commitment, they are more likely to be dedicated to sport for their own performance. Perhaps individual sport athletes, though highly dedicated to their track, swimming, or wrestling teams, may not be quite as bound by the rigid mandates of cohesive behavior that football or hockey players are. This interpretation is reflected by the fact that dozens of professional individual sport athletes have come out publicly both while playing and after retiring, while only five have come out in professional team sports.[6]

Sport scholar Bruce Kidd agrees with Griffin. He observes, "the preferences we express for different sports . . . are in part statements about what we value in 'a man' and what sort of relations we want to encourage between them" (1990, 37). Undoubtedly our valuing of team sports (which require brute strength and excessive risk) over individual sports (which normally require more endurance and finesse) can also be said to reflect the cultural value of masculinity over femininity.

Furthermore, evidence gathered from this research suggests that team sports may be more homophobic than individual sports because the number of team sport athletes I was able to locate for this research was fewer than that of individual sports. What is interesting about this is that even though I could not find as many team sport athletes to interview as individual sport athletes, I learned that their treatment did not significantly vary from the treatment of openly gay individual sport athletes.

In his research on gay Canadian athletes, Brian Pronger (1990) asserts that homophobia may also be stratified between combative sports and noncombative sports (which he calls struggle sports). He predicts that sports requiring physical contact between men (whether team or individual) will yield a higher degree of homophobia than others. In this manner, one would expect wrestling (an individual sport) to have a higher degree of homophobia than swimming (an individual sport absent of contact). Michael Messner (1992) concurs, believing that a higher degree of homophobia is necessary to negate the sexualized contact between men in combative sports.

Similarly, Pronger maintains that sports that are judged for aesthetic appeal might be lower in homophobia than sports in which competitors directly struggle against each other. In this case, one might judge that swimming might be more homophobic than diving, while sprinting might be more homophobic than figure skating. In each case, humans judge the latter and clocks the former. I add that aestheticism is akin to femininity, whereas the rigidity of time is more aligned with masculinity. Indeed, circumstantial evidence supports this theory, as there is evidently a higher rate of openly gay figure skaters and divers than tennis and golf players.   .

Another classification of sports may be made between sports that have originated and are popular in Europe, as opposed to those that have originated and are popular in the United States. This might be due to the lower rates of cultural homophobia in Europe (Widmer et al. 2002). European sports, therefore, might not have the same footprint of homophobia and they may not be coached in the same homophobic manner even when played in America.

For example, football, basketball, baseball, and hockey are all of North American design and they remain the four most popular sports in America. Conversely, rugby, water polo, and soccer originated and are more popular in Europe. Whereas each group of sports requires physical contact and coordination of effort between players, one could speculate that football might be higher in homophobia than rugby, that baseball might be higher in homophobia than soccer, and that hockey might be higher in homophobia than water polo. Supporting this contention, research by Price and Parker (2002) showed that an openly gay English rugby team, playing in an ostensibly heterosexual league, found that while rugby was imbued with homophobic and sexist rituals and language, the heterosexual teams were nonetheless willing to compete against the all-gay team despite the fact that the gay team's ranking was above the fiftieth percentile.

Similarly, American water polo can only be described as a vicious sport because the surface hides illegitimate violence from players who scratch, kick, and squeeze the testicles of opposing players below the water's surface. Whereas such violence might spawn a baseball team to brawl, one heterosexual water polo athlete tells me:

> Yeah, some guy might grab your balls under water during the game sending you to the sidelines, and then we will drink beer together at a party that night and talk about the game . . . its just part of the game. It's expected, and you don't call someone a fag because they did it.

I asked, "Do you ever hear them say fag or faggot?" "You know, I never hear that," he responded. "One of my good friends is gay, and he goes to all our meets and hangs out and parties with my [NCAA D1] team, and nobody cares, he's just one of the guys." To corroborate this, I contacted his gay friend, who told me, "The guys know fully well that I am gay, and they still want to hang out with me. They ask me about what it's like being gay, and some have even gone clubbing with me. They've hung out with my friend Chris before too; and he is *quite* gay." He later contrasted this experience with having tried to befriend members of the baseball team at the same school. When I asked how that went, he responded, "Let's just say that they were hostile toward homosexuality."

OTHER FACTORS

There are, of course, other factors that might influence the degree and type of homophobia present on a team. One might predict that all-male schools and religious schools might have higher rates of homosocial pressure, as well as athletic programs that garner a high degree of media attention. Having had an openly gay athlete on a team before is also likely to decrease the degree of homophobia on a team. Another variable that seems important in the world of sports is the level of play.

Griffin (1998) has suggested that the higher the caliber of competition, the less accepting sport might be. This, however, is hard to conceptualize from my research. For example, whereas high school athletes are inundated with a higher degree of homophobia as a result of increased homophobia of their cohort, university athletics are generally thought to be more competitive than high school athletics. This may mitigate the level of homophobia between these two levels. Essentially, it was hard for me to determine that there was a quantifiable difference between the homophobia exhibited between high school and university settings.

While it might be tempting to suggest that professional team sports are more homophobic than high school team sports (because my study was able to find openly gay high school team sport athletes but not openly gay professional team sport athletes), the sheer difference in numbers available nullifies this comparison. These factors prevent a clear hierarchy of homophobia from developing between high school, college, and professional sports; and all that can really be said is that professional team sports are more homophobic than professional individual sports.

Still, the majority of social discussion of homophobia in sport concerns itself with professional sports. This may be partially due to the obsession that Americans have with professional sports and also because knowledge of professional sports is more accessible in popular media. Therefore, the next chapter in this book serves to juxtapose professional sports with the previous chapters. It draws from both secondary and original sources in order to illustrate how matters work in professional sports, where there may be less elbow room and more narrow conceptions of masculinity.

9

The Center of Masculine Production: Gay Athletes in Professional Sports

ONE ATHLETE'S STORY:
STEVEN, CLOSETED NFL PLAYER

The name Steven Thompson is an alias, but it represents a real, gay National Football League player who is currently playing and one whose front as a gladiator betrays his inner anxiety and fear.[1] "I'm not brave. I'm gutless really," he told sport writer Mike Freeman in his book *Bloody Sundays* (2003, 142). "I do feel alone, and sometimes like a coward. I get frustrated and angry, but I also know that now is not the time for me to call a team meeting and say, 'What's up everybody? I'm gay.' Now is not the time, and unfortunately that moment will not come in my lifetime" (151). Thompson fears that should he come out or if word leaks out or people simply figure out that he is gay, he will suffer public ridicule, be singled out for violence, or be driven out of the sport by a hostile workplace. Surprisingly, his psychologist agrees with him, reinforcing the hegemony of silence and telling him that it is okay to remain shackled by fear.

At one point, Thompson flirted with coming out. But as alcohol fueled hostility during a San Francisco dinner, the heterosexual teammate he thought would safely harbor his proclamation clamored, "Somebody should kill those fucking faggots," squashing Thompson's belief in his broadmindedness. Thompson recoiled even more when another teammate said, "We are in Fagville" (141).

Thompson had heard San Francisco referred to as Faggot City before, and he was certainly no stranger to homophobic discourse. He had heard his parents use the terms frequently when he was a kid, and frequently heard faggot as a name for one who doesn't play through pain in the NFL. Thompson, a better than average player, has inflicted pain and received a great deal of pain himself. He has, after all, played in the NFL for many years. But Thompson laments upon the emotional not the physical when it comes to coming out. "I know keeping this secret is eating me up inside." He says, "But right now, I don't care. I love this game so much I won't do anything to jeopardize it" (151).

One might question such devout love for a violent game; a game that, paradoxically, is positioned in ideological opposition to his hidden identity. One might ask why Thompson would choose to live in a social space predicated upon demonizing the identity he relates to. But perhaps, for all its homophobia, pain, and homonegative violence football somehow provides Thompson a shelter from something he fears more than marginalization. Indeed, his willingness to remain closeted indicates that whatever he fears about coming out, the consequences of doing so are judged as being worse than living the segmented life of a closeted superstar. Whatever the answers, he is not the only one in this position, he claims to know other closeted NFL players too, in what he calls, "an underground network of gay NFL players" (152).

PROFESSIONAL SPORTS

As of the writing of this book, there has yet to emerge an active, openly gay professional athlete from a team sport in the United States or Canada, and only five have come out of the closet after retiring.[2] Indeed, there has never been an openly gay American basketball, baseball, football, soccer, volleyball, or hockey player to come out while playing, and one survey maintains that it isn't likely to happen anytime soon.[3] When one considers that the average career in professional sports is about three years, it may seem remarkable that none have come out while playing. Collectively, tens of thousands of professional athletes have gone through team sports without coming out, being outed, or otherwise reliably been determined gay. This chapter examines why.

It examines the center of sports, the world of professional sports and professional closets. It highlights the institutionalization of homophobia in professional athletics and asks questions about the relationship between professional sports and gay athletes. One question it does not address, however, is whether gay athletes at this elite level of sport *exist*. We know they do. Three of them are represented in this book. Rather, some of the important questions that this chapter examines are in what numbers do they exist, why don't they come out, and how will they come out.

THE RELATIONSHIP BETWEEN PROFESSIONAL ATHLETES AND HOMOSEXUALITY

There is no shortage of publicized homophobic comments from professional team sport athletes, both voluntary and involuntary. Some of the most famous comments include NFL player (Reverend) Reggie White, who told the Wisconsin state legislature in 1998 that the nation has strayed from God by allowing homosexuality to "run rampant."[4] Later, White violated NFL policies by appearing in a full-page antigay ad run in the *Washington Times*, while wearing his Green Bay Packers uniform.

In December 1999 baseball player John Rocker included homophobia along with a litany of other prejudices in a *Sports Illustrated* interview:

I would venture to say the Mets fans aren't even humans. There are some, uh, you know, 80 percent are some kind of Neanderthals. . . . Imagine having to take the 7 train to the ballpark, looking like you're riding through Beirut next to some kid with purple hair next to some queer with AIDS right next to some dude who just got out of jail for the fourth time right next to some twenty-year-old mom with four kids. It's depressing. . . . The biggest thing I don't like about New York are the foreigners. I'm not a very big fan of foreigners. You can walk an entire block in Times Square and not hear anybody speaking English; Asians and Koreans and Vietnamese and Indians and Russians and Spanish people and everything up there. How the hell did they get in this country? (cited in Pearlman 1999)

In 2002 NFL player Jeremy Shockey made an appearance on the Howard Stern Show in which he said, "If I knew there was a gay guy on my college football team, I probably wouldn't, you know, stand for it." He added, "I think, you know, they're going to be in the shower with us and stuff, so I don't think that's gonna work."[5] In 2002, Garrison Hearst of the San Francisco '49ers, said, "Aww, hell, no! I don't want any faggots on my team. I know this might not be what people want to hear, but that's a punk. I don't want any faggots in this locker room" (cited by Kaufman 2003).

When interviewed by the Sacramento Bee, one anonymous San Francisco Giants player said, "If I found out someone is gay in here, I'd run (him) out. It would be uncomfortable for me and for him in the shower. It would be ugly" (cited by Kaufman 2003). And in 2003, Colorado reliever Todd Jones, commenting on the Broadway play *Take Me Out* (a fictional story of a gay baseball player) said, "There was no place for an openly gay player in the big league."[6] Finally, an anonymous NFL player told reporter Mike Freeman, "If there was an out-of-the-closet homo on the team, everyone would be worried about if he was looking at you or wanted to fuck with you" (2003, 143).

Perhaps the most illuminating comments came with a 1998 issue of *Outside the Lines* on *ESPN*, where several professional athletes were asked about their views on gays in professional sport. Darrell Green of the Washington Redskins said, "I won't be voting for it. I am on the other side . . . we don't have any more space in our locker room.'" Offensive guard Tre Johnson said, "It would put everybody on edge. Everybody would ostracize that person. Everybody's fears and insecurities would come to the forefront, and being in this testosterone-ego environment that we are in, that person would get hammered." Similarly, Minnesota's Chris Carter said, "I think it would be tough for a lot of the athletes that I play with to think that, 'Wow, I am showering, I am performing on the field, I am bleeding, I am fighting with a person that is a homosexual. . . . I know there would be people definitely taking shots at him. I feel very confident that that would happen." Illustrating the closed-loop nature of homophobic reproduction and the association of homosexuality with weakness in sport, NFL running-back coach Johnny Roland said, "You try to sell your team on being a rough, tough, hard-nosed football team . . . and I would assume if that person was of that persuasion, I am not sure of the quality of his toughness."

These comments illustrate the near-total institution that pressures athletes into a narrow worldview. They help illustrate why Michael Messner calls this level of sports the center, and how some athletes are not able to disentangle gender from sexuality. Admittedly, the comments also raise an eyebrow regarding Freudian reaction formation, suggesting that perhaps some of these comments are made by deeply closeted gay men themselves, who might be exaggerating their hatred of homosexuality. But even athletes who maintain that they are not homophobic and wouldn't have a problem with gay players express concern over the level of homophobia in sport. John Salley, a former Detroit Piston's NBA player, said that homophobe baseball player John Rocker "would be accepted into the NAACP [before] a gay guy on a team" (Freeman 2003, 143), and J. T. Snow of the San Francisco Giants told a reporter, "I don't think he [a gay athlete] would be accepted. The guy would have a target on his back" (Ford 2004). While teammate Jay Witasick said, "I don't care about a person's [sexuality] . . . but I think it would be very tough."[7]

One reason there are so many widely publicized homophobic comments from professional team sport athletes is that professional team sports garner the majority of cultural attention. I jest that you can always tell an *individual sport* coach (compared to a team sport) because he begins reading the morning paper's sports section from the back. But just because team sport athletes are most frequently reported making homophobic comments does not mean that these comments are germane only to them. Olympic gold medalist Greg Louganis recalls in his autobiography (1996) that rivals formed a "Beat the Faggot Club," and research on professional ice skating found that homophobia drove a number of men from the sport (Adams 1993).

But as discouraging as these comments can be, they are, in the large picture, just *a few* publicized attitudes. Homophobic comments are certainly more likely to be reported by the press than homopositive comments, so these comments may not accurately reflect the degree of homophobia in professional team sports. While we can safely maintain that the institution of sport is, in general, highly homophobic, we cannot suggest that all players subscribe to such, for there is also strong support for gay athleticism voiced by heterosexual team sport athletes.

Details magazine quoted New York Mets manager Bobby Valentine as saying that professional baseball is "probably ready for an openly gay player," adding, "the players are diverse enough now that I think they could handle it" (Buzinski 2002). Indeed, after the comments, *New York Post* gossip columnist Neal Travis speculated that Valentine's comments were a "pre-emptory strike" designed to clear the path for the eminent outing of a Met's player since there had been (and remains) persistent rumors about Mike Piazza's sexuality. Piazza reacted by immediately telling the press that, "I'm not gay," but he was also sure to show that he was also not homophobic, announcing, "In this day and age, it's irrelevant. I don't think it would be a problem at all" (Buzinski 2002).

After Billy Bean came out in 1999, he received a number of supportive phone calls from his ex-teammates. San Diego Padre Brad Ausmus told the *New York Times*, it "wouldn't have made any difference to me when we played together . . . and it doesn't matter now."[8] Padre manager Jim Riggleman called Bean "a class act" (cited in Bean 2003, 217). Lenny Harris of the Dodgers and Benny Ruiz of the Detroit Tigers also called to support him. Perhaps most touching, Detroit Tigers Chief Executive Officer John McHale Jr. called Billy to say, "I just want you to know that you were once and always will be a member of the

Tigers. You have my support and the support of this organization. Once you wear the Old English D on your chest, it can never be taken away" (cited in Bean 2003, 241).

To their credit, many professional athletes show progressive views on sexuality. One quarterback says that he would have no problem playing with an openly gay man. "I play with wife beaters and drug abusers. Why would I have a problem playing with a gay man?" (Freeman 2003, 145). Although the quote should be equally noted for its subversive critique of sport as much as its careless conflation of homosexuality with deviant and illegal behaviors, the player's attitude greatly contrasts what we hear most from professional players.

A more accurate assessment of the attitudes regarding homophobia in professional sports comes to us in the form of a 1998 unpublished quantitative analysis by sports agent Ralph Cindrich (who gave me permission to use it). Results show that 63% of his respondents said that it does not matter to them what the sexual preference of their teammates are, and 76% said they would be comfortable playing next to a gay teammate. In addition, 58% said they would even be comfortable having a locker next to a gay teammate, and 50% would be uncomfortable calling gay men faggots or other derogatory terms. Only 16% said that if a gay man propositioned him, he would react with a physical assault (keep in mind that there is likely to be a discrepancy between those who say they would react physically and those who would).[9] The survey was conducted anonymously over the telephone, and all of his 175 athletes were interviewed, giving us a large quantity of respondents by which to make generalizations.

Baseball fan Dug Funnell, a nonacademic baseball fanatic, has unknowingly given us a quasi-quantitative study to examine regarding homophobia in professional baseball by sending out over five thousand letters to baseball players, managers, owners, front-office officials, and broadcasters in the past fifteen years. His actions reflect a political tool to reduce the homophobia found within the sport. Part of his letter reads,

> Baseball has kept players on who have been charged with assault, felonies, solicitation, statutory rape and illegal financial doings. And not to forget all the players who admitted to selling, buying and using illegal drugs. The message here is—drugs, rape, assault and solicitation are more acceptable than being gay. What's wrong with this picture? (2002)

Dug received about one hundred letters back. "Dug, my message is: Be yourself," wrote Turk Wendell, a relief pitcher who pitched in the

World Series with the New York Mets. "Don't be sensitive . . . about not getting responses from players; most of them are jerks. They forget where they came from and what got them there." Wendell, who sent a handwritten, three-page response, was not the only player who sent support. Pitcher Jerry DiPoto, said:

> I agree with your point of view 100%. Baseball and the world in general are imperfect places. I know it is a difficult thing to ask, but I will ask you to remember that baseball is a game made up of individuals. Don't condemn the game itself or question your passion for the game because of the ignorance or bigotry of the masses. There are a number of individuals who feel just as you and are fair-minded. . . . I can't ever know just how difficult the world can be for a gay man. I just try to make it a little more livable for all of us. I hope that your letter opens some eyes around baseball because, as you said in your letter, "baseball is a reflection on life in America."

And Dodger Steve Sax returned a letter saying, "I try to use my position as a public figure to do what I can to make the world a better place."

Management has also responded to Funnell. He has received letters of support from, among others, Peter McGowan (San Francisco Giants owner); Lee Thomas (then the Philadelphia Phillies general manager); Dave Dombrowski (Florida Marlins general manager); Mike Illich (Detroit Tigers owner); Larry Himes (Chicago Cubs special assistant to the general manager) and John Harrington (Boston Red Sox owner). Interestingly, Larry Lucchino, president and chief executive officer of the San Diego Padres, the very team Billy Bean was playing for in 1995, responded:

> Philosophically, it is important that the New Padres make a conscious and sustained effort to reach out to all societal constituencies. Part of the enduring beauty of baseball is that it can be enjoyed by people of all races, religions, ethnic groups, ages and sexual preferences. It is a game that might best be described as being fundamentally *inclusive* and in no way, intentionally *exclusive*. Stated simply, baseball can ill-afford to be discriminatory at any time, in any way.

Although the above statement should be critiqued for representing baseball as being "inclusive," it highlights what Funnell maintains is a growing support for gay athletes in sport. He says that over his fifteen-year letter-writing campaign he has been able to gauge the level of homophobia in professional baseball and suggests that, while overall, "baseball hates a faggot," the climate has "warmed somewhat" (all cited in Funnell 2002). Indeed the climate may have. Another quantitative study of attitudes in professional baseball supports this. In 2004 the *Tribune* newspaper company surveyed 750 professional baseball players and found that 74% said they would not be bothered by having a gay teammate, and only 15% said they would be.

Although the study did not ask if players would *support* a gay teammate, the results show that three-fourths of professional baseball players are, at least on this one question, not ostensibly homophobic.

While most of the popular analysis focuses on the agency of homophobic players, ex-professional baseball player Billy Bean suggests, for example, that Major League Baseball has been defunct in creating an atmosphere of tolerance and has therefore silently promoted homophobia.

> The Major League Baseball Players Association, of which I'm a member, should make the case for sexual orientation non-discrimination, as other unions routinely do. As the association has made clear, baseball is a workplace, not a playground. In states and municipalities with gay-rights laws on the books, baseball clubs may actually be violating antidiscrimination statutes by allowing a hostile workplace. (2003, 238–39)

Social attitudes in baseball have also been tested via a September 7, 2003 article in Cleveland's largest newspaper, *The Plain Dealer*. The story chronicles a Japanese baseball player, Kazuhito Tadano, who was signed to a $67,000 contract .to a Minor Cleveland Indians team. Tadano, who is just twenty-two, appeared in a gay pornographic movie when he was a nineteen-year-old college student without a scholarship in Japan. He says that he engaged in sex with another man not because he is gay but because he was paid more for it than for engaging in heterosexual sex. But because pornography is illegal in Japan, Tadano was blackballed, so he tried out for several American minor league teams, and after being turned down by the Arizona Diamondbacks because of the incident, the Cleveland Indians picked him up.

In the article, Indians director of player development John Farrell said, "From what we were able to determine, his involvement in the film was a one-time isolated incident." Tadano addressed his minor league teammates, "I want to apologize to the fans and all the people who have supported me. I made a big mistake," he said. After his five-minute speech, one athlete said:

> I told everyone that I felt we needed to support this guy. I thought we should give him a chance to be our teammate and friend. You could

tell he was sincere and embarrassed. I've sat in the bullpen with him and he's a good guy. We've all messed up in some shape or form in our life.

Tadano's story highlights some of the mechanisms that occur with gay athletes at the lower levels. First, Tadano's masculine capital is raised because he is a talented pitcher who would have easily made the professional ranks of Japanese baseball had he not been banned. Furthermore, he had the support of a few key people, both players and club staff (likely because he is good). Finally, other players may have accepted him because he willingly reproduces the ascription of orthodox masculinity in that he has renounced his homosexual activities as "embarrassing," and apologized for them, couching his same-sex experience as *a mistake*. In a January 27, 2004 article on ESPN.com, he said "I'm not gay. I'd like to clear that fact up right now." Still, in a truly progressive stand, Farrell told the press that while he doesn't care to see the pornographic film, "his sexual orientation is not an issue with us," and that "it's a moot point with his teammates."

Finally, Tadano appears to be skillful enough that he might make it to the Indians' Major League team soon. Indians shortstop Omar Vizquel said, "I'd have no problems being on the same team as him. Baseball is baseball is baseball. If a guy can play, he can play. There are probably gay baseball players . . . what people do away from the field is their business."

Tadano's case and Funnell's letters and the *Tribune's* survey illustrate that the institution of baseball is at least growing more aware of the fact that they could have players among their ranks. But before I leave the topic of gay athletes in professional sports, I also feel it is important to address the fact that whereas the core of homophobic reproduction is centered among the athletes in sport, it may also trickle out of that center to ancillary members of the institution (referees, agents, physical trainers, team doctors, newspaper reporters, managers, etc.). These members of the institution may be less likely to be protected from homophobia than the very athletes who generate it, because they do not have access to raise their value to their teams in the same fashion that athletes do. Those who hold ancillary positions to the sporting arena cannot quantify their performance as easily as do the athletes. For example, a friend of mine (who is a closeted baseball umpire) says that he fears being fired because nobody would trust a gay umpire. The story of professional umpire David Pallone (1990) exemplifies this.

Pallone, who was fired for unsatisfactory performance shortly after coming out maintains that his termination had nothing to do with his performance, and everything to do with his sexual orientation. But the largely unquantifiable nature of his position leaves him less recourse when faced with this type of discrimination than an athlete who can clearly show he is the best on the team.

The contextual juxtaposition between the athletes (who enforce the homophobia) and the ancillary participants (who are victimized by it), highlights that those who possess higher social currency are permitted to transgress societal boundaries while those who do not are allowed no transgressions. In this manner, professional sports represent the same king-of-the-hill style hierarchies found in jock-ocracies, those on the field are given social prestige, and the ancillary members are suppressed.

This section has shown that while we can safely assume that professional team sports remain a bastion in the reproduction of hypermasculinity and homophobia for both those at the center and in the periphery, we can also suggest that homophobia in these ranks is not seamless and that the orthodox form of masculinity is beginning to be contested. While we can accuse professional sports of institutionalizing homophobia, we can also begin to see cracks in that very reproduction. That is to say, there are fissures within the system, discourse more conducive to sharing this arena with gay athletes is beginning to develop. Still, coming out in the world of professional sports will be no easy task. Gay athletes have grown up in a near-total institution predicated upon homophobia, and challenging the system might first mean confronting some of the fears they have built up throughout their socialization and existence in a highly homophobic arena.

PROFESSIONAL-SIZED FEAR

Team sport athletes (gay and straight) often represent a paradox in masculinity. Whereas they are assumed to be fearless because they are associated with orthodox masculinity, whereas they are thought to possess emotional strength, independence, and courage, in actuality, they are also quite scared. They are neither emotionally strong, independent, nor courageous. Team sport athletes cowardly adhere to the strictest of gender roles, and if Michael Messner is right about professional sports being the center of masculine production, then professional athletes are the most likely to do what they are told.

Professional athletes may be afraid of deviating even slightly from the masculine ascription, because the terrain outside masculine boundaries is viewed as a contentious and stigmatized space. Essentially, team sport athletes exhibit toughness only on the outside. They are members of the cult of athleticism, tithing their agency and vow-ing complacency to team norms. They are not freethinking and free speaking; rather their ideologies are largely shaped by the cult, and they express uniformity in thought and action—benevolent to the ide-ology of orthodox masculinity.

In order to make salient this point, I frequently challenge the ath-letes in my courses to come to class wearing a dress. Generally saying, "We think that athletes are brave because they put up with physical brutality, and in that aspect they are. But when it comes to bravery of self-expression, or fearing stepping outside predetermined masculine boundaries, they are the most afraid. Let's see how much you truly don't care what other people think of you." I chide them, "Come to class in a dress." Highlighting my point Thompson says, "I love play-ing football more than I love myself and my sense of pride and well-being" (cited in Freeman 2003, 143).

In short, athletes who best represent hegemonic masculinity are often afraid to be anything but hypermasculine. Following masculine mandates has been shown to damage self-esteem, which in turn has been shown to make athletes more accepting of abuse from coaches and teammates (cf. Coakley 2002). Perhaps the ultimate example of an athlete following masculine scripts and of doing what he is told comes to us from Billy Bean who so adhered to the expectations of his team-mates that he skipped the funeral of his lover in order to make a base-ball game!

Billy Bean's sacrifice (missing his lover's funeral for a baseball game) might seem extreme to those from outside the institution of baseball. However, sacrifice is the hallmark of sport, and for those with enough talent and desire to emulate masculinity enough to make it to the elite levels of sport, the near-total institution requires them to sac-rifice health, education, stability, security, friendship, family, and gen-der expression for the sake of athletic elitism and the social merit that accompanies it. Ironically, whereas athletes are willing to sacrifice all types of personal freedoms for athletic success, they are not willing to sacrifice athletic success for personal freedom.[10]

When it comes to sacrificing personal freedom for physical safety, gay team sport athletes find themselves in another paradox. Whereas athletes are commonly thought to be intimidating, closeted gay ath-letes fear that the level of violence, in an already violent sport, might intensify if it were known that they were gay. So even though they are not supposed to be capable of being intimidated, they are. And there might be some reason for this: openly gay athletes might genuinely be targeted for extra (illegitimate) violence by other athletes. Retired gay football player Esera Tuaolo said:

The one thing I could never do was talk about it. Never. No one in the
NFL wanted to hear it, and if anyone did hear it, that would be the end
for me. I'd wind up cut or injured. I was sure that if a GM didn't get
rid of me for the sake of team chemistry, another player would intentionally hurt me, to keep up the image. (cited in Freeman 2003, 155)

Furthermore, Thompson tells of a situation on his NFL team in which
his coach described a player from another team who was suspected of
being gay, by saying, "He's soft, real soft, and some of you guys know
what I'm talking about. He gets hit, he folds up like a bitch. So smack
him around and he will give up." The coach added, "Just don't bend
over when you're near him" (cited in Freeman 2003).

There is no doubt that intentional violence occurs in these spaces.
Minnesota Viking player (and Reverend) Reggie White said:

Sometimes you have to hit somebody to get them out of the game cuz
if you get them out of the game then it gives you a better opportunity
to win. When you see Emmit Smith pull a hamstring a week before
the game, you're thinking good this is my job and my job is to go out
and do whatever I need to win. (cited in Kaufman 2003)

Similarly, Thompson said that when playing against this team he
noticed the player in question was getting more than his fair share of late
hits, cheap shots, spit on, and kicks to his stomach. After one play in
which the player suspected of being gay was left on the ground, Thompson went to help him up. "Don't help that fag up!" a teammate exclaimed
(Freeman 2003). Thompson didn't, and never helped him up again.

PROFESSIONAL PRESSURE

In addition to being afraid of breaking with the cult of masculinity and
being victimized by violence, gay athletes might also be pressured to
remain closeted by their fears of having their athletic performance
decreased as a result of social pressures from coming out. In professional sports, careers are made and destroyed by a finite number of
chances. Gay athletes who have come out after retiring and those who
are still closeted both express that coming out would have a significant
effect toward bringing unwanted pressure to their athletic experience.
They suggest that the stress of coming out, combined with the already
exacting pressures to perform at the world-class level, would make
coming out highly distracting to a team that is "playing" for million-
dollar contracts. Billy Bean told *Sports Illustrated*:

It would be very difficult for a player to come out today. This guy has to play in stadiums with 40,000 people. What's he going to hear if he strikes out? Overnight this guy's career will have nothing to do with his athletic ability. It's not a safe time to do it. (cited in Menez 2001)

In the October 2002 issue of *Out* he added:

To put your sexuality at the forefront of your life when you're a professional athlete, that's really hard. The sport has to be at the forefront. To sacrifice that, that's a huge thing. When you are at the top of your game you do realized how hard it was to get there, and you do know how short-lived that can be. And overnight you are changing the focus of your game. It doesn't take a long time to slide off that scale. (cited in Konigsberg 2002, 81)

But this attitude is just one side of the coin. They fail to account for the effect that the distraction, depression, anxiety, and fear of being outed against one's will might also have on a player; something which he articulates in his autobiography.

My confusion was hard to shake, even at the ballpark, which always had been my sanctuary. I would stand in center field, my every move scrutinized by 40,000 screaming fans, worrying about my parents' reaction to the inevitable tabloid headlines about the queer ballplayer when I should've been focusing on the location of the next pitch or on getting the best possible jump on a hit my way. Striding to the plate, I'd catch myself wondering about how my otherwise sturdy, dependable body could possibly harbor such desires. . . . I regressed to the stage of a rookie. (2003, 103)

He later says, "My emotional turmoil was obviously contributing to my inability to concentrate on the field. My self-confidence, the foundation of any player, was shot" (107).

Similarly, retired gay NFL player Esera Tuaolo said:

I would get a sack, force a fumble, stuff a play on the goal line. And hours later, in the middle of the night, I'd wake up sweating, clutching my chest and gasping for breath. Maybe someone who knows saw that, I'd think to myself. Maybe they'll call the coach, or the owner, or the papers. Sometimes I'd spend hours lying awake, praying for the anxiety attack to end, hoping my head would stop spinning on top of my banged-up body.[11]

The contradictory statements lead one to wonder just what the effect of stress is on an athlete, and whether the stress of remaining closeted is more deleterious to performance than the stress of dealing with pressures as an openly gay athlete. While I cannot sociologically assess the situation for professional athletes (because there are not enough to study), the insights I have gained from studying openly gay high school and college athletes might help illuminate the complexity of the situation.

Openly gay high school and college athletes tell me that they too faced crippling fears of being discovered. However, these same athletes unanimously expressed an empowerment as a result of coming out. They reported an intoxicating sense of agency in controlling one's social space. Similarly, Olympic gold medalist Mark Tewksbury even tells me that his performance dramatically improved after telling his coach that he was gay. "I dropped 1.3 seconds off my backstroke in just ten months because I freed so much of my energies after finally telling my coach that I was gay. I had been working for years to gain tenths of seconds, but after I told him I dropped 1.3!"[12] Other gay athletes have also expressed similar performance related gains after coming out. Bob dropped his 800-meter time from 1:56 to 1:51 shortly after coming out, a substantial improvement that he attributes to his feeling less socially restricted. "I was just looser, more relaxed," he said. "Like a giant weight was removed from my back."

Ultimately, it is the not knowing what *might* happen after coming out of the closet that cripples gay athletes. However, after coming out of the closet, their tactics change. General panic is replaced with strategic and empowered thinking. This sense is nearly universal among the athletes I interviewed. When they came out publicly it was almost always coupled with the desire to have come out sooner. Conversely, athletes who come out covertly report less empowerment from being out. Indeed, these athletes often maintain a general sense of anxiety about who knows and what they might think and they find themselves stuck in the second-class citizenship of don't ask, don't tell.

While remaining closeted, or managing a compartmentalized identity (choosing to be out in some arenas and not in others) is most certainly *stressful*, it does not necessarily mean that the stress will result in poorer performance. Terry (the professional football player) and Aaron (the professional hockey player) report stress from managing their identity in this manner, but they do not report that their choice to remain in the closet has had a deleterious effect on their performance. And although they cannot know this with certainty, because they have not tried coming out, I do not feel comfortable enough drawing broad conclusions about the effect of coming out in sport and performance with professional athletes.

GAY ATHLETES AND THE SPORT-MEDIA COMPLEX

While professional athletes share many similarities with athletes from the lower levels of sport, they do maintain a unique relationship to the sport-media complex that the others do not. That is to say, being an openly gay athlete at the professional level might bring extra social circumstances in terms of how they relate to and gain from their sponsors, agents, and managers, and whether they are given access to prime playing positions and time, which foster their careers.

In the 1998 issue of ESPN's *Outside the Lines*, leading sports agent Leigh Steinberg, on whom the movie *Jerry Maguire* is based, said, "A gay team sport athlete would have a harder time finding sponsors than a convicted felon." He added, "I think it would be much easier, in many senses, to be convicted of robbery and serve time, than come play in major-league baseball or the NFL, and be gay." He continued:

> I think it would have a devastating effect in terms of the marketability of any athlete to come out and talk about gayness. The whole concept of endorsements is an attempt by a company to appeal to the broadest possible audience. The thought that a company would want to step into the middle of that controversy, especially with the very heavy fundamentalist Christians who are making this a public issue, is just not there.

But significant change has been underway since 1998. The U.S. Supreme Court ruled that sodomy laws were unconstitutional, gays and lesbians have gained popularity in the media, and in terms of sport, Billy Bean and Esera Tuaolo have brought the issue of gays in sport to the forefront of sports media. In light of these advancements I interviewed Steinberg again. "Would you still make that statement?" I asked.

> Oh, absolutely. . . . Clearly Ray Lewis was involved with a potential attempted murder charge, yet he has come back from that to do a large number of national ads. Jason Kidd was involved with domestic violence, and he has come back to be a popular national figure. Clearly there are athletes who are involved with domestic violence, murder, drunk driving and an array of scrapes with the law, and they have been able to assume the mantel of popular endorsers, and we have yet to see an out-of-the-closet gay team sport athlete. Much less someone involved with the endorsement of product.

In a note of reflection, he paused, "although I did see Esera Tuaolo playing a banjo in an ad for *Chili's*." He cracked an acknowledging smile that progress is indeed being made. Still, it is the fear of losing or not gaining new product endorsements that this billion-dollar sports agent cites as a major reason why so few athletes have come out in professional sports, and why none have come out in professional team sports.

However, the lay analysis of corporate sponsors dropping gay athletes doesn't hold up to empirical investigation. When examining this issue of sponsorship, it is less important to cite the high rate of homophobia in sport and more important to examine the culture of homophobia in the corporate world. Research shows that the higher a company's Fortune 500 rank, the more likely they are to offer same-sex benefits to their employees (Human Rights Campaign 2003). Nike, for example has a 100 percent score with the Human Rights Campaign, meeting all seven of the Human Rights Campaign's (HRC) points of consideration for a conducive climate for gay and lesbian employees.

Presumably, most corporate sponsors wish to avoid a politically incorrect media fiasco and a possible boycott should they pull an endorsement away from an athlete who has come out of the closet. Indeed, companies strive to improve their performance on the Human Rights Campaign Corporate Quality Index, which measures the gay friendliness of corporation on seven measures, including benefits for same-sex partners. Their 2003 report states,

> The initial publication of the HRC Corporate Quality Index in 2002 sparked strong public interest and caught the attention of corporate executives. Within a week of its release in August of 2002, more than 30 companies called the Human Rights Campaign to inquire about how to obtain a rating, or improve the one they had.

To show why I maintain that corporate sponsors would not be reluctant to sponsor a gay athlete, I turn to the case of U.S. national 800-meter track champion and silver medalist of the 2002 World University Games, Deric Peterson. Deric approached me about wanting to come out publicly about his bisexuality and found a warm reception. I encouraged him to do so, as he would not only be U.S. track and field's first openly gay athlete but would also be the first professional black athlete to proclaim that he is something other than heterosexual. Before meeting with me to write the story, I advised him to contact his sponsor, Adidas, to see what they thought of the idea of a story appearing about him in the July 2002 issue of *Genre* (a mainstream gay men's magazine). Deric called Adidas and told them he was contemplating doing this story and reported to me, "They said, 'Great, that's not a problem at all.' They don't care. It's not like people are going to run to the store to return their Adidas."

Furthermore, a well-recognized professional gay athlete who comes out of the closet while actively playing is also quite likely to receive a great deal of sponsorships, *precisely because he is gay.* In 2001 ESPN conducted a poll, asking: "If a player on your favorite professional sports team announced he or she was gay or lesbian, how would this affect your attitude towards that player?" Only 17% said they would turn against the player; 63% said it would make no difference, and 20% said they would become a bigger fan, leaving one to conclude that coming out would help the athlete gain 3% of fan support (cited in Buzinski 2002, August 19).

Indeed, there are many corporations that look to create brand loyalty with gays and lesbians: Subaru, Ikea, Miller, Absolute Vodka, Calvin Klein, Armani Exchange, Abercrombie & Fitch, and others all court the gay dollar, both because they are interested in the bottom-line and (sometimes) for political advocacy. Furthermore, other research of mine shows that gay athletes are incredibly brand loyal, saying that they would pay more for a gay-friendly athletic brand than not.[13] All one needs to do is flip through any gay magazine to see a host of advertisers that attempt to court the gay consumer. In this respect it's no accident that Esera Tuaolo landed a national Chili's commercial, or that even openly gay high school football player Corey Johnson advertised for a furniture company. After conveying this thought to Leigh Steinberg, he replied, "You might be right. In fact, I think that there has probably never been a time so right for an athlete to attempt to come out. The climate will be the most hospitable that it has ever been to make the attempt."

THE EMPLOYER

Another career obstacle a gay player might have to face is the potential discrimination through his employer(s). Freeman's interview with Steve Thompson uncovers a startling system of covert discrimination against gays in the NFL. He quotes a football coach who claims to have been close to signing a talented player until the franchise's security personnel revealed that the player was gay. This coach, his general manager, and team owner decided not to offer him a contract.

> Basically, this player was not being covert about it. It was pretty well known, I was told by our security people, that he was very visible at these gay bars, and we were worried that it would get out, end up on ESPN, and ruin the guy, and then just like that there goes all that money you invested. (2003, 144)

The coach says that they are not the only franchise to have such security measures.

According to Glenn Burke's (1995) autobiography *Out at Home*, when famed Los Angeles Dodger Coach Tommy Lasorda grew tired of the *friendship* between his gay son (of which Lasorda still denies) and Burke (who helped Lasorda win his third World Series title), Dodger management offered to pay for a honeymoon for Burke if he would agree to a marriage of convenience in order to conceal his sexuality. When Burke refused, he was traded to the Oakland A's for an aging outfielder. When the A's manager, Billy Martin, learned of his sexual orientation he called him a faggot in front of the rest of the team and took the first chance to cut Burke from the A's. Billy Martin made public statements about not wanting a homosexual in his clubhouse.[14]

These quotes relate to stories I've heard about gay players from various sports being told that they must stay away from the gay scene. It also makes salient that when the don't ask, don't tell policy is not adhered to, the employer feels justified in employment discrimination, similar to the U.S. military. One NFL coach said, "Call me prejudiced or whatever, but I have to look out for the morale of the team, and a known gay man could destroy it" (Freeman 2003, 145). The identical argument was used to keep black players out of professional sports and seems ludicrous when compared with athletes like Lawrence Philips, who despite having dragged his girlfriend by her hair down a flight of stairs, remains employed by the NFL.

When presented with the same scenario, another NFL coach told Freeman, "Basically, if he kept the fact that he was gay quiet and didn't flaunt it, and he was good, I'd sign him. But he'd have to stay in the closet, and he'd have to be real good to counter the risk of signing him" (144).

All professional team sport athletes have contractual obligations in which the player is not allowed to cause damage to the reputation of the team. Even college athletes have clauses in their scholarship contracts that say they will represent the school well at all times. Indeed, one closeted professional coach told me that his contract specifically prohibits him from coming out publicly with his sexuality. As bizarre as it sounds, those around the issue of gays in sport have consistently heard rumors about rules prohibiting MLB players from coming out. Similarly, a player in the All-American Girls Professional Baseball League was kicked out after she cut her hair short, a violation of an agreement that players would keep the appearance of feminine heterosexuality (144).

When I asked Leigh Steinberg, who now deals exclusively with NFL players, he responded:

I can't think of anything contractually that would [pauses]. . . . There is language that covers drugs, arrests, and bribes, gambling, conduct reasonably judged by the commissioner to be a detriment to football. But in a football contract there is nothing that even vaguely would cover sexual preference.

But sports writer Mike Freeman discusses a secret society of investigators who look for and report on gay NFL players who frequent gay bars. Jim Buzinski at OutSports.com tells me, "Yeah, I know, I hear a lot about that in baseball too. It's not that the NFL hires these people, rather some of the individual clubs do." It's not that a club would come right out and say, "We are firing you for being gay," but one might imagine that a gay player could face covert action. If a player were to come out, he might be scrutinized to a different standard than his heterosexual teammates.

Athletes are also dependent upon their club for contract renewals, playing positions, and a host of variables that help shape their career. If an athlete were not given these chances, his career could be stymied. Therefore, a gay athlete might fear that coming out will give him less than favorable treatment by his club. Indeed, there seems to be a perception of those who own and control the sport that a gay athlete has less right to public proclamations of his sexuality than a heterosexual athlete.

Steinberg is adamant that it would be unfair for a professional athlete to come out publicly without first telling his club:

It's unfair because the club is the employer, and it has consequences for the club. It's making a presumption about the club's position and subjecting them without time to prepare, and that's not fair, and not only is that not fair but it destroys a chance for partnership in dealing with whatever the issues are.

But even with advance notice, athletes at the professional level would undoubtedly be subject to the same factors that influence the hospitality of their team toward their sexuality. That is to say, his experience would be made better or worse depending on his status as an athlete, his degree of masculine capital, the attitudes of his teammates, and the attitudes of the club and its owner. Steinberg says:

There is a broad continuum in the respect of ownership and management of individuals who own teams. They run the gamut from politically progressive individuals with fairly high degrees of sensitivity with social issues to political troglodytes that are extremely reactionary. So that it would really depend on someone like Robert Daly who runs the Dodgers, who owns a motion picture company and would have a much different take, or Robert Craft who owns the New England Patriots, who is a community leader who is politically sensitive. These are men who are in tune to the times. But there are those who are really out of it.

Athletes contemplating coming out of the closet publicly might find yet another obstacle in his manager and/or agent. "I can't imagine that there would be very many agents representing athletes who would be excited by or supportive by that decision," Steinberg says:

> And if we are talking about an athlete who has considerable endorsement revenue, the reaction of the agent would probably be knee-jerk in attempting to protect those endorsement relationships by counseling the athlete to not rock the boat. Most agents would probably calculate the downside to their own practice of representing and being associated with a gay athlete. And the publicity that might come to their practice, and the potential negative within their own client base, and the public antipathy that might be engendered through the proceeding brouhaha.

Sports agents *might* also fear the guilt-by-association process regarding homosexuality, fearing that their own heterosexuality may be questioned, and that their business might consequently suffer. One can certainly imagine how such fears might influence agents to be resistant of athletes coming out publicly. This fear may come across to closeted gay athletes both formally and informally in dealing with their agents.

When I asked Steinberg about what he would do should an athlete tell him that he was contemplating coming out of the closet, he said:

> My first inclination would be to determine whether the motivation of the athlete was pristine. I would be tempted to bring a psychologist into the mix to probe whether the motivation of the athlete was sincere and genuine; and secondarily, whether he was psychologically equipped to handle what would come later.

He continued with "what might come later," and the picture is daunting:

> I think I would be tempted to bring some psychological insight into the mix, to make sure that my athlete was prepared and that those family members, friends and intimates of the athlete, who might be affected

by the successive events, were also sufficiently prepared . . . you know even, to the extent that there would be a physical security issue that needed to be covered, in other words there might be potential unbalanced individuals who may try to do my athlete harm. Whether there would be a need for bodyguards or extra security at his home. I mean I might be exaggerating all of this but I certainly want to think through whether or not certain religious groups that are extreme—you know what the consequences might be just to be prepared.

This one-sided scrutiny deserves several pages of critique; it serves the perfect example of covert discrimination that structurally intimidates gay athletes from feeling free to come out. Steinberg does, however, correctly maintain that a franchise owner's motivations are not going to be centered on the emotional well-being of the gay athlete, rather, "It's going to be to protect the value of the franchise, the day-to-day popularity of the franchise and to the extent that they have a popular franchise with a supportive fan base. Why would they do anything to alter that?"

CRACKING THE CENTER

There are three basic theories as to how a professional gay team sport athlete might come out, with the first being that the athlete could emerge from the lower levels. My research shows some support for this. Those who come out of the closet in the lower ranks of sport are almost unanimously the best of their teams and regions. Although openly gay high school and collegiate athletes face many of the same homophobic attitudes that pro players do, when most high school athletes come out, there is no risk of losing sponsorship or financial contracts, no media harassment, and they're provided more formalized protection under education laws. Additionally, because they are largely out of view from the professional media and community attention, high school and college athletes are likely to have a core of gay friends outside of their sport, whereas professional athletes, who are public figures, may be too afraid to be seen with gay friends or in gay areas. Therefore, it is *possible* that a gay athlete will emerge from the closet in high school, gain social support, self-esteem as an openly gay collegiate athlete, and finally graduate to professional sports, being out the entire time, because once you're out, you can't go back. I do not, however, think this *too* likely.

The second theory maintains that a gay athlete will voluntarily come out of the closet while actively playing the sport. If this is the case, my research suggests that it would most likely occur from an athlete who maintains high masculine capital. That is to say, because most of the athletes in my study who came out publicly to their high school and collegiate teams were the best on their teams, we might predict that the same would be true for a professional athlete. Steinberg agrees, saying,

> Everything depends on the status of the player, because the true superstar is treated in sports in an entirely different way than anyone else. So that the superstar player is catered to, so if the superstar player decides that he is going to do it, then the franchise is going to adjust to it.

He continued:

> It took a Jackie Robinson to integrate baseball, and the most helpful thing for breaking the barrier in respect to gay acceptance in sports would be a truly gifted gay athlete who would come out of the closet. Because it is the true superstar who has the leverage and power to motivate a franchise to look beyond his sexual preference, to motivate his teammates to look beyond his sexual preference. And to forever break the stereotype because in most of the cases, athletes who have later come out of the closet tend to be marginally performing athletes. What truly would shatter stereotypes would be a superstar athlete who would be so clearly gifted and high-performing that it would parallel the old cliché, "I don't care if he is black, yellow, or purple" as long as he can hit .350, or throw thirty-five touchdown passes, or make a three-pointer.

It is possible that if such an athlete were to come out publicly, that the media, the players, and the entire complex around the notion of gays in sport might begin to quickly dissipate. Steinberg agrees:

> Exactly, I think the intriguing aspect of this all is that this stigma and paranoia will exist until someone breaks the stereotype. And once the first athlete does, I believe that it will be largely broken forever. And whatever that breakthrough, and whoever that breakthrough is will be the Jackie Robinson of gays or homosexuals. And if it's the right athlete, one who like Robinson has a strong stomach and has the ability to withstand a certain amount of derision with some nobility, if it is the right athlete who can carry himself with dignity and class while performing at a high level, this heritage of, you know, fear and paranoia will be shattered forever.

None of this, however, is to say that once a highly valued team sport athlete comes out while playing professionally, that the discrimination against them will dissipate. Indeed, Jackie Robinson broke the color barrier well over fifty years ago, but black athletes are still underrepresented on the benches (suggesting that the only way a black athlete will make a team is to be better than, not just as good, as his white teammates), and they are vastly underrepresented in positions of leadership and positions that are central to the outcome of the game (suggesting that white team owners don't trust black athletes with the same responsibility), such as pitcher, catcher, or quarterback.[16] And while the situation that Steinberg speaks of may be the most ideal circumstances in which an openly gay athlete will come out in sports, I contend that it is not the most likely. I maintain that it is far more likely that someone will be outed against his will.

At one point Americans largely believed that there could be no homosexual invaders in the pristine training ground of masculinity. Gay men were simply considered too weak, too effeminate, or not interested in competitive, and violent, contact team sports to be present. However, America's ignorance on the subject has changed. We know that gay men exist in all social spaces, and whereas we once did not want to believe that one of our sports heroes could be gay, today many fans are hell-bent on knowing who is gay. I recommend examining the web page www.outsports.com in order to see just how much discussion and just how much media attention is devoted to this issue. It is, without doubt, the most frequently asked question I get when I lecture.

The intriguing social phenomenon exists in the fact that playing competitive team sports, even at the highest level, no longer automatically disqualifies one from being suspected of being gay. That is to say that the veneer of heterosexuality team sports once provided men is beginning to slip. Because of this, it is truly only a matter of time before a gay athlete, who is living in a semisecret life, is outed against his will. Unlike how the media once respected President Roosevelt's infirmities by not showing them on film or discussing them in print, today's media would exploit them.

In May 2001 Brendan Lemon, editor-in-chief of *Out* magazine, claimed to have been dating a professional gay baseball player, and with the paparazzi-style media surrounding professional team sport athletes, I assumed that some savvy journalist would simply tail Lemon until he discovered just who the athlete was. While this never materialized (one of many reasons why I doubt the truthfulness of Lemon's claims), it is by the same process that I can foresee someone being outed involuntarily.

The final theory of how a professional gay athlete might come out while playing has not been widely discussed. To explain it, I propose the following situation. Suppose a savvy minor league player was called up to the majors—given his one shot at his dream of playing professional ball—but his season went poorly, and it was doubtful he would remain in the big leagues for long. Knowing that his salary was about to be slashed, that history would fail to recognize him, and that his fleeting professional career would not provide enough celebrity status to reap an income of endorsements or public speaking engagements after playing, he might feel inclined to make a public statement that he is gay.

At a minimum, the proclamation would bring his name from relative obscurity to the front page of every sports paper, talk show, and magazine in the world. As an international celebrity he would be steeped in media coverage, invited to talk shows and offered book and movie contracts. He would become an instant hero in the gay community and would command large financial gains for his endorsement of a multitude of products. The proclamation would even bring him job security, as the club would fear that if they did not bring him back the following year the public would interpret the decision as homophobia, in the same manner Ellen's dismissal from ABC was interpreted years ago.

While I maintain that this final method of a professional athlete breaking the sexuality barrier is not as ideal as it would be to have a household name come out, I propose that it is entirely more realistic since there are so many more no-names than there are star athletes in professional sports. While I maintain that the homophobic landscape would not be altered as it would if it were an athlete with high masculine capital, the media attention it brought might very well spark another athlete to come out, in the same manner that Roy Simmons did after David Kopay announced that he was gay.

10

Doing Something about It

It is difficult to write a book that is true to the academic understandings of this research but that is also accessible to people without training in academic discourse. I have tried to explain important concepts and terminology to help explain the findings; however, it is hard for me to get away from academic discourse because it helps explain complex social issues that are based in a history of research. This chapter, however, is written in a nonacademic fashion. It summarizes the findings and places them into a practical guide. In other words, it uses academic ideas but accessible language to help gay athletes, gay coaches, and others concerned with the status of gays in sport make a difference.

RESEARCH FINDINGS

I began my sociological investigation into the relationship between gays and sport after coming out of the closet as an openly gay high school coach in 1993. The awful experience had left me with an intellectual angst about the relationship between sport, masculinity, and homophobia and the desire to better understand their connection. In fact, it motivated me to earn a PhD in sociology. I began research for this book in 1998, five years after I had come out of the closet. During this time, homophobia in the general society had greatly decreased but I suspected that it remained unaltered in sports. Thus, I set out to examine the level of homophobia in team sports by interviewing openly gay athletes.

Whereas I fully expected to hear stories from athletes that would resemble my awful coming out experience, much to my surprise I found things were very different. Sports were not as homophobic as I thought. There were a number of stories in which heterosexual teammates celebrated their gay teammates' sexuality by renewed bonding efforts of solidarity in the face of institutional discrimination. There were stories like the one of heterosexuals donning gay pride socks in order to support their gay teammates during a state championship race, and two heterosexual men pushing beds together and flanking the gay athlete in the middle. More so, I found that gay athletes were particularly accepted into sport if they were good. Quit simply, the better an athlete was the better experience he seemed to have. One athlete put it this way, "You don't mess with the best."

Perhaps the most striking finding was that none of the forty athletes were physically assaulted after coming out to their teams (that should reduce some anxiety among readers), and no athletes have been assaulted since this book's final revisions, or at least none that I have heard of. Still, this doesn't mean that all is well for gay athletes in sport. Average athletes found themselves in something I describe as a don't ask, don't tell policy. They found themselves sort of stuck between being one of the guys and not. Their teammates were often more awkward around them, and most of this was likely do to the fact that they didn't want to discuss matters of homosexuality. Interestingly, many gay athletes bought into this silence themselves. They often justified it by saying that sports weren't the place for discussions of sexuality, even though their heterosexual teammates talked about their sexuality all the time. So the athletes, gay and straight, just went about not talking about it, sort of like trying not to talk about an elephant in the living room.

Still, not all openly gay athletes followed this policy, and when gay athletes did talk about their sexuality, they often opened up the door for their teammates to ask questions, joke about, and to celebrate their teammates' diversity. I showed that once highly homophobic heterosexual football players even undid years of socialized homophobia after they met and befriended gay men in their new sport of cheerleading. Some heterosexuals seemed to rejoice, sometimes in comical fashion, about their teammate's sexuality, like when Corey Johnson's team sang "YMCA" in his honor. It seems that when athletes avoided the don't ask, don't tell culture they reported having a totally different experience than athletes who did not. Corey Johnson's story exemplifies this.

These positive results are perhaps a reflection of the decreased cultural homophobia and increased media representation that gays have gained in recent years. A variety of media, religious, and political events have worked to greatly reduce homophobia, and matters continue to get better. It is also important to remember that there is a cohort effect here. In other words, there is a large generational difference. The younger generation is much more accepting of homosexuality than the older generation, perhaps because younger people are more likely to have liberalizing influences like MTV. All of this suggests that the relationship between homosexuality and athletics is growing less tense with each passing year.

Despite the fact that gay athletes are more welcomed in sport than they used to be, masculinity in America remains predicated upon athleticism, and boys and men still use sport as an arena in which they compete with each other in order to bolster their sense of manliness. I found that, for better or worse, gay athletes were just as eager to participate in this culture of hypermasculinity and competitiveness. I also show that homonegative language is still very common in sport. Homophobic words are frequently used by coaches and other athletes as a way to "motivate" athletes, but it was also found to serve as a way to deny the homoeroticism of sport. In other words, there is a certain amount of sexual energy among groups of athletic men, and at some level even heterosexual men recognized this. Using homophobic terms serves as a tool to express their heterosexuality and deny any same-sex arousal.

In this book I also showed that many gay males were attracted to sport because being an athlete helps hide their sexuality from the public. In other words, being an athlete provides some protection against homosexual suspicion. Not only that, but sports are alluring to gay men because they are an arena in which men get to be around a great number of other highly sexualized and often very good-looking males.

Finally, I suggest that there are several ways in which gay athletes and heterosexual athletes can influence the experience that an openly gay athlete will have on a team. In other words, the culture of homophobia in athletics is somewhat changeable. The purpose of the rest of this chapter is to help you learn how to do this. It is primarily designed to help closeted athletes come out and to navigate the sometimes homophobic waters of team sports. However, the information and suggestions provided will also help heterosexual athletes, coaches, and administrators shape a more inclusive culture in athletics.

Factors in a Positive Coming Out Experience

It should be no surprise to know that the better you are the easier coming out is. This research clearly shows a strong correlation between an athlete's ranking and the quality of experience he has as an openly gay team member. In short, the better an athlete is, the more value he possesses to his team, and therefore, the more his teammates are likely to accept and celebrate his sexuality because they are afraid of losing his talent. Conversely, the worse an athlete is, the less important he is to his team's success, so the less likely his teammates are to accept and celebrate his sexuality.

This is an old finding in sport. We all know, for example, that coaches are much more willing to overlook problem athletes if they are good than they are to overlook problem athletes who sit on the bench. Not infrequently, bad athletes get one mistake before being kicked off a team, while good athletes seem to have nine lives. The reason coaches and athletes are willing to overlook the stigma of being gay is because a good gay athlete can help the team avoid the worse stigma of being losers. Thus, what counts more than anything in sport is the victory. Now, I am not trying to say that the only way you will have a positive experience on your team is if you are good, but rather that the better you are, the better your chances are of retaining team support.

Another important factor was the popularity of the athlete. If the gay athlete had a good number of friends before coming out, he was more likely to have a good experience after coming out. Essentially, the more friends you have the better. Friends have a vested interest in each other's success, and the more friends you have, the more popular you are in peer culture. Having a few good friends, especially those who are central to the operation of the team (say, those who score the most points), can also help improve the chances of having a successful coming out because they can help mitigate the homophobia of other athletes. It is one thing to call an athlete a fag when he is alone, and quite another to call him a fag when he is backed up by several loyal friends. Conversely, if you are already alienated or marginalized on the team, if you are already unpopular with your teammates, then coming out of the closet will most likely give your teammates a reason to further marginalize you.

Because athletes generally learn their attitudes regarding masculinity and homosexuality in a top-down fashion, that is, they are easily influenced by older boys and particularly the coach, this research suggests that the more liberal your coach, the better your chances of having a positive experience. If you are not sure where your coach stands on the issue of homosexuality, you might be wise to feel him out on the issue by asking him how he feels about gay marriage, or whether he thinks there are any gay athletes on his team. And while there isn't much you can do about your coach's attitude, you can influence him to support you (when you do decide to come out to him) by appealing to his masculine script of *protector*. In other words, if you approach your coach with, "Coach, you know how you always tell us that we can talk to about stuff? Well I really need to talk to you. I need your help." By approaching him in this manner, you appeal to his self-worth and avoid a direct confrontation, which is usually better than simply saying, "Coach, I'm coming out of the closet whether you like it or not." I might also recommend lending him this book after you tell him.

If your coach does not support you, you may consider publicly challenging him on his position. Some of the athletes in my study did this by reporting their coach to higher authorities. While this will not gain your coach's support, it may be effective in curbing his tendency to use homophobic diatribes. If your coach is gay-friendly, you should probably talk to him and enlist his support to mitigate any problems that might arise from homophobic teammates when you finally come out to them. On the other hand, if your coach is not gay-friendly, try the reverse approach: Build up the positive support from your teammates before telling him. However, it may be best simply not to tell the coach at all. It is certainly possible for you to play on the team, talk about your boyfriend, and other gay issues without having a face-to-face confrontation with the coach. The advantage to this strategy is that if your coach does have a problem, he will have to bring it up, not you.

The more liberal your school is, the easier it will be to come out. Christian schools don't seem to tolerate gay students as well as public schools, but this is not a general rule: The athlete who found himself sleeping between two heterosexual men because they wanted to prove to him that they were not homophobes, rowed for a Christian school. Also, the more liberal your state, the easier it will be. Currently, seven states have laws protecting gay and lesbian students in public education: California, Connecticut, Massachusetts, Minnesota, Vermont, Washington, Wisconsin, and the District of Columbia. These laws give high school students legal clout and help protect them from institutionalized homophobia.

Another influence seems to be the size of the school. Whereas one might think that being in a smaller school would enable you to have more friends, and therefore more supporters, this does not actually play out. In fact, it seems that the bigger your school, the easier it will be. Perhaps this is because larger schools provide more anonymity. Larger schools also provide you with a greater chance of having other openly gay people to connect with. This effect might also reflect the fact that larger schools tend to be found in urban settings, where attitudes toward homosexuality have been shown to be better anyhow. Conversely, small schools, especially ones in which sports are all the rage (like Columbine High School) tend to be considerably more homophobic. This might also be related to geographical region. Other research of mine has shown that the South is more homophobic than other regional locales. Yet another variable of significance (perhaps the most obvious) is that the more muscle-bound you are, the fewer problems you will have. Surely, I do not need to say more about that.

Before we leave this section, I must also say that there is one variable that has a great deal of power in shaping your acceptance onto the team but was impossible for me to quantify. There seems to be a strong confidence effect: The more confident you are, the fewer problems you will have. Maintaining an air of sophistication and ease with who you are, avoiding any suggestion that your confidence is wavering, and possessing a fearlessness about confronting prejudice, all have a way of staying off homophobia. I have even found this to be the case when the gay athlete is considerably smaller than a homophobic athlete. Essentially, it seems that bullies are often looking for easy targets. A positive attitude may help ensure that you will be far less likely to have problems after coming out. Be sure to understand that this isn't a matter of projecting a tough guy image; in fact that would be unwise because this might be perceived as a physical challenge to a bully. And under the unofficial rules of masculinity, a challenge to fight cannot be denied without losing masculine capital. Rather, what I refer to is simply possessing a matter-of-factness about who you are. If you are unashamed and you hold your head up high, you send a message that you are beyond intimidation. At the end of this chapter I even give some sample scripts to help with this.

HOW TO COME OUT TO YOUR TEAM

Over the years I have had the privilege of helping a great number of gay boys and men come out to their families, their friends, and even to their teams. Helping so many gay individuals has enabled me to better understand how to come out effectively in order to maximize the chance of a successful reception and to minimize the stress. Note that while I am specifically gearing this section toward the gay athlete coming out to his teammates, the information equally applies to coming out to friends and family.

The first step is to begin by building a support system outside your team. Friends outside of your team will be able to counsel you, listen to you, and help you keep things in perspective. It is also important to establish contacts in the gay community first. Having a social support system of gay friends will help you deal with problems that might arise, and it is just comforting to know that you are not the only one who has been through the coming out process. Also the more successful experiences you have coming out, the more confident you will present yourself with each subsequent episode. Thus, coming out to people away from the athletic setting (people who are less likely to be homophobic) will help you possess an air of confidence as you come out to your teammates.

I recommend that you first come out to your coach or person with the most vested interest in you. Do not, however, do this spontaneously. Be sure to tell the person ahead of time that you have something important to talk about and that you want to schedule an appointment in the next few days. Perhaps you can say something along the lines of, "Hey John, I need to talk to you about something really important with regard to my life. How about we meet for lunch after practice on Thursday?" You might also want to alleviate any worry he might have that the meeting is about him by saying, "Don't worry its not about you, I just need your help with something." By doing it this way, you give him the idea that the nature of your meeting is serious and this will start him speculating about what it could be. While considering various possibilities, he will invariably ask himself what he would say in response to each. In other words, you're giving him time to prepare. Hopefully, there may have been enough clues so that he may guess that you are going to come out to him, and then he will have the opportunity to formulate a response that represents his true feelings.

It is also important to set a meeting a few days in advance because coming out is an unforgettable event. Every openly gay or lesbian has a number of stories about their coming out experience. Some are wonderful scenarios, while others still upset us. Essentially, the moment you come out to someone (particularly if it is one of the first people you come out to) is burned into your memory. I clearly remember the first few people I came out to but have a hard time remembering the coming out scenario of the tenth through ten-thousandth person.

The point is that giving your teammate or friend the opportunity to think about what the nature of the meeting is ahead of time, might help ensure that he gives you a response that will facilitate positive memories.

I also recommend setting your meeting in a public place, like a restaurant. This provides a certain insurance against the highly unlikely event that you elicit a violent response. Of all the coming out stories I've heard over the years, this tactic proved important only one time. Although he did not feel that it was necessary, Mike was glad he took my advice because his father exploded into a tirade and marched out of the restaurant when Mike told him the news. Several weeks later (when they began to talk again), the father said, "It's a good thing you didn't tell me at home, I would have hit you." I also recommend that you come out while eating. Biochemists have shown that feelings of fondness are produced for those you eat with.

When you actually tell him you are gay be sure to do so in a positive and upbeat manner. Remember that this is not about sorrowfully admitting your homosexuality; it is about a celebration of the fact that you no longer desire to hide the secret and that you have chosen your friend to confide in. Remind him how much this means to you, and tell him that you hope he is honored to be the first person that you have told. Be sure to set him up for a positive response. Say something along the lines of, "Okay, John, you know I asked you here for a reason, I have something to tell you. I know you are going to take it well because you're such a cool guy." Or, "I know you are not going to have a problem with this because you are so open-minded." Avoid saying something like, "I know you're not going to like this, but. . . ." I recommend you do this because people often receive messages according to the way they are delivered, and they often respond to messages according to how they are expected. Telling someone that you are gay in a positive, unashamed manner is more likely to produce a favorable result. In other words, come out with a sense of secure pride. Show no question about whether you should or shouldn't come out, and no remorse about your decision to come out. There is absolutely no shame in being gay, so show it. Remember, you aren't looking for sympathy, you are simply telling your teammates and friends as a celebration of your newfound honesty.

It is also important to remember that you've had a long time to think about coming out and that it has taken years to get to the point in which you are comfortable doing it. Your teammate, however, has had only a few moments to digest the matter. So, in the event that matters don't go well, be sure to give him a few days to digest it. Understand that your friend has an image in his head of who you are and that he has to readjust it now that he has learned that you are not heterosexual. It often takes time to change the image, and this change is often experienced as something of a loss.

Essentially, while a proclamation of your sexuality should be a celebration of your sexual identity, the revelation that you are gay is also likely to be taken as a loss to your teammates of who they thought you were. This is actually quite similar to the experience one feels after losing a major competition. We tend at first to deny the loss and then grow angry about it before entering into depression. In time, depression slowly becomes acceptance. Your teammates may go through these stages with your coming out as well. For example, someone might deny your revelation by saying, "No, you're not" or "But what about that one girl?" He might grow angry at you for not having told him earlier, only to later grow depressed that you "are not who I thought you were." Chances are he will eventually come around to accept you and your new public identity.

I also recommend that you tell only one teammate at a time. By telling teammates one at a time, you improve the chances of receiving a better response. When it comes time to tell the next team member, be sure to *tell the next teammate together*. Much of the homophobia athletes express is not because they truly hate gays, rather they think that if they do not act in homophobic ways, they will not be acting within the boundaries of normative masculinity. In other words, it is actually easier for them to be homophobic than not. By coming out to athletes who you think you have the greatest chance of success with first, you can begin to build a small group of support that will help you when it comes to telling less supportive teammates. When these less supportive teammates are approached by you and your allies, it will be harder for them to express having a problem with your sexuality. In fact, people, in general, are very likely to state that their opinion conforms to the group. In one famous study, a room full of confidants all unanimously agreed that the shorter of two lines was actually longer. When confronted with the fact that the rest of the people in the room believed that the shorter of the two lines was actually longer, the subject also agreed.[1] In other words, people will say they think one way, even if they don't, when they sense that everybody else is thinking that way.

Avoiding the Bisexual Trap

Athletes often ask me for specific advice on what exactly to say when they come out. When it comes to this, I have found that the most important thing is to be sure to tell them that you are gay and not that you are bisexual, even if you are. Gay athletes frequently pretend that they are bisexual in the coming out process because telling someone that you are bisexual seems easier than telling them you're gay. I certainly did. Saying that you are bisexual is a way of saying, "I am different from you, but I am not all that different from you." While this might seem advantageous, some people will feel that they can sway you into being straight. Or they will ask you to suppress your gay side but emphasize your straight side. This is something that bisexual people face on a daily basis. They are constantly confronted with people who want them to choose one side, and of course, most people generally want them to choose heterosexuality. This is particularly true with parents.

Telling people that you are bisexual (even if you are) also makes it easier for them to go into the policy of don't ask, don't tell regarding your attractions for people of the same sex. It allows them to talk about your heterosexual side and to avoid your homosexual side. If, however, you tell people that you are gay up front, they eventually lose hope that you will like the opposite sex, and they are forced to accept your same sex desires sooner. I recommend you follow this advice, even if you are bisexual. Tell them that you are gay. Wait for them to accept the fact that you like men, then after they have done this, you can go back and tell them why you approached it in this manner. Don't be surprised, however, if they begin to push you toward acting on your heterosexual desires more. This is a form of biphobia that is common.

After Coming Out

One of the most encouraging findings from this research was that none of the athletes in the study were physically assaulted. In fact, most of the openly gay athletes in the study found that they heard the word *fag* on their teams much less often after coming out. That's the good news. However, you are likely to run into a lot of heterosexism in the form of not wanting to know about your business. Generally what happens is the teammates say, "Okay, fine. You're gay, but we don't want to hear about it or talk about it." In fact, heterosexual teammates will often continue to act as if nothing has changed. This often means that they will pretend that you are heterosexual and often ask you what you think of certain women. While it might be tempting to partake in these discussions in order to feel like you fit in with the boys, and while this might somehow seem a nod to acceptance, in reality it reflects a don't ask, don't tell policy so that your sexuality does not have to be treated on a par with theirs. In other words, it is a strategy to deny your sexuality.

Perhaps one of the interesting things about don't ask, don't tell was that gay athletes were found to be as culpable as heterosexual athletes in its promulgation. For example, gay athletes frequently say to themselves, "If they want to know about my love life, or what it's like being gay, they will ask," while his friends are thinking, "If he wants us to know about his gay life, he will tell us." One can easily see, in this situation, how both sides unwillingly dupe the other into thinking silence is preferable to open communication.

To help avoid a don't ask, don't tell culture, one simple rule must be followed: Athletes must be able to talk openly about their sexuality. You can do this in a number of ways. For example, you can talk about the guy you are seeing, you can talk about the club that you went to the other night, or you can tell your teammates about the problems or pleasures of having recently come out to other people. It is important to understand, however, that avoiding don't ask, don't tell is a two-sided coin. Your teammates might desire the policy, even if you don't, which sets the stage for tension. How can you best ward this off? When the guys say, "Hey, what do you think of her?" I recommend something like, "Yeah, I thought you knew I'm interested in him, not her?" Or, perhaps another response would be, "Her? I'm more interested in her brother." You see, when you talk about your sexuality you also send a message to your teammates that they too can talk about it and you would be amazed what type of questions straight boys will ask when they feel they have the opportunity! Be honest with them; let them ask questions and encourage them to talk more about it. In doing so you will educate them, provide an atmosphere that fosters others to be able to come out of the closet, and you will feel better about being out yourself.

DEALING WITH UNCOMFORTABLE SITUATIONS

Athletes frequently tell me that they remain closeted because they are afraid of uncomfortable situations that might arise as a result of their sexuality. However, it's important to remember how uncomfortable you have been made by being closeted. Ask yourself how often you feared your teammates finding out or worried about not being accepted if they did know? How much emotional energy have you spent dwelling over whether to come out or not? It is important to know that one of the most consistent findings in this research was that openly gay athletes almost always feel that they wish they had come out of the closet sooner—I know I did.

At any rate, although it would be unreasonable to believe that there would be absolutely no problems or awkward moments associated with your coming out and being out on an athletics team, it would be equally as unreasonable to assume that it will be the end of your world. This was certainly not the case with the forty athletes in this research, and by the time you read this book, cultural homophobia will have decreased even more.

When it comes to hot-button issues, the locker room seems to be the most talked about site of contention. Interestingly, however, in my interviews with openly gay athletes, locker room situations were rarely problematic. This is partially because athletes rarely shower at schools anymore. Most finish their workout and wear their practice clothes home. Still, gay athletes often fear that their teammates will think they are sexually attracted to them and that they are scoping them out in the locker room. The absurdity of the notion that all gay men are attracted to all men notwithstanding, the truth is that, statistically, you will be attracted to men in the locker room. After all, you are gay. This doesn't mean that you have to change your actions however. And if the discussion comes up with your teammates about whether or not you are attracted to them or about their discomfort with you in the locker room, remind them that there are other men in the locker room, mostly closeted gay men, that could also be checking them out. Depending on your relationship with them, you might say, "How do I know you're not checking me out?" Later in this chapter, I will talk more about how to respond to questions of whether or not you are attracted to your teammates.

The simple answer to the locker room question is to do nothing different than you have done before coming out of the closet. If you've been changing with them all along, then you continue to change with them. If you've been showering nude, you continue to do so. The only thing that has changed is that they now know you are gay. If they have a problem with that, they can avoid the locker room, rather than you avoiding it. If you start giving into situations like this, you will find yourself increasingly marginalized from the team. Just go about doing what you've always done and they will get over it sooner or later.

In addition to locker rooms, overnight trips seem to be a point of tension among gay and straight athletes because beds are usually shared. I often say that this is where the theory of accepting gay athletes is put to the test. This situation, however, is something that is absolutely out of your control. Therefore, again, I recommend that you do nothing different than before. If the coach normally makes the decisions on who stays with whom, let him do that. If you normally share a bed, then don't volunteer to take the floor. Remember, just because you are gay doesn't mean that you should be treated as a second-class citizen. The more normal you act, the easier it will be for your teammates to accept you for who you are.

The same can be said with using the bathroom. I know it sounds funny, but after I came out of the closet as a coach, I quickly found that my athletes were afraid to stand at the urinal next to me. Before I came out, we would stop the van at a rest-stop and all sprint to the bathroom, but afterward it became something of a game. Athletes would watch to see what I was doing; if I sprinted, they walked, and if I walked, they sprinted. If they came into the bathroom while I was at the urinal by mistake, they'd suddenly have to wash their hands, or they would find some other way to avoid having to stand at the urinal next to me. These behaviors changed in time, as my athletes slowly lost their fear of having me check them out. The key, again, is to do exactly the same things that you did before you came out of the closet.

The last major point of contention seems to revolve around the display of public affection. I can keep my advice short on this issue: If you have a partner, don't deny his existence. Your allegiance should be to your lover, not your teammates. Bring him to the banquet; introduce him to those who do not know him; hold his hand in public; kiss him hello, and treat him like a heterosexual would treat his girlfriend. Anything less is degrading. If others are intimidated by this, let it be their problem.

On Being Attracted to Your Teammates

I can almost guarantee that if your team is not into don't ask, don't tell, the subject of whether or not you are attracted to your teammates will come up. Sooner or later, someone is bound to say, "Hey, do you find any of us attractive." Most of the athletes I talk to have trumped potential romantic and sexual liaisons with their teammates by saying, "No, I just think of you as my teammates. I don't see you in that way." Or, "You guys aren't my type," even if they are. I do not recommend this approach for several reasons.

Primarily, I do not think you need to avoid this discussion because as a society, we need to get over our discomfort with the issue of gays being attracted to straights. But I also recommend against a flat denial of sexual attraction because we don't know who is straight. The individual asking you the question might actually have an ulterior motive. In asking "Are you attracted to me?" he may actually be hoping that you are. Thus, if you say yes, you may increase his chances of coming out if he is gay, or you raise his self esteem if he is straight. If you say no, he may slither further into the closet. I do not, however, recommend that you state whether or not you are attracted to him, without first undergoing the following dialogue:

Him: So, do you find any of us attractive?

You: Some yeah. How come?

Him: Oh, I'm just wondering. Like who do you find hot?

You: Well, I don't need to say just who. But I'd sure hope that if they knew I was attracted to them they would take it as a compliment.

Him: Oh yeah, totally. So do you think I'm good looking?

You: Well do you really want to know? I mean if I say yes would it make you uncomfortable? And if I say no, would it lower your self-esteem?

Him: Nah, dude, I can handle it either way.

Here is another example:

Him: So, you think any of the guys on the team are attractive?

You: Well, let's do it this way. If they want me to think that I think they are attractive, then yes, they are hot. But if they don't want me to think them attractive than no they are not.

This approach also prevents you from having to flatly deny that you could be attracted to your teammates and gives them a chance to think about whether they want more information from you or not.

When Things Don't Go Well

In the event that things don't go well when you come out of the closet, I highly encourage you to document everything that happens. You never know when you might need evidence to support your behaviors, or even if you might need the evidence in a future lawsuit. This is particularly true for coaches who come out. Thus, if you are harassed, kicked off the team, assaulted, or in any way treated unjustly because you are gay (or for any other reason), write down everything that transpired. Be sure to include the names of the principal agents, who said what and to whom and list any witnesses. Sign the letter and find a friend to sign and date the letter as well. This helps prove that you wrote it on the day in question, in case you need proof later. Keep a file and if anything suspicious happens, put it in the file.

Also be sure to get official support. From the minute you suspect things are not going well, get a lawyer or a gay faculty member or look for your local Gay Lesbian Straight Education Network (GLSEN) chapter (see the links on my website, www.EricAndersonPhD.com). Also be sure to know your rights. Find out what the specific laws are for your state, and remember that as of the printing of this book, California, Connecticut, Massachusetts, Minnesota, Vermont, Washington, and Wisconsin as well as the District of Columbia have educational laws that protect high school students. And if you are in high school, be sure to use your parents if they support you; you'd be amazed at what a phone call can do. Also feel free to use the press. Administrators hate negative press and things can change rather quickly when the press gets a sniff of a student or coach getting his rights trampled.

If you are confronted with violence, get out of there. Don't try to be macho or stand your ground. Report it to the police and your county's human relations committee. Finally, be sure to report hate crimes, threats, or harassment. High schools and college administrators are usually horrible at dealing with such problems, but you have to go through these channels to start. Remember you can also go outside the school, to the local human relations agency and the police. If you are harassed in college, forget the athletic administrators, go straight to the ombudsmen or the sexual harassment officer. Remember that harassing you for being gay *is* sexual harassment.

THE IMPORTANCE OF COMEBACKS

Having prepared responses to questions and insults is a valuable tool when coming out. Men try to cut each other down with insults as an attempt to raise their own masculine capital. Having a few witty statements prepared is likely to defuse some of this. Also, if you find yourself being seriously harassed, a few witty comments might be able to change the tide. Humor has a particularly powerful effect on decreasing a tense situation. Furthermore, using humor against someone who is troubling you will help you win other people onto your side.

Here are some examples of ways in which others typically try to get at gays; and some prepared comebacks that you can memorize. Memorize the responses that best fit your personality.

Fag

No, that's proud fag.
Good, I'm not the only one.
What, you didn't think I knew that?
Yeah, we established that when I came out.

Thanks for the compliment.
Careful, it's contagious.

Dude, why do they have to make an issue out of it?

Last I checked it was the Christian right making the issue.
You're right, straights do make an issue out of it.
Now who is calling it to people's attention?
Didn't you hear? I was voted most likely to make an issue out of it.

You're cool, I mean you're gay but you don't act gay.

And you're cool and straight, but you don't act straight.
Yeah, I pride myself on acting as average as possible.

I'm not a homophobe I just don't think gays should be able to marry.

I don't think straights should be able to get divorced.
Yeah, you wouldn't want them being treated equally or anything.
Yeah, me either, heterosexuals have messed marriage up just fine
    without us.

Specific Issues for Gay Coaches

If you are a gay coach who is contemplating coming out to your team,
first get a formal evaluation. Try not to tip the administration off when
doing this. Perhaps you can say you are applying to be a Big Brother
and need a letter attesting to your quality of character or that you are
applying for a scholarship or something. Having this formal evaluation (hopefully, it is good) will help you make a better case if things get
ugly. Similarly, be sure to copy your personnel file. The law requires
that you have access to it. Copy everything in it, just in case things
seem to disappear after you come out.

If you come out after the season is over, you make it easier for
them to fire you than if you come out just as the season gets underway.
Also perhaps some of their vehemence (if there is any) will end by the
time the season is over. Be sure to make an appointment with the
administrator to come out; don't do it spontaneously. If you suspect
that he is a homophobe, request that a secretary be there to take notes
on the meeting. This will keep him on his toes. It's also important to
tell the administration before the athletes. Let them know you are
informing them as a professional courtesy. Show no shame, guilt, inde-
cision, or remorse. Keep it as matter of fact as you can so that the
administration sees no signs of being able to manipulate you or to try

to talk you out of coming out to your team. Also make sure that you discuss with them what they will say to any parents or others who call to complain. An appropriate answer would be, "Our coaches' sexual orientation, gender, race, or religion is simply not an issue."

When it comes time to come out to your team, be sure to tell your seniors first. You want the ones who know you the best, the ones who have the most respect for you, to know first. That way, they will support you when the younger athletes find out. I'd recommend telling them one at a time, in the same manner I described earlier for teammates. Try to do it in a matter in which you can't be accused of making an issue out of it, even though that's a meritless heterosexist statement at best. Nonetheless, wait until one of them asks what you think of a girl or asks if you have a girlfriend, then you can say matter of factly, "Hey John, let's talk for a few minutes after practice." Set them up for success like I described that athlete's doing earlier by saying, "I know you're going to be cool with this . . ." and then tell them the truth.

Afterwards, change nothing in your routine. Do things exactly the same as you did before you came out of the closet, with the notable exception of being able to discuss your sexuality openly. However, a sensible precaution is to avoid any situation in which you could be accused of wrongdoing. I'm not an advocate of being so cautious that you lose your humanity, but it is foolish to leave your guard down completely. Remember, an accusation is usually synonymous with guilt in this culture.

HANDLING THE PRIVACY ISSUE

Lets face it, the only time we hear your sexuality is private is when we are referring to homosexuality. Heterosexuality is a very public issue, but homosexuality is supposed to be private? This is part of the operation of heterosexual hegemony, and many gay people fall victim to it by silencing themselves. If administrators, parents, or kids ask, "Why do we need to know your sexual orientation?" you simply answer, "Why do I need to know yours?" You need to help explain to them that people declare they are heterosexual everyday in a multitude of ways. Simply saying, my wife or my girlfriend is a proclamation of sexuality. We only notice it, however, when it is a proclamation of homosexuality.

For example, if a heterosexual coach says, "Oh my wife and I went to San Diego and saw a great art exhibit," all the focus is on *San Diego* and *Art exhibit*. But, if I say, "My boyfriend and I went to San Diego and saw a great art exhibit," the focus is on *my boyfriend*. Both are equal proclamations of one's sexual orientation, but only one gets noticed. So the short of it is that one's sexual orientation is not a private matter.

I make this poignant through an exercise in my lectures. The first few minutes of the first lecture I tell my students that I believe they should have the right to know something about me. I give them a five minute autobiography and include the fact that I am married to my wife Molly of seven years. I show photos of my dog and tell them what I like and don't like. I also make sure to say that I hate the Lakers. After the introduction, I ask them if they had any problems with what I said. Inevitably, someone raises their hand to say that they "like the Lakers." I then ask if anyone had a problem with me telling them about my wife, dog, and favorite foods. Nobody ever does. Then I say, "Great. Now let me tell you the truth."

I repeat the story identically (all five minutes worth) but when I get to the end I tell them about my partner Grant. I then follow it up with, "If you didn't have a problem with me telling you about the fictional Molly then you won't have one with the real Grant. And if you do, you have some homophobia to live up to." Interestingly, many of the gay students later tell me that they, just like the rest of the students, also saw nothing wrong with me talking about my wife, but that they felt uneasy when I talked about my partner. One student said, "It's just like, okay, you can talk about it, but should you be so in your face about it?" It was the perfect question to illustrate that when it comes to heterosexism, homosexuals, just like heterosexuals, are often all too complacent in accepting it.

WARMING DOWN

Perhaps more than understanding how masculinity works and what the relationship between gay athletes and sporting culture is, the six years of research into these issues has taught me that just when you think you have it figured out, things change. I suspect that when it comes to cultural homophobia in the United States, and especially when it comes to the relationship between gay athletes and sport, it is nearly impossible to put your finger on what is exactly occurring. Things just seem to change too fast.

In recent years, there has been a flurry of gay awareness in the media, a litany of gains (and many declines) in regard to gay marriage, and the rapidly growing allure of the term *metrosexual*. In short, American men, gay and straight, seem to be in a flux when it comes to asking what it means to be masculine, what the value of orthodox masculinity is, and how gay men fit into it.

It is clear that sport lags behind whatever cultural gains are made in the population at large, and that the structure of sport helps resist these gains. Still, young athletes are raised in a culture that is much more understanding of homosexuality. Thus, perhaps the cultural lag between the popular culture and sport will shorten. One thing remains certain, sport, like any institution, is not immune to social change. If the whole world around sport is changing, sport will also have to change, or it will lose its significance in culture, and be viewed as an archaic way of thinking.

Notes

1. Although the term *American* is technically not correct, since it can refer to any country in North or South America, I use it synonymously with the United States in this book.

2. Jeni Loftus (2001) and Widmer et al. (2002) both show significant reductions in the amount of cultural homophobia in the United States.

3. My experience as America's first openly gay high school coach is the subject of my 2000 autobiography *Trailblazing: The true story of America's first openly gay track coach.* The second edition, *Trailblazing: America's first openly gay high school coach,* is currently in print with Identity Press (2003).

4. I earned my PhD at the University of California, Irvine in 2004. This book was not my dissertation research.

5. *Queer Eye for the Straight Guy* premiered on Bravo in 2003. The premise of the show is to feature a heterosexual male who desires to be more "metrosexual" by taking advice on fashion and culture from five gay men. The metrosexual is reputed to represent a softer, more expanded version of heterosexual masculinity. See Hyman (2004) and Flocker (2004) for more about metrosexuality.

6. Gay youth generally create an anonymous screen name to enter gay chat rooms and to instant-message with others. After feeling comfortable enough, they often begin a slow process of revealing their identity. Eventually,

their online community leads to public meetings. Gay youth today are therefore provided with greater opportunity to communicate anonymously and openly with other youth than they were prior to the Internet.

7. Gert Hekma (1998) discovered in interviews with gay athletes that after they came out of the closet there was a high rate of dropping out of sport. Rates of openly gay athletes who drop out of sport were not, however, compared to rates of heterosexual athletes dropping out of sport.

CHAPTER 1. WARMING UP

1. Mariah Burton-Nelson (1995) explores the role sport plays in the reproduction of patriarchy in her book *The Stronger Women Get, the More Men Love Football*. Here she hypothesizes that as women have increasingly gained access to institutions that were once reserved for men, men have responded by emphasizing the physical differences between men and women.

2. Older conceptions of masculinity hold that gay men are not really masculine, and are therefore incapable of participating in highly masculinized activities like contact team sports. For example, a 1999 study of rookie NFL players anonymously questioned men about the possibility of gay men existing on their teams. The results showed that 54 percent of the men surveyed felt that there were no homosexuals on their team. The unpublished research was sponsored by sport agent Ralph Cindrich who has granted me permission to use the data in this book. The research itself was conducted by telephone interviews with Campos Market Research. This attitude, however, may be changing. Research that I currently have under review (2004) with *Social Problems* indicates that heterosexual men are beginning to disentangle sexuality from masculinity. Essentially, heterosexual men today maintain that gay men can be "just as masculine" as heterosexual men, and many heterosexual men look down upon feminine-acting men. One informant even said, "Gay men should remember that they have a dick too, and they should act like it."

3. Brian Pronger created the first substantial theoretical thinking on the issue of gay men in sport with his groundbreaking book, *The Arena of Masculinity*. For more postmodern theorizing around this issue, I recommend his (2000) chapter, "Homosexuality and sport: Who's winning?" in J. McKay, M. Messner, and D. Sabo's *Masculinities and Sport*.

4. General Social Survey data is cited in Loftus (2001).

5. Ibid.

6. I have also shown that once highly homophobic football players (who later become cheerleaders) can quickly undo their socialized homophobia after befriending gay men on their collegiate cheerleading squads. This research is currently under review with *Social Problems*. For more information on how personal contact helps reduce homophobia, see Cullen et al. (2002).

7. *Los Angeles Times*, April 11, 2004.

8. The softening of American masculinity may be seen among heterosexual male cheerleaders who used to play football. This other research of mine, shows that after joining cheerleading, many highly masculinized heterosexual men rethink their perceptions of masculinity and offer a softer version that is based less in homophobia and misogyny. This research is currently under review with *Sociological Perspectives.*

9. In his (2004) book *The Metrosexual Guide to Style,* Michael Flocker credits writer Mark Simpson with coining the term *metrosexuality* in the early 1990s (although I am not able to find its original source). The term *metrosexuality* became popular when a marketing research firm called RSCG published its findings in 2003.

10. According to Realitytvworld.com, the show was the most watched television program among eighteen to forty-nine year olds at the 10:00 pm slot in early September 2003.

11. Ralph Cindrich, *The Cindrich Survey 1999, Campos Market Research.* Because of the sensitivity of the material, this survey is not widely available but Ralph Cindrich has granted me permission to use it for this book.

12. I am currently working on a survey for attitudes regarding homosexuality among NFL players for 2004 and would encourage readers to check my website, www.EricAndersonPhD.com, for the results of such.

13. For information on grounded theory, see Corbin and Strauss (1990), Glaser and Strauss (1967), and Dilorio (1989).

CHAPTER 2. SPORT, MASCULINITY, AND HEGEMONIC OPPRESSION

1. For more information on the multiple constructions of masculinity, see Chen (1999), Staples (1998), Baca-Zinn (1998), Connell (1987), Connell (1995), and Majors (1990).

2. One example of this is that openly gay athletes commonly feel that public discussions of their homosexuality are in violation of "flaunting" or "making too big an issue" out of one's sexuality. This was discovered in my first examination of gay male athletes in my (2002) article, "Openly Gay Athletes: Contesting Hegemonic Masculinity in a Homophobic Environment."

3. Robert Connell is largely credited with beginning the discussion of hegemonic masculinity in his 1987 book *Gender and Power.*

4. For more information on the conflation of homosexual sex with a homosexual sexual orientation, see Humphreys (1975), Lancaster (1988), Plummer (1999), and Smith (1998). For more information about the manner in which heterosexuality may be broadening to include limited forms of same-sex sexual interaction with other men in America, either see my research that is currently under review with *Social Problems* or my (2004) dissertation.

5. In addition to this discourse being found in my research for this book, it was also found by Bernard McGuigan (1995).

6. For more information on the difficulty of maintaining a heterosexual identity, also see Kimmel (1994).

7. For more information on the feminist perspective on the construction of masculinity, see Lorber (1994), Kimmel (1996), Chodorow (1978), and David and Brannon (1976).

8. In his book, *Real Boys*, psychologist William Pollack discusses the trappings of American masculinity and how it affects boys. He describes the strict antecedents of being a "real boy" as producing depression in youth. He encourages Americans to reconstruct what it means to be a boy or man as the way to relieve boys of their depression.

9. Sociologist Michael Messner interviews heterosexual collegiate and professional athletes for his research on the problems of masculinity in sport in his book *Power at Play*.

10. Billy Bean's autobiography, *Going the Other Way*, is as much a fascinating and disturbing glimpse into the life of a professional baseball player as it is a disturbing account of the difficulty in being closeted.

11. For more on human capital see Becker (1964).

12. See Richard Majors (1990) for more information about the manner in which black men have constructed a masculinity that emphasizes flashy athleticism and muscular fitness as a way of resisting white dominance in at least one social arena (athletics) within their control.

13. For a very good account of the relationship between masculinity and homophobia, see Kimmel (1994).

14. Barrie Thorne's *Gender Play* provides a thoughtful ethnography of boys and girls and how they are not simply passive agents of top-down socialization, like sex-role theory maintains. Rather, Thorne showed that boys and girls maintain considerable agency in the construction of normative gender practices.

15. Further research would have to be conducted to see if the reduction in homophobia at the national level has trickled down to elementary school children.

16. Shawn McGuffey and Lindsey Rich (1999) document elementary school-aged children and their use of homophobia to police masculine behaviors and construct peer hierarchies even before they know what homosexuality is.

17. Graduate student Kirby Schroeder, at the University of Chicago, is working on a dissertation in which he examines compulsory homosexuality amongst heterosexual men at a military college. Michael Robidoux (2001) has written an excellent ethnography of hockey players and the construction of masculinity.

18. This is similar to the findings of Hondagneu-Sotelo and Messner (1994) or Majors (1990), who both found that marginalized men may display masculine bravado in an attempt to act powerful when actually in a state of powerlessness.

19. For an excellent article on the subject, see Plummer (1999).

20. For an excellent discussion on the use of homophobia as a tool of sexism, see Suzanne Pharr (1997).

21. For an excellent videotape on the problem of masculinity in America, I recommend Jackson Katz's *Tough Guise.*

CHAPTER 3. THE RELATIONSHIP BETWEEN GAY ATHLETES AND SPORT

1. This does not mean that I am in contact with sixty gay athletes at one given time. Because of the length of my study (five years), I am generally only in contact with a few at any one time. Like heterosexual athletes, gay athletes also drop out of sport at a rapid rate. Gay athletes, however, can be found by using online search engines like America Online. Note that gay athletes rarely write *gay* in their profiles—I generally use words like "football," "boys," and under the column for marital status I often look for "don't ask." Perhaps the best search engine for young gay male athletes is to utilize the "bois" section on XY.com. Here you know that every athlete is gay. Finally, for nonschool athletes, one might best use the gay athlete registry found at my website, www.EricAndersonPhD.com.

2. Of course, gay men are not the only ones to threaten the institution of sport as a homogenous masculine arena. The emergence of women into sport has also challenged notions of physical masculine superiority. Sport collides with the male body in representing power, but power is not determined by male biology. Male power is embedded within the institutions of a patriarchal order and expressed through the male body. Should women express this physical power, or men not express theirs, they are thought to be transgressive in relation to sport and masculinity.

3. For an excellent account of the manner in which a gay subculture is resisted within sport, see both Pat Griffin's (1998) *Strong Women, Deep Closets* and Wolf and others' (2001) "How Much Difference Is Too Much Difference? Perceptions of Gay Men and Lesbians in Intercollegiate Athletics."

4. The search for inclusion into existing social structures is also highlighted by the gay and lesbian community's plight for inclusion into the institution of marriage. Assimilating to the dominant power structure may be more alluring than reinventing it because there are institutional rewards for such an endeavor.

5. The Gay and Lesbian Athletics Foundation is an international organization that brings together scholars, athletes, and fans in a forum to discuss the issue of gays in sport at all levels; www.glaf.org.

6. The fact that gay athletes are choosing (or perhaps structured into) the assimilationist route is not surprising; it is the path our community has traveled in all other institutions. Indeed, we may shake things up a little as we progressively engrain ourselves into the dominant social structures of American society, but for the most part we demand to be treated equally and to be viewed as being perfectly normal with the exception of who we sleep with. We (myself included) demand the right to gay marriage, rather than questioning the institution as being oppressive to women and unnecessary in modernity. We have fought long and hard to be treated equally on all fronts.

7. Combining football, basketball, hockey, baseball, volleyball, soccer, and rugby.

8. I fully recognize that straight and gay kids may be fully unaware of their sexuality in childhood anyhow.

9. See L. Shawer (1995). For more information on the subject of gays in the military I recommend using the Center for the Study of Sexual Minorities in the Military at the University of California, Santa Barbara. Their website is: http://www.gaymilitary.ucsb.edu.

10. See Laumann et al. (1994). It should also be noted that while Laumann, et al. may have found the rates of same-sex sex decreasing, other research of mine suggests that it may be higher. Among one group of men I studied, five out of ten heterosexual men informed me that they had engaged in some form of same-sex sexual activity. This study is currently under review with *Social Problems*.

11. Regarding hazing, Gershel and Katz-Sidlow (2003) show that little is known about the prevalence of hazing behaviors among adolescent athletes. Their survey of 1,105 6th through 12th grade athletes found that 17.4% had been subjected to practices that qualify as hazing. Many of these teenagers did not comprehend the abusive and potentially dangerous nature of hazing.

12. As reported in www.newsday.com, Professor Hank Nuwer is a Professor at Franklin College in Indiana.

Chapter 4. Systems of Masculine Reproduction

1. For information on the friendliness of Fortune 500 companies toward gay issues, see www.HRC.org.

2. For more information on homosexuality in public schools, see www.GLSEN.org

Chapter 5. Coming Out in Sport

1. Using sport as a means out of poverty is common in both inner cities and reservations. See Coakely (2002) for more information regarding black

athletes and the inner cities and Anderson (in press) for an ethnography of the Navajo's use of basketball in reservation life.

2. Statistics derived from the Los Angeles County Gay and Lesbian Center show that there were 238 hate crimes against gays and lesbians in Los Angeles County in 2002, of which 59% were violent.

3. Note that Matthew Shepard was not an athlete and did not know his killers.

4. Like many firsts, including my title as the nation's first openly gay high school coach, Corey wasn't really the first-ever to do such; in fact, I had already interviewed three high school football players before his story hit the press. Rather, both Corey and myself are the first that the media recognized. For more information on my story, see Anderson (2003).

5. In addition to this being found in my research in the United States it was also found in the Netherlands, Hekma (1998), and in Great Britain, Price (2000).

CHAPTER 6. MITIGATING GAY STIGMA

1. For a nuanced account of the history of black athletes in American sport, I recommend Arthur Ashe (1988), a two-volume set.

2. Black athletes are "stacked" in sport because they are only put into positions where they are said to be better than all potential white men for that position.

3. Unlike a black athlete, a closeted athlete is able to attempt to advance up the masculine hierarchy by improving upon his athletic abilities; he can literally slip under the gaydar by choosing to remain closeted. In other words, he is given the chance to enter sport as a second-class athlete, and then try to work his way up to superstar status, while a black athlete may be prevented from entering sport as a second-class athlete.

4. National figure skating champion Rudy Galindo came out in 1995, and eight-time national diving champion David Pichler came out before he made the 1996 Olympic team. Former world bodybuilding champion, Mr. Universe, Bob Paris came out two years before retiring in 1984 and Gold medalist and world record holder swimmer Bruce Hayes came out during the gay games in 1990 (in which he broke two more world records). For a list of out gay athletes, see my website, www.EricAndersonPhD.com.

5. After coming out Mark also learned that five of his other teammates (those he had trained for years with) were also gay. This may have also facilitated a safer space for him.

6. See Price and Parker (2002) for a shorter version of these findings. I recommend contacting the author for the original research that appeared as Price's dissertation, titled *Rugby as a Gay Men's Game*.

Chapter 8. Factors That Influence Acceptance

1. Other research of mine (Anderson 2004) on collegiate male cheerleaders found that about 80 percent of men who cheer identify as heterosexual, and that about 80 percent of those men used to play high school football.

2. For more information on the intersectionality and construction of race, see Omi and Winant (1986).

3. For an excellent collection of articles on gender and identities, see Ferree et al. (1999).

4. I recommend Cochran and Mays (1998) for a discussion of this.

5. The Cindrich Survey 1999, *Campos Market Research.* Because of the sensitivity of the material, this survey is not widely available and was never published. However, sports agent Ralph Cindrich has granted me permission to use it for this book.

6. A list of professional gay athletes can be found on my website, http://www.EricAndersonPhD.com.

Chapter 9. The Center of Masculine Production

1. The quotes from Thompson are from the book *Bloody Sundays,* written by a respected *New York Times* sports columnist. Although I can have no guarantee that the interview he conducted with Thompson is true, I have no reason to doubt its authenticity either.

2. David Kopay came out first in 1975 (football), followed by Roy Simmons (football) also in 1975, Glenn Burke (baseball) came out publicly in 1994, Billy Bean (baseball) in 1999, and Esera Tuaolo (football) in 2002.

3. Of those who visit the Gay and Lesbian Athletics Foundation Website, 61 percent think that a professional team sport athlete won't come out between the next five years and never; see http://gayconference.org/index.php.

4. This quote came from an article in "Behind Closed Doors: 'Faith-Based' Summit Meets" from the website GayToday.com; see www.gaytoday.badpuppy.com/garchive/world/042701wo.htm.

5. This quote came from a September 10, 2002 radio interview on the Howard Stern Show, after Shockey was asked by Gary Del 'Abate if he thought there were any gay players in the NFL.

6. This quote came from a May 28, 2002 article, "Giants Doubt A Gay Player Would Fit In," http://www.outreach.com.au/asp/news.asp?item=208.

7. Ibid.

8. This quote came from Billy Bean's excellent (2003) autobiography *Going the Other Way,* p. 217. In the book he discusses not only what it was like

to be a professional and closeted gay baseball player, but he illustrates the difficulties that any ball player would have in the near-total institution of professional baseball.

9. These statistics came to me from a 1999 study of rookie NFL players anonymously questioned about the possibility of gay men existing on their teams. It was conducted by *Campos Market Research*. Because of the sensitivity of the material, this survey is not widely available but Ralph Cindrich has granted me permission to use it for this book.

10. It should be noted that this statement is somewhat misleading because the athletes I've interviewed are those who have chosen to remain in sport. Athletes who have dropped out of sport are not represented by my study. Therefore, I can't really say what percentage of athletes are willing to sacrifice personal freedom for athletic success.

11. This quote was found in the November 11, 2002 issue of *ESPN: the Magazine*, http://espn.go.com/magazine/vol5no23tuaolo.html.

12. Mark Tewksbury tells me that he estimates that he gained six years of training improvement by coming out of the closet to his teammates and coach.

13. For more information on gay athletes and product loyalty, see my online article, "All the Right Clothes" at www.EricAndersonPhD.com.

14. For more information on this see Glenn Burke's hard to find autobiography titled *Out at Home*.

15. The media would certainly be interested in reporting suspicions of a professional athlete's suspected sexual orientation.

16. For a good summary of this, see Coakley (2002).

CHAPTER 10. DOING SOMETHING ABOUT IT

1. For a scholarly analysis of this and other research into conformity see Rod Bond and Peter Smith (1996).

References

Acker, Joan. 1990. Hierarchies, jobs, bodies: A theory of gendered organizations. *Gender & Society*, 4 (June): 139–58.

Adams, Henry E.; Wright, Lester W.; and Lohr, Bethany. 1996. Is homophobia associated with homosexual arousal? *Journal of Abnormal Psychology*, 105(3): 440–45.

Adams, M. L. 1993. To be an ordinary hero: Male figure skaters and the ideology of gender. In T. Haddad (Ed.), *Men and masculinities*. Toronto: Canadian School Press.

Anderson, Eric. 2002, July. In the macho world of track and field one man breaks out of the pack. *Genre*, 17.

———. 2002, December. Openly gay athletes: Contesting hegemonic masculinity in a homophobic environment. *Gender & Society*, 16(6): 860–77.

———. 2003. *Trailblazing: America's first openly gay high school coach*. Fountain Valley, CA: Identity Press.

———. 2003. All the right clothes. www.EricAndersonPhD.com.

———. 2004. *Masculine identities of male nurses and cheerleaders: Declining homophobia and the emergence of inclusive masculinity*. Dissertation, University of California, Irvine.

———. In Press. Colonial sports and the Navajo. *The International Journal of the History of Sport*.

Ashe, Arthur Jr. 1988. *A hard road to glory: A history of the African American athlete 1919–1945, volume 1.* New York: Warner Books.

———. 1988. *A hard road to glory: A history of the African American athlete since 1946, volume 2.* New York: Warner Books.

Baca-Zinn, Maxine. 1998. Chicano men and masculinity. In Michael Kimmel and Michael Messner (Eds.), *Men's lives.* Boston: Alyson and Bacon.

Bailey, Michael J. 2003. *The man who would be queen: The science of gender-bending and transsexualism.* Washington DC: Joseph Henry Press.

Bean, Billy with Bull, Chris. 2003. *Going the other way: Lessons from a life in and out of major-league baseball.* New York: Marlowe and Company.

Becker, Gary. 1964. *Human capital.* Chicago: University of Chicago Press.

Bissinger, H. G. 1990. *Friday night lights: A town, a team, and a dream.* Reading, MA: Addison-Wesley.

Bond, Rod and Smith, Peter. 1996. Culture and conformity: A meta-analysis of studies using Asch's (1952b, 1956) line judgment task. *Psychological Bulletin,* (119): 111–37.

Bourdieu, Pierre. 2001. *Masculine domination.* Palo Alto: Stanford University Press.

Brannon, Robert. 1976. The male sex role—and what it's done for us lately. In R. Brannon and D. David (Eds.), *The forty-nine percent majority.* Reading, MA: Addison-Wesley.

Britton, Dana M. and Williams, Christine. 1995. "Don't ask, don't tell, don't pursue": Military policy and the construction of heterosexual masculinity. *Journal of Homosexuality,* 30(1): 1–21.

Bryant, Michael. 2001. Gay male athletes and the role of organized team and contact sports. Unpublished Master's Thesis, Seattle Pacific University.

Burke, Glenn and Sherman, Erik. 1995. *Out at home.* New York: Excel Publishing.

Burn, S. M. 2000. Heterosexuals' use of "fag" and "queer" to deride one another: A contributor to heterosexism and stigma. *Journal of Homosexuality,* 40(2): 1–11.

Burstyn, Varda. 1999. *The rites of men: Manhood, politics, and the culture of sport.* Toronto: University of Toronto Press.

Burton-Nelson, Mariah. 1995. *The stronger women get, the more men love football: Sexism and the American culture of sports.* New York: Avon Books.

Butler, Judith. 1990. *Gender trouble: Feminism and the subversion of identity.* New York: Routledge.

Buzinski, Jim. 2002, May 21. Is there a gay NY Met? http://www.outsports.com/columns/gaymet20020521.htm.

———. 2002, August 19. I'm not homophobic but my buddy is: New survey examines attitudes towards gays in pro sports. http://www.tampabay-coalition.com/files/820FansImNotHomophobicButMyBuddyIs.htm.

———. 2004, January 27. Florida settles with lesbian athlete. http://www.out-sports.com/campus/20040227zimbardisettlement.htm.

Carrington, Christopher. 1999. *No place like home: Relationships and family life among lesbians and gay men*. Chicago: University of Chicago Press.

Cashmore, Ellis and Parker, Andrew. 2003. One David Beckham: Celebrity, masculinity, and the soccerati. *Sociology of Sport Journal*, 20(3): 214–31.

Chen, Anthony. 1999. Lives at the center of the periphery, lives at the periphery of the center: Chinese American masculinities and bargaining with hegemony. *Gender & Society*, (13)5: 584–86.

Chodorow, Nancy. 1978. *The reproduction of mothering*. Berkeley: University of California Press.

Clarke, G. 1998. Queering the pitch and coming out to play: Lesbians and physical education in sport. *Sport, Education, and Society*, 3(2): 145–60.

Coakley, Jay. 2002. *Sport in society: Issues and controversies*. Boston: McGraw-Hill.

Cochran, Susan, and Mays, Vickie. 1998. Sociocultural facts of the black gay male experience. In Michael Kimmel and Michael Messner (Eds.), *Men's Lives*, 4th ed. Boston: Allyn & Bacon.

Connell, Robert. 1995. *Masculinities*. Berkeley: University of California Press.

———. 1987. *Gender and power*. Palo Alto: Stanford University Press.

Corbin, Juliet and Anselm, Strauss. 1990. Grounded theory research: Procedures, canon, and evaluative criteria. *Qualitative Sociology*, 13(1): 3–21.

Crosset, Todd. 1990. Masculinity, sexuality, and the development of early modern sport. In Michael Messner and Donald Sabo (Eds.), *Sport, men and the gender order: Critical feminist perspectives*. Champaign, IL: Human Kinetics.

Cullen, J. M.; Wright, L. W.; et al. 2002. The personality variable openness to experience as it relates to homophobia. *Journal of Homosexuality*, 42(4): 119–34.

Curry, Timothy. 1991. Fraternal bonding in the locker room: A profeminist analysis of talk about competition and women. *Sociology of Sport Journal*, 8(2): 119–35.

David, Deborah and Brannon, Robert. 1976. *The forty nine percent majority: The male sex role*. Reading, MA: Addison-Wesley.

Dilorio, Judith. 1989. Feminism, gender, and the ethnographic study of sport. *Arena Review*, 13(1): 49–59.

Ferree, Myra Marx; Lorber, Judith; and Hess, Beth. 1999. *Revisioning gender*. Thousand Oaks: Sage

Fine, G. A. 1987. *With the boys: Little league baseball and preadolescent culture*. Chicago: University of Chicago Press.

Flocker, Michael. 2004. *The metrosexual guide to style: A handbook for the modern man*. New York: DaCapo Press.

Ford, Nancy. 2004, August 20. People will talk. http://www.txtriangle.com/archive/1034/entertainment.htm.

Foucault, Michel. 1977. *Discipline and punish: The birth of the prison*. New York: Vintage.

———. 1984. *The history of sexuality, volume 1: An introduction*. Translation by Robert Hurley. New York: Vintage.

Freeman, Mike. 2003. *Bloody Sundays*. New York: William Morrow.

Funnell, Dug. 2003. Holding up a mirror to baseball's homophobia. http://www.outsports.com/difference/funnell.htm.

Garner, Brian and Smith, Richard. 1977. Are there really any gay male athletes? An empirical study. *The Journal of Sex Research,* 13(1): 22–34.

Gerdy, John. 2002. *Sports: The all American addiction*. Jackson: University Press of Mississippi.

Gershel, J. C.; Katz-Sidlow, R. J.; et al. (2003). Hazing of suburban middle school and high school athletes. *Journal of Adolescent Health,* 32(5): 333–35.

Glaser, Barney and Straus, Anselm. 1967. *The discovery of grounded theory: Strategies for qualitative research*. New York: Aldine De Gruyter.

Glassner, Barry. 1999. *The Culture of fear: Why Americans are afraid of the wrong things*. New York: Basic Books.

Goffman, Irving. 1959. *The presentation of self in everyday life*. New York: Double Day.

———. 1961. *Asylums*. New York: Anchor Books.

———. 1963. *Stigma: Notes on the management of spoiled identity*. New York: Simon and Schuster.

Gramsci, Antonio. 1971. *Selections from prison notebooks*. London: New Left Books.

Greendorfer, Susan. 1992. A critical analysis of knowledge construction in sport psychology. In Thelma Horn (Ed.), *Advances in sport psychology*. Champaign, IL: Human Kinetics.

Griffin, Pat. 1998. *Strong women, deep closets: Lesbians and homophobia in sport*. Champaign, IL: Human Kinetics.

Hargreaves, Y. 1996. *Sport, power, and culture: A social and historical analysis of popular sports in Britain*. New York: St. Martins Press.

Hekma, Gert. 1998. "As long as they don't make an issue of it . . .": Gay men and lesbians in organized sports in the Netherlands. *Journal of Homosexuality,* 35(1): 1–23.

Herdt, Gilbert. 1981. *Guardians of the flute: Idioms of masculinity*. New York: McGraw-Hill.

Herek, Gregory. 1998. Psychological heterosexism and anti-gay violence: The social psychology of bigotry and bashing. In Michael Kimmel and Michael Messner (Eds.), *Men's lives* (254–56). Boston: Allyn and Bacon.

Herek, Gregory and Berrill, K. 1992. *Hate crimes: Confronting violence against lesbians and gay men.* Newbury Park, CA: Sage.

Hondagneu-Sotelo, Pierrete and Messner, Michael. 1994. Gender display and men's power. In H. Brod and M. Kaufman (Eds.), *Theorizing masculinities* (200–18). Thousand Oaks, CA: Sage

Human Rights Campaign. 2003. http://www.hrc.org/worknet/cei/cei_report 2003.pdf.

Humphreys, Laud. 1975. *Tearoom trade: Impersonal sex in public places.* New York: Aldine De Gruyter.

Hyman, Peter. 2004. *The reluctant metrosexual: Dispatches from an almost hip life.* New York: Villard.

Ibson, John. 2002. *Picturing men: A century of male relationships in everyday life.* Washington, DC: Smithsonian Books.

Kaufman, King. 2003, January 8. Football: America's favorite homoerotic sport. http://www.salon.com/news/sports/col/Kaufman/2003/01/08/homoerotic/.

Kaufman, Moises. 2001. *The Laramie project.* New York: Vintage.

Kidd, Bruce. 1987. Sport and masculinity. In Michael Kaufman (Ed.), *Beyond patriarchy: Essays by men on pleasure, power, and change.* Toronto: Oxford University Press.

———. 1990. The men's cultural centre: Sports and the dynamic of women's oppression/men's repression. In Micheal Messner and Donald Sabo (Eds.), *Sport, men, and the gender order: Critical feminist perspectives* (31–44). Champaign, IL: Human Kinetics.

Kimmel, Michael. 1990. Baseball and the reconstitution of American masculinity, 1880–1920. In Michael Messner and Donald Sabo (Eds.), *Sport, men and the gender order: Critical feminist perspectives.* Champaign, IL: Human Kinetics.

———. 1994. Masculinity as homophobia: Fear, shame, and silence in the construction of gender identity. In H. Brod and M. Kaufman (Eds.), *Theorizing Masculinities.* Thousand Oaks, CA: Sage.

———. 1996. *Manhood in America: A aultural history.* New York: The Free Press.

King, J. L. 2004. *On the down low: A journey into the lives of "straight" black men who sleep with men.* New York: Broadway Books.

Kinsey, Alfred. 1948. *Sexual behavior in the human male.* Philadelphia: W. B. Saunders.

Konigsberg, Bill. 2002, October. Billy Bean. *Out.*

Kopay, David and Deanne-Young, Perry. 1977. *The David Kopay story*. Co: Arbor House Publishing.

Lancaster, Roger. 1988, April. Subject honor and object shame: The construction of male homosexuality and stigma in Nicaragua. *Ethnology*, 27(2): 111–25.

Laumann, Edward; Gagnon, John; Michael, Robert; and Micheales, Stuart. 1994. *The social organization of sexuality: Sexual practices in the United States*. Chicago: The University of Chicago Press.

Loftus, Jeni. 2001. America's liberalization in attitudes toward homosexuality, 1973 to 1998. *American Sociological Review*, 66(5): 762–82.

Lorber, Judith. 1994. *Paradoxes of gender*. New Haven: Yale University Press.

———. 1998. *Gender inequality: Feminist theories and politics*. Los Angeles: Roxbury Publishing Company.

Louganis, Greg with Marcus, Eric. 1996. *Breaking the surface: The autobiography of Greg Louganis*. New York: Penguin.

Loy, John. 1995. The dark side of Agon: Fratriarchies, performative masculinities, sport involvement, and the phenomenon of gang rape. In Bette Karl Heinrich and Alfred Rutten (Eds.), *International sociology of sport: Contemporary issues* (263–81). Stuttgart: Verlag Stephanie Naglschmid.

Majors, Richard. 1990. Cool pose: Black masculinity and sport. In Michael Messner and Donald Sabo (Eds.), *Sport, men and the gender order*. Chapaign, IL: Human Kinetics.

McGuffey, Shawn and Rich, Lindsey. 1999. Playing in the gender transgression zone: Race, class, and hegemonic masculinity in middle childhood. *Gender & Society*, 13(5): 608–10.

McGuigan, Bernard. 1995. *Queering the pitch: The experiences of gay athletes in mainstream sport and gay games V*. Unpublished Dissertation, Exeter University. Netherlands: Amsterdam.

Menez, Gene. 2001, May 22. The toughest out. http://sportsillustrated.cnn.com/features/scorecard/news/2001/05/22/sc.

Messner, Michael. 1987. The meaning of success: The athletic experience and the development of identity. In Harry Brod (Ed.), *The making of masculinities: The new men's studies*. Allen and Unwin.

———. 1990. Boyhood, organized sports, and the construction of masculinities. *Journal of Contemporary Ethnography*, 18(4): 416–45.

———. 1992. *Power at play: Sports and the problem of masculinity*. Boston: Beacon Press.

———. 1999. Becoming 100 percent straight. In Michael Kimmel and Michael Messner (Eds.), *Men's lives*, 4th ed. Boston: Allyn and Bacon.

———. 2000. Barbie girls vs. sea monsters: Children constructing gender. *Gender & Society*, (14): 765–84.

———. 2002. *Taking the field: Women, men, and sports*. Minneapolis: University of Minnesota Press.

Messner, Michael and Sabo, Donald. 1990. *Sport, men and the gender order: Critical feminist perspectives*. Champaign, IL: Human Kinetics.

Miracle, Andrew and Rees, Roger. 1994. *Lessons of the locker room: The myth of school sports*. New York: Prometheus Books.

Nardi, Peter. 1999. *Gay men's friendships*. Chicago: University of Chicago Press.

Nichols, Jack. 1975. *Men's liberation: A new definition of masculinity*. New York: Penguin.

Omi, Michael and Winant, Howard. 1986. *Racial formation in the United States*. Boston: Routledge.

Outside the lines. 1998, December 16. ESPN.

Pallone, Dave. 1990. *Behind the mask*. New York: Penguin.

Pearlman, Jeff. 1999, December 23. At full blast. http://sportsillustrated.cnn.com/features/cover/news/1999/12/22/rocker/.

Pharr, Suzanne. 1997. *Homophobia: A weapon of sexism*. Berkeley, CA: Chardon Press.

Pitts, Brenda. 1990. Let the games begin! A case study of sports tourism, commercialization and the gay games V. Paper presented at the second conference of the gay games: Queer Games? Theories, Politics, and Sport, Amsterdam.

Plummer, David. 1999. *One of the boys: Masculinity, homophobia, and modern manhood*. New York: Harrington Park Press.

———. 2001. Policing manhood: New theories about the social significance of homophobia. In C. Wood (Ed.), *Sexual positions: An Australian view*. Melbourne: Hill of Content/Collins.

Pollack, William. 1999. *Real boys: Rescuing our sons from the myth of boyhood*. New York: Henry Holt and Company.

Price, Michael. 2000. *Rugby as a gay men's game*. Unpublished dissertation, University of Warwick.

Price, Michael and Parker, Andrew. 2002. Sport, sexuality and the gender order: Amateur rugby union, gay men, and social exclusion. *Sociology of Sport Journal*, 20(2): 108–26.

Pronger, Brian. 1990. *The arena of masculinity: Sports, homosexuality, and the meaning of sex*. New York: St. Martin's Press.

———. 1995. Gay jocks: A phenomenology of gay men in athletics. In Michael Kimmel and Michael Messner (Eds.), *Men's lives* (3rd edition). Boston: Allyn and Bacon.

———. 1999. Outta my endzone: Sport and the territorial anus. *Journal of Sport and Social Issues*, 23(4): 373–89.

————. 2000. Homosexuality and sport: Who's winning? In J. McKay, M. Messner, and D. Sabo (Eds.), *Masculinities and sport*. Thousand Oaks: Sage.

Rathgeber, Brad. 2003. Unpublished paper presented at the Gay and Lesbian Athletics Foundation, Boston.

Robidoux, Michael. 2001. *Men at play: A working understanding of professional hockey*. Quebec: McGill-Queen's University Press.

Rotundo, Anthony. 1994. *Transformations in masculinity from the revolution to the modern era*. New York: Basic Books.

Rubin, Gayle. 1984. Thinking sex: Notes for a radical theory of the politics of sexuality. In Carole Vance (Ed.), *Pleasure and danger: Exploring female sexuality*. Boston: Routledge.

Sabo, Donald; Miller, M.; Melnick, Michael; and Heywood, Leslie. 2004. *Their lives depend on it: Sport, physical activity, and the health and well-being of American girls*. East Meadow, NY: Women's Sports Foundation.

Sabo, Donald and Panepinto, Joe. 1990. Football ritual and the social reproduction of masculinity. In Michael Messner and Donald Sabo (Eds.), *Sport, men and the gender order: Critical feminist perspectives*. Champaign, IL: Human Kinetics.

Schwartz, Martin D. and DeKeseredy, Walter S. 1997. *Sexual assault on the college campus: The role of male peer support*. Thousand Oaks, CA: Sage.

Sedgwick, Eve Kosofsky. 1990. *Epistemology of the closet*. Berkeley: University of California Press.

Shawer, L. 1995. *And the flag was still there: Straight people, gay people, and sexuality in the U.S. military*. New York: Harrington Park Press.

Smith, George. 1998. The ideology of fag: The school experience of gay students. *Sociological Quarterly*, (39)2: 309–35.

Smith, Michael. 1983. *Violence in sport*. Toronto: Butterworths.

Staples, Robert. 1998. Stereotypes of black male sexuality. In Michael Kimmel and Michael Messner (Eds.), *Men's lives*, 4th ed. Boston: Allyn and Bacon.

Talbot, M. 1988. Understanding the relationships between women and sport: The contributions of british feminist approaches in leisure and cultural studies. *International Review for the Sociology of Sport*, (23): 31–39.

Thomas, Judy L. 2000, January 29. Catholic priests are dying of AIDS, often in silence. *Kansas City Star*, http://www.nestar.com/projects/.Thorne, Barrie. 1999. *Gender play: Girls and boys in school*. London: Rutgers University Press.

Thorne, Barrie. 1998. Girls and boys together . . . but mostly apart: Gender arrangements in elementary school. In Michael Kimmel and Michael Messner (Eds.), *Men's lives*, 4th ed. Boston: Allyn and Bacon.

Thurow, Lester. 1985. *The zero-sum solution: Building a world-class American economy*. New York: Simon and Schuster, 1985.

West, Candice and Zimmerman, Don. 1987. Doing gender. *Gender and Society*, 1(2): 125–51.

Whitson, Dave. 1990. Sport in the social construction of masculinity. In Michael Messner and Donald Sabo (Eds.), *Sport, men and the gender order: Critical feminist perspectives*. Champaign, IL: Human Kinetics.

Widmer, Eric D.; Treas, Judith; and Newcomb, Robert. 2002. Attitudes toward nonmarital sex in 24 countries. *Journal of Sex Research*, 35(4): 349–65.

Wilson, Brian. 2002. The "anti-jock" movement: Reconsidering youth resistance, masculinity, and sport culture in the age of the internet. *Sociology of Sport Journal*, 19(2): 206–33.

Wolf Wendel, Lisa; Toma, Douglas; and Morphew, Christopher. 2001. How much difference is too much difference? Perceptions of gay men and lesbians in intercollegiate athletics. *Journal of College Student Development*, 42(5): 465–79.

Woodward, Rachel. 2000. Warrior heroes and little green men: Soldiers, military training, and the construction of rural masculinities. *Rural Sociology*, 65(4): 6–40.

Woog, Dan. 1998. *Jocks: True stories of America's gay male athletes*. Los Angeles: Alyson Books.

——— . 2002. *Jocks 2: Coming out to play*. Los Angeles: Alyson Books.

Index

SUNY series on Sport, Culture, and Social Relations

CL Cole and Michael A. Messner, editors

Ralph C. Wilcox, David L. Andrews, Robert Pitter, and Richard L. Irwin (eds.), *Sporting Dystopias: The Making and Meanings of Urban Sport Cultures*

Robert E. Rinehart and Synthia Sydnor (eds.), *To the Extreme: Alternative Sports, Inside and Out*

Eric Anderson, *In the Game: Gay Athletes and the Cult of Masculinity*

Pirkko Markula (ed.), *Feminist Sport Studies: Sharing Experiences of Joy and Pain*